Bridges to the Future

Bridges to the Future

Prospects for Peace and Security in Southern Africa

EDITED BY
Hans-Joachim Spanger and Peter Vale

Taylor & Francis Group
LONDON AND NEW YORK

First published 1995 by Westview Press

Published 2018 by Routledge
52 Vanderbilt Avenue, New York, NY 10017
2 Park Square, Milton Park, Abingdon, Oxon OX14 4RN

Routledge is an imprint of the Taylor & Francis Group, an informa business

Copyright © 1995 by Taylor & Francis

All rights reserved. No part of this book may be reprinted or reproduced or utilised in any form or by any electronic, mechanical, or other means, now known or hereafter invented, including photocopying and recording, or in any information storage or retrieval system, without permission in writing from the publishers.

Notice:
Product or corporate names may be trademarks or registered trademarks, and are used only for identification and explanation without intent to infringe.

A CIP catalog record for this book is available from the Library of Congress.

ISBN 13: 978-0-367-00931-1 (hbk)
ISBN 13: 978-0-367-15918-4 (pbk)

Contents

Foreword, Desmond M. Tutu — vii
Preface — ix
Acknowledgments — xv
About the Contributors — xvii

1 Appreciating Updike's Syndrome: Southern
   African Security in the 1990s, *Peter Vale* — 1

2 Regional Economic Co-operation and the Development
   Challenge in Southern Africa, *Robert Davies* — 13

3 Time to Decide: Rethinking the Institutional Framework
   of Regional Co-operation in Southern Africa, *Peter Meyns* — 33

4 Organizing Collective Security: African Experiences,
   Ivor Richard Fung — 61

5 Crisis Prevention and Conflict Management in Southern
   Africa in the Post-Cold War Era, *Willie Breytenbach and
   Pál Dunay* — 91

6 Security Dilemmas in Southern Africa: A Case for
   Confidence-building Measures? *Hans-Joachim Spanger* — 107

7 Establishing Democratic Defence Forces in Mozambique:
   A Case Study, *Joao Bernardo Honwana* — 147

8 Towards a Security Regime in Southern Africa: Some
   Working Suggestions, *Hans-Joachim Spanger and Peter Vale* — 167

About the Book and Editors — 189
Index — 191

Foreword

For half a century, Southern Africa has represented the very worst of exploitation of people by fellow human beings. Colonialism, racism, apartheid—these were the terms which people all over the world used to explain the seemingly endless series of conflicts which marked the region's post-World War II history. But as this century ends, Southern Africa has come to be associated with the terms which suggest the very epitome of humanity's epic stuggle to create a better world. Compromise, reconciliation, multiculturalism—these terms are increasingly used to understand and explain the course, and the cause, of Southern African affairs.

The long years of struggle have produced something which is worth preserving, but—as with most things in life—it was not without its price. Physically, Southern Africa has been badly damaged; political structures have been tried and found wanting; the region's economy is crippled; and—most important of all—the dignity of its people has been terribly assaulted. While the current mood promises a new beginning, the region's past has left an indelible mark on its future prospects.

The task before the region is all the greater, because the 1990s have witnessed an increased marginalization of our continent. It is as if the world no longer cares. As Southern Africans take control of their own destiny, they will have to draw on the promising beginnings, but build with a great sense of urgency and focus. They will not succeed if they are not prepared to be open and honest—this means that citizens and leaders alike should have the courage to criticise and to take criticism.

South Africa's role in regional affairs has been watched with interest. As the strongest state in Southern Africa, it will need to marry its own interests to the region's. This will not be easy, because each of the states of the region, like individuals themselves, have expectations of, and from, South Africa. Managing these promises will be the single most important challenge to those who make the country's foreign policy.

This collection of essays grapples with the manifold problems which Southern Africa faces as one millenium ends and another opens. The authors erect theoretical and practical signposts which point the way to peace and security in the region, but—again, like life itself—only so-called ordinary people can make a difference.

Desmond M. Tutu, D.D., K.F.C.
Archbishop of Cape Town
Chancellor, University of the Western Cape

Preface

Like most projects in international relations, this book is part of a wider process—securing peace and security in Southern Africa. Without both, as the world knows, the region will not prosper. Understanding and explaining all this has not always been easy, however. Therefore, the energies which contribute to projects like this are often wasted.

A decade ago, the region was caught in bloody conflagration. The struggle to end apartheid had reached a pivotal, though inconclusive, stage. Although pitched battles raged throughout South Africa, it was increasingly clear that the liberation movements—led by the African National Congress (ANC)—were unable to break the stranglehold of minority rule. But the many who defended apartheid were also caught in a dilemma. Their continued hold on power was controlled by an ever increasing body count. In a world of mass communication, this price was too high.

For the countries of Southern Africa, the deepening stalemate within their neighbourhood was immensely destructive. Encouraged to see the conflict in their country in vulgar Cold War terms, South Africa's powerful military lashed out across the country's borders. The fight over apartheid exacted a terrible toll from the region: in the 1980s it is estimated to have cost in excess of 60 billion US dollars, and—infinitely more important—it took 1.5 million Southern African lives.[1]

As the 1980s ended, however, the region was caught in quandaries which lay beyond the apartheid issue. South Africa's political bankruptcy was matched, in real and often quite quaint ways, by the failure of the states around it. In some of these—Mozambique and Angola are far and away the best examples—the struggle over apartheid has rendered worthless the nation-building project. In others—best epitomised, perhaps, in Malawi—a 1960s-style African dictatorship persisted into the 1980s. Lesotho, in turn, suggested post-colonial Africa's inability to deal with traditionalism and modernization. In Zimbabwe, the region's youngest member and potentially its brightest star, the limitations of African-style socialism were increasingly evident. The inability to implement a vision for the region was therefore compounded by the deepening crisis of the Southern African state. This was not only the region's predicament. Subsequent developments have confirmed it was the world's.

In the midst of this destruction, prospects for peace and security in Southern Africa looked dismal. Efforts to establish a truce with the apartheid regime—as the much heralded, though short-lived, Nkomati Accord demonstrated—were futile. But the predatory governments which held on to power in the name of opposition to minority rule also thwarted the prospects for peace and security. Only the total destruction of apartheid could end the region's misery. The stalemate within South Africa, therefore, held the region's progress captive. However, South Africa's power alone suggested long time-frames: there was little prospect that peace and security could be realized before the century closed.

Throughout these years, the region's hopes for a better life were confined to the musings of academics—mainly based in the North—who considered the lost opportunities in Southern Africa from a safe distance. The truly historic efforts to advance the cause of peace and security—of which the Southern African Development Coordination Conference (SADCC) is the outstanding example—were based on the theoretical insights provided by Northern-based intellectuals. This is not to discount the contributions to hopes for peace by a range of Southern African leaders: for the courage of perseverance, Kenneth Kaunda of Zambia stands out. Nor does it dismiss the immense contribution of millions of Southern Africans who made sacrifices, away from the glare of politics, in the hope of a peaceful region.

For all intents and purposes, Southern Africa's search for peace and security—like many intractable international issues in the 1980s—was tied to the Cold War. In 1989, when the Cold War ended, it marked the dividing line between decades of fruitless efforts to secure the region and a new era when, with luck, the region might build towards peace and security. But events in history are seldom marked by absolute dividing lines. The ending of the Cold War was only the high point in a set of circumstances which forced authorities in Moscow (and elsewhere) to understand that the future could not be secured along the lines of the past.

Events in Southern Africa helped feed this process. The resurgence of Cuban involvement in Angola during 1987 and 1988 changed the capacity of South Africa's military to wage war on the region's people. This, in turn, stimulated the forces which changed the wider course of international relations. Many believe, for instance, that the battle for Cuito was decisive in international relations—it certainly changed the course of the region's history. A short two years later, a wave of optimism was sweeping the region. Identifying the moment at which this surge commenced is not difficult—February 1990. F.W. de Klerk's opening speech to South Africa's Tricameral Parliament signalled a moment from which there would be no fundamental retreat, despite innumerable tactical withdrawals. Thus, as South Africa was charted for change and reconstruction, so was the region.

The optimism of the 1990s has changed the terms of the debate on the region's future. Additional items have been added to the lexicon of issues which are thought to be essential to guaranteeing the region's future: participatory democracy and open economies are certainly the most important. Through this, new passageways to the region's future have opened, and debating the region's prospects for peace and security has become near commonplace. As Kadar Asmal, destined to become a minister in South Africa's Government of National Unity, in early 1994 noted:

> I am bound to report ... that, based on the number of visitors to our offices, the topic of regional security in Southern Africa has become the academic flavour of the month across the world! But the guns which have ... (recently) ... boomed from the hills around the Maseru ... and the acid rain in the Eastern Transvaal attest to the urgency of finding answers to these and other questions. We do not have the time, nor the resources, to simply ask more questions.[2]

The Midgard Conference, held in Namibia in May 1993, upon which this collection of essays was forged, is only one in a series of discussions on peace and security in the region.[3] But Midgard was unique; this, too, is reflected in the contents of this book. At Midgard, senior military men were drawn together for the first time in academic debate. As importantly, senior officers who had defended apartheid in the past met South Africans who had sought to destroy the system. And—perhaps most consequentially—these South Africans met under the watchful eye of their neighbours. The concerns which underpinned the debates at Midgard Conference have been highlighted, updated and amplified in this collection. Through this, the obstacles to peace and security in the region have been thrown into sharp focus.

The first of these impediments involves the complexities of South Africa's reintegration into the region. This deliberate understatement underpins one of the most important challenges in Southern Africa's long-term future: the problems which flow from the preponderance of a single state. Any discussion on the region's prospects for stability is meaningless without an appreciation of this. Statistics demonstrate the dilemma—South Africa occupies only 16.6 percent of the total land mass of the Southern African Development Community (SADC) region and has only 30 percent of the population of SADC, but it generates a GNP 255 percent more than SADC's. Without accommodating these imbalances into the region's geometry, Southern Africa—even if stable—will be caught between the fact of peace and the hope of prosperity.

Like history itself, each of the region's existing institutions carries the burden of the past. Each was constructed at a distinct moment, and, to survive, each will have to overcome its individual legacy. Evidence suggests that only SADC has shown itself capable of changing without losing the gravitational pull which holds it together. But, if the truth be told, the process is far from completed. SADC's most important test remains ahead: can it shed the preoccupation with development which shielded it during apartheid and reach towards the new challenges which link development with security?

The second obstacle involves an international environment in which shock is the normal state of affairs. Despite the terrible prospect of nuclear war, the Cold War was a compliant period. Sudden jolts to the international system were rare and, as a result, early warning systems—through the United Nations and elsewhere—were almost ritual. Exactly the opposite is true in the 1990s. Almost every corner of the world has experienced security quakes of seismic proportions. These shocks have severely tested the international system and the capacity of multilateral organizations to rise to the challenge of uncertainty. Additionally, the ability of large powers—such as the United States—to mould the world in their image has been found wanting. Without tested shock absorbers, the challenge for Southern Africa—and all regions—is to engineer mechanisms which manage deep-seated trauma.

The enormity of this task has been highlighted by two recent experiences in other parts of the continent—the horrors of Somalia and Rwanda. Both emphasize the paradox of the contemporary state, and the immense tragedy around both suggests how enormously difficult it is for Africa to deal with the exigencies of the times. This is why the slow erosion of the political and security situation in Lesotho has been monitored with such concern throughout Southern Africa.

Few doubt that Southern Africa shares a common future. How it manages the move towards this will be a function of how quickly the region can develop internal shock absorbers. This suggests that the multilateral process in Southern Africa will have to develop beyond the "natural" barriers represented by states. Overcoming this—the third obstacle—will not be easy. Enormous political energy has been devoted to building states within colonial boundaries in Africa. And yet, all the evidence suggests that these are artificial creations. Managing the problems of the post-Cold War world has added increased weight to our understanding that regional approaches to security issues offer the best—

perhaps the only—hope of success. Without real visionary leadership, however, it will not be easy to shift thinking.

The final obstacle which needs to be demarcated from the others, because it is of structural importance, is order—without it, as countless conflicts over the globe indicate, anarchy will dictate political outcome with tragic consequences. But managing change in an orderly fashion in Southern Africa will not be easy. As the 1980s progressed, it was increasingly clear that centres of economic activity were changing. Africa, all the evidence suggests, was falling further and further behind the rest of the world. Today, it is commonplace to argue that Africa is marginalized from the mainstream of the international community. Declining economic performance and the consequent inability of governments to deliver in a number of important socio-economic areas have increased the prospects for crime throughout Southern Africa. In many cases, crime and political disaffection have combined to form an increased sense of insecurity. Through all this, the region's orderly transition is sapped. The hard truth is that without economic growth and its corollary, vigorous redistribution, the region's prospects for peace and security will be dimmed, if not dashed.

These four obstacles informed the policy proposals which conclude this book. For many, these will not go far enough; for others they will outstrip even the modest academic licence, as envisaged in the ideas leading to the Midgard Conference. This is as it should be, of course. Advancing the debate runs the risk of undermining an essential ingredient of both peace and security: the necessity to build confidence between partners. Despite the changes which have occurred in Southern Africa in recent years, suspicions run deep. To help anchor the region, therefore, those involved in thinking about its future should prescribe the "do-able." If they do so, then this particular part of the wider process on the region's prospects for a better future will not have been in vain.

Hans-Joachim Spanger
Peter Vale

Notes

1. *South African Destabilization: The Economic Costs of Frontline Resistance to Apartheid*, African Recovery, Press Summary (New York: United Nations, October 1989).

2. "South Africa in Africa." Keynote Address by Professor Kader Asmal, Professor of Human Rights, University of the Western Cape, and Member of the

National Executive Committee, African National Congress, at the African Centre for Development and Security Studies (ACDESS) Conference, Windhoek, Namibia, Thursday, 27 January 1994.

3. For an account of the proceedings, see Hans-Joachim Spanger and Peter Vale, *Security, Development and Co-operation in Southern Africa: The Midgard Conference*, PRIF Reports, No. 31 (Frankfurt: Peace Research Institute, 1993).

Acknowledgments

Innumerable institutions have supported the process which has enabled our collaborative work to deepen. In particular, mention has to be made of the Midgard Conference on "Security, Development and Cooperation in Southern Africa," held in May 1993 in Namibia, which would not have been possible without the support of the Foundation Development and Peace, Bonn. Midgard Conference not only proved an important step forward in the joint efforts to secure peace and security in Southern Africa, it also encouraged us to pursue the idea of this volume.

Many caring people contributed to the successful completion of this book. We are especially grateful to Margaret Curran (Oxford) and Gerard Holden (Frankfurt), as well as to Minnie Venter from Cape Town, who successfully tackled the task of translating and language editing. Similarly, we wish to thank Valmarie Haywood of the Centre for Southern African Studies, University of the Western Cape, who typed and re-typed drafts of various chapters, and Alexander Kelle from the Peace Research Institute Frankfurt, who prepared the typescript for publication.

The editors want to remember Norman (Shezi) Msimang who attended the Midgard Conference and who tragically perished in a car accident six weeks later. We hope that this collection will help achieve the goals for which he, and many others, have laboured.

H.-J.S.
P.V.

About the Contributors

Willie Breytenbach is professor of African Studies at the University of Stellenbosch, South Africa. In the early 1980s, he was in the Ministry of Constitutional Affairs and acted as Secretary to the Cabinet of President P.W. Botha. A graduate of the University of Pretoria, Breytenbach has published widely and consults on developments in South and Southern Africa.

Robert Davies was elected to South Africa's parliament in May 1994 for the ANC. Previously Co-Director of the Centre for Southern African Studies, University of the Western Cape, he has written widely on Southern African issues and acted as a consultant to SADC. Davies graduated in economics from Rhodes University, South Africa, and in international relations from the University of Southampton, United Kingdom. His doctorate was from the University of Sussex.

Pál Dunay is associate professor at the International Law Department, Eötvös University, Budapest. From 1989-1990 he served as legal advisor to the Hungarian delegation to the talks on Conventional Forces in Europe. He holds a doctoral degree in international law and has published extensively on conventional arms control, European security and international conflict resolution.

Ivor Richard Fung is a political affairs officer at the United Nations Department of Political Affairs; since 1992 he has been Acting Director of the United Nations Regional Centre for Peace and Disarmament in Africa. Previously, he worked as Executive Assistant to the President of the International Peace Academy in New York. He has a doctorate in international relations from Columbia University and has published on security on the African continent.

Joao Bernardo Honwana, colonel (rtd.), is a senior researcher at the Centre for Conflict Resolution, University of Cape Town, where he works on civil-military relations, the integration of armed forces and weapons proliferation in Southern Africa. Formerly a fighter pilot, he was National Commander of the Mozambican Air Force and Air Defence from 1987 to 1992. He holds an M.A. in War Studies from King's College, London.

Peter Meyns is professor of international relations and development studies at the University of Duisburg, Germany. He has frequently been to East and Southern Africa on research and teaching assignments (e.g., University of Dar es Salaam in 1968-1969; University of Zambia in 1979-1982). Chairman of the African Studies Association in Germany, he has published widely on issues of development and regional co-operation in Southern Africa.

Hans-Joachim Spanger is senior fellow at the Peace Research Institute Frankfurt. In 1987-1988 he was a research associate at the International Institute for Strategic Studies in London. He holds a doctoral degree in political science and has written several books and many articles on international security, arms control and North-South relations.

Peter Vale is a graduate of the Universities of the Witwatersrand and Leicester, and was a research associate at the International Institute for Strategic Studies, London. In the 1980s, he was Director of Research at the South African Institute of International Affairs and later a professor at Rhodes University, Grahamstown. In 1990, he became Founding Director of the Centre for Southern African Studies, University of the Western Cape. He has written extensively on Southern African issues, South African foreign policy and the theory of international relations.

1

Appreciating Updike's Syndrome: Southern African Security in the 1990s

Peter Vale

An old world is collapsing and a new world arising; we have better eyes for the collapse than for the rise, for the old one is the world we know.
John Updike

The end of communism has forged the Russian Doll: a world in which complex economic, security and political issues are embedded within others. To open one is to reveal another in a series which knows no end. A full fifty months after the Cold War divide was breached at Berlin's Friedrichstrasse, the international community is no closer to understanding the course of events—not to mention prioritising them—than it was on that exhilarating November evening in 1989. That no corner of the world was untouched by those dramatic events is the only thing we appear to know with absolute certainty.

This chapter assesses the ebb and flow of international change on Southern Africa—a region which has been profoundly affected. In order to explain the region's new security agenda, it borrows from elsewhere, but these comparisons are secondary to its Southern African interest. The argument isolates two sets of security concerns which have followed upon the crumbling of the Berlin Wall; this distinction helps both analyst and activist recognise the unfolding of events in Southern Africa and places these, where this is possible, within a theoretical perspective. But first a note about methodology.

A feature of the ending of the Cold War has been the disarray which it has caused in the ranks of social scientists, especially security buffs. In profound ways, all possible truths have been tested with the result that social science methodology has increasingly been found wanting. Established approaches to security questions have been largely overturned as both institutions and individuals have struggled to make sense of a world without the bipolar divide. This chapter is no exception to this general rule; its approach is, therefore, largely eclectic, but its central focus remains evaluating Southern African security concerns in the 1990s and beyond.

The first set of security concerns is drawn together under the rubric of international change; a second and separate rubric is global transformation. Because the difference appears hazy, it is helpful to see the first as short-term change and the second as structural shifts in international society.

International Change

The speech made by South Africa's President F.W. de Klerk on 2 February 1990, which freed the country's leaders and its politics from self-imposed deadlock, could not have been made were it not for the collapse of communism. So the ending of the Cold War has had obvious effects on Southern African affairs. But the root causes predate the events at Friedrichstrasse. The withdrawal of the Soviet Union from Southern Africa, which commenced in the mid-1980s, was an event of monumental importance. Not only did it pave the way for peace in Namibia, but it opened the path to an end to apartheid rule. De Klerk readily acknowledged all this by claiming that the series of steps which were to follow his speech signalled the triumph of market forces and the failure of socialist experiments. The ending of the Cold War and the transformation of Southern Africa, therefore, are intimately associated.

De Klerk's speech and the undertakings which followed—the unbanning of exiled political movements and the release of Nelson Mandela, to mention only two—generated huge political energy in South and Southern Africa. Within weeks, the African National Congress and the South African government were locked in a series of talks which were destined to end, more than four years later, when South Africa went to the polls. Formal talks between the chief protagonists and the negotiations themselves seemed a roller-coaster ride: each setback was portrayed as a cataclysm; each breakthrough thought to bring the country to shining success.[1] Away from this heart-stopping thrill, South Africans from every level of society were engaged in a network of intensive talks. In four years scarcely a day passed without South Africans engaging in a serious discussion on their complex socio-economic problems.

Southern African affairs were also caught up in the changing times. Political players and academics began a series of complex bilateral and multilateral interchanges of which the gathering at Midgard, which gave rise to this book, was only one in a series of meetings. The ending of the Cold War therefore generated creative responses amongst political players throughout Southern Africa. In South Africa these were measured in the abandonment of the armed struggle by the ANC and the reluctant and slow termination by South African forces of the destabilization policies which had a decade earlier brought Southern Africa to the point of collapse.

Embedded deep within the core of Southern Africa, other evidence of international change is also found. A fundamental dilemma involves the centrality of South Africa's power in the region. Had there been no apartheid, the world-wide passion associated with race discrimination would arguably not have arisen. In these circumstances, South Africa would have been relegated far from the centre of contemporary international life. This proposition obviously rests on a fragile premise, but it helps to support this important observation—South Africa is not a central player in international relations. For all practical purposes, South Africa's geographical setting has placed it far from the centres of international power. This has affected its past and promises to influence its future, as we shall see, in various ways.

It is important to enter a caveat here: Western countries protected South Africa throughout the post-World War period. This was especially so in the 1980s when the United States and the United Kingdom were particularly forgiving in the face of the widespread revolt in South Africa and the mounting evidence that the ANC was not fundamentally wedded to Soviet or any other form of communism. The central point is, however, that when sanctions were eventually imposed against South Africa, the international community scarcely blinked. There were no serious economic dislocations, no major wars and no substantial sociological fall-out. To paraphrase the American poet T.S. Eliot, South Africa's isolation occurred with a whimper, not a bang!

The importance of the racial question did, however, mean that the international community continued high-level engagement with South Africa's government. Its centrality in a series of wider international debates about the nature of race in the contemporary world enabled South Africa to play international affairs in a league far above its economic standing or geographical setting.

Let us pause here to consider this irony. The ending of the Cold War led, as we have noted, to the withdrawal of external powers from the region. This, in its own turn, amplified the appeal of regional powers. As a result, South Africa—long the chief regional tormentor—has suddenly found itself at the core of a desperate need to reconstruct Southern Africa. As the world searches for a series of answers in the aftermath of the ending of the Cold War, the race issue and the need for regional reconstruction are unlikely to disappear. Because of this, South Africa will be closely watched; and it is likely, therefore, to be continuously viewed as a symbol of race relations and regional restraint (or aggression) for years to come.

Deep within the trauma of race relations in South Africa are two central dilemmas of modern constitution-making. Both have implications for the region's security. The first involves the quandary presented by majority (and in this case, black) power and minority (here represented by whites) fear. As apartheid was contested especially in the 1970s and 1980s, this predicament was an essential part of the international propaganda over the country's future. More recently, the intense debate over South Africa's post-apartheid constitution, as in many other post-Cold War situations, reflected the almost timeless dimension of essentially the same quandary: powers of majority, rights of minorities. The second dilemma derives from the monetarist revolution of the 1980s, particularly political participation and economic opportunity. This is increasingly central in debates on the reconstruction of societies in the aftermath of the Cold War. Put within the South African context, what real hope exists that majority rule will guarantee bread on the table in a world in which the theology of the market is dominant?

The resolution of these dilemmas is tied up in a complex series of political shifts which are certain to emerge, perhaps in a decade or so, through social contract between the many parties within South African society. This, of course, does not devalue their immediate importance or mean they have no relevance for situations elsewhere. For instance, the deepening cry of discrimination in Brazil, where direct accusations of apartheid are linked to questions of exploitation, are increasingly commonplace.

If Southern Africa is a symbol of racial conflict, it has also become a symbol of post-Cold War efforts to peacefully settle conflicts. The liberation of Namibia is the definitive case: long portrayed as an intractable conflict between the races over wealth, power and South Africa's regional ambitions, the conflict over the status of South West Africa was resolved by careful diplomacy. Of course, the agreement between the superpowers to withdraw from the region helped speed the Namibian outcome. Additionally and crucial for the region's security,

Namibia's decolonization coincided with the ending of the Cold War. The deepening convergence of interests and the relative lack of "new" international issues made it easy to settle in Namibia. Emerging political plurality and the potency of market forces was not still tarnished by the series of events which were to come to Bosnia and the Soviet Union. This is why the emergence of Namibia as an international player must surely be regarded as an archetypal "end of history" settlement.

Understandably, the hopes engendered by the Namibian experience were projected on neighbouring South Africa; however, the course of the political settlement in this country has been less smooth and uncertainty more politically charged. For one thing, the deteriorating security circumstances in Bosnia and elsewhere and the economic strains felt in other transforming societies directly inform debates around South Africa's search for peaceful outcomes. Chiefly, however, efforts to settle the South African conflict have revived the spectre that at the very base of regional tension lies the question of ethnicity. If this is so, then Southern Africa—again, through the South African issue—becomes a symbol of world-wide ethnic conflict. The ending of the Cold War has yielded a new set of realities around the question of ethnicity. A recent study observes that

> the drive towards ethnic-national self-determination is one of the greatest challenges facing the international community in the 1990s. From the Balkans to Burma, from the Caucasus to the Horn of Africa, communal groups are asserting claims of self-determination by force.[2]

Three structural issues will play into efforts to resolve the tensions associated with ethnicity in Southern Africa. First, the region has a variegated collection of groupings within its boundaries and they speak a rich variety of languages. If Southern Africa is to find peace, these groupings will have to find a place in its political mosaic. Secondly—and almost more importantly—the region, through apartheid, has an unhappy history of using ethnicity as a principle of political organisation. Addressing this—another of apartheid's devastating legacies—will take courage and vision. Thirdly and most destructively, the region's ethnic mix has been made a lethal cocktail by the proliferation of weapons. This, too, is a reflection of what is happening elsewhere where the combination of political passion and weapons have crowded out peaceful efforts to solve conflict.

In Southern Africa the fusion of ethnic rights with the right to self-determination has created much confusion around the idea of "democracy." Southern Africa's problem—a universal one, to be sure—is how to define political communities; this, too, poses a threat to its security. Both groupings in South Africa—the Inkatha movement and the white right, for example—assert the right to self-determination on the basis of ethnic separateness. This approach is tied to a list of determining features: extraction, language, religion, culture.[3] In their theoretical setting, these should both set people apart and bequeath to them separate institutions and organs of government. The obstacle is that inevitably they are too narrowly defined.[4] As a result, they exclude peoples from other groupings who live in the same territory and, conversely, incorporate members of the same grouping who do not wish to be part of the community. These undemocratic forces of ethnicity are not conducive to the purported desire for democracy in Southern Africa. But opinions over the vitality of ethnicity within South Africa differ. An astute observer, van Zyl Slabbert, writes that the country has

> a surprisingly low level of racial and ethnic intensity. If anything, ethnic mobilization in South Africa tends to correspond to the paraphernalia of traditionalism rather than the technological advantages of modernity.[5]

Were this not the case, the physical map of the region might be programmed to change. Like the Soviet Union, South Africa might collapse under the strain of pressures for ethnic self-determination. A linked concern is that individual Southern African countries—Lesotho is a good example, as we shall see—might be absorbed into a greater South Africa. Through all this, the shifting currency of sovereignty—another feature of the ending of the Cold War—has played into the security calculations of Southern Africa. To understand the wider importance of this to the region, however, we must shift our focus to the second set of security concerns.

Global Transformation

Evidence of the ending of the Cold War is everywhere to be found. But the crumbling of the Berlin Wall itself—like the ending of communism—was little more than a line in the sand. Actually, the tell-tale signs of deep change in the international system were to be seen in the furthest corners of global society as early as the mid-1970s. In Southern Africa, as we have noted, a series of theoretical and practical concerns over sovereignty and self-determination raged throughout the 1980s. The intensity of the conflict between these in the region has been compounded in the 1990s by three political shibboleths.

The first is the belief that the borders of the region are unchallengeable. In Africa this was canonised by the Organization of African Unity, which ruled that colonial borders were inviolate. As a result, African countries have struggled to keep together under the most debilitating circumstances even when, as in Biafra, their people suffered huge deprivation.

Secondly, the widely held view is to be taken into account that irredentist pressures in Southern Africa are all purely indigenous and, therefore, that they represent deep-seated fractures in the politics of the region. The propagation of at least three political movements—Inkatha, Renamo and UNITA—in the region in the 1980s were the result of extra-regional involvement: primarily, the use of the region as a site for Cold War conflicts. Reaching accommodation with these three movements has proved immensely difficult and, at the time of writing, there seems no evidence that this can be achieved. Legacies of the Cold War therefore promise to linger in Southern Africa—as they have elsewhere, incidentally—for decades.

The third myth is almost uniquely South African and has its roots in the first two: that the primary goal after the ending of apartheid is to build a nation-state. This, as we have already explored, leads to the continuing, confusing and often contradictory debate over the most appropriate constitutional arrangement. But at its very edges, the same debate extends beyond South Africa's borders touching the viability—even necessity—of smaller states in Southern Africa. The best example of this has been the debate over the future of Lesotho which, in January 1994, led to conflict in that country. In essence, Lesotho's sovereign future turns on two near-irreconcilable questions. In a world in which the currency of sovereignty is on the wane, would not the country's best option be to join South Africa? But given South Africa's own messy transition might it not be better to sustain the country's independence as far as this is possible?[6]

This debate over Lesotho's future would be aimless if the physical borders of Southern Africa were secure. Often little more than lines on a map, the bypassing of border-controls is fast developing into one of the region's most serious security issues. Faced with war—especially in Mozambique and Angola—and deep-seated change, Southern Africa's people have responded in a time-honoured way. They are voting with their feet. This move has engendered a range of parallel concerns, many of which are subterranean: the killer diseases—malaria, TB and AIDS (this order is important in the Southern African context)—are crossing borders at an alarming rate. And the region's cities, originally designed to accommodate colonial governments only, are growing at an equal speed. Their size and their hold on the politics of the countries in which they are situated is often indirectly proportional to their capacity to administer themselves. Southern Africa's cities are a cause for long-term insecurity in every sense.

But the inherently destabilizing features of migration are to be found elsewhere in the region. Here, the destructive seepage of small arms across the region's borders is a central concern. While weapon proliferation has become a feature of the post-Cold War world, its manifestation in Southern Africa has threatened to destroy the entire process of change. Put bluntly, there is simply no way to ensure that a weapon which is used in the killing fields of Mozambique's southern province of Maputoland has not been used in the violence of South Africa's Natal province. In this, Southern Africa's openness to international trade weakens it—the region has become a target in the global arms trade with a chain of arms-traders up Africa's east coast from the Cape to Somalia.

In many important ways, the proliferation of arms feeds the ambitions of dissident movements. There can be no more potent regional cocktail than the ambitions of a power- and ethnically inspired demagogue who has access to small arms. This is the combination of circumstances, as we have seen in the former Yugoslavia, which turns the right to differ into the fight to differ. Ominously, there seem no possible means available to develop even crude control mechanisms. In Southern Africa, efforts to achieve this during transitional periods have been subjected to intense political pressures. Only a legitimate government with the necessary recourse to law and its effective enforcement may be able to ensure gun control in South Africa. The qualification is important. As the American lesson so graphically teaches, gun control reaches into every possible corner of a national psyche.

As is happening in Eastern Europe, efforts to stem the control of arms bump up against another legacy of the Cold War—the local arms industry. South Africa developed an important and technologically sophisticated arms industry.[7] Hopes that the new government would find the will to break up the arms industry seem to have been thwarted by the understanding that this industry represents an important asset in the country's industrial armoury. South Africa, it now seems certain, will continue to sell weapons on the international market.

The final issue in this triangle of defence and military related security concerns touches on the future of the region's armies. Although dwarfed by South Africa's military power, the countries of the region represent a potent force. That this military is skewed towards land-based forces makes its adaptation immensely difficult. Within South Africa itself, the intense debate over the redirection of the country's military forces has concentrated on the army with little or no attention paid to the future mission of the air-force and the navy. Obviously, it is these latter arms of the service which could assist with the wider issue of national development.

Little of the debate on the future of the region's security has been devoted to the emerging issues around human security. In this area, the region is at odds with work elsewhere in the world. The crumbling of the Berlin Wall has hastened the redirection of security studies away from the strictly military. Attention has moved towards the issues of the global commons: managing the wider questions which face the planet at the end of this millennium. Closely linked to this are the series of issues which impinge on the emerging paradigm of global human security—"the absence of threat to human life, lifestyle and culture through the fulfilment of basic needs."[8] These two thrusts confirm the observation that

> many old concepts must now be radically revised. Security should be reinterpreted as security for people, not security for land. Development must be woven around people, not people around development—and it should empower individuals and groups rather than disempower them. And development cooperation should focus directly on people, not just on nation states.[9]

In Southern Africa, these "new" security issues have been mainly ignored as analysts and activists have grappled to create the means to "manage" traditional security concerns. Even more alarming has been the singular determination of the region's academic community to ignore the longer term as they grapple to engineer short-term changes in favour of retaining large military establishments. But making the necessary political accommodation for long-range security issues within Southern Africa is inevitable. In this region, as in other parts of the world, global change will have profound implications beyond the immediate. To these long-term challenges we finally turn.

The Challenge of Co-operation

A central and primary concern in securing Southern Africa's future is improving regional communications. This is a manifold problem which will require a directed multilateral approach. The region's communications are weak; currently, the most reliable means of transport is a century-old rail network, which reaches from Cape Town to the banks of the Zaire River. It is augmented by an electricity grid which has a similar reach but which, like the railway lines, is under the domination of South Africa. Regional airlines are poor and unpredictable. And more importantly, they run on north-south axes; this makes it devilishly expensive and time-consuming to cross the region in an east-west direction. The telephone lines run on similar axes. It is easier (and far quicker) to telephone London or New York from Cape Town than Dar es Salaam or Nairobi. As a result, intra-regional co-operation is difficult. Existing networks around which regular international intercourse turn are dated and, because so, the region is further impoverished. More modern means of communication associated with the miracle of the microchip are imperative if the region is to secure its long-term future.

This sense of weakness is confirmed by the overall understanding that, in very obvious ways, Southern Africa is increasingly marginalized from the international mainstream. In part, this is the product of the region's distance from centres of international power, but, more probably, it lies in the scarcity of resources and in the region's poorly-skilled manpower. Add to this the overall lack of resources devoted to research and development and it is obvious why science and technology in the region is impoverished. This, in turn, fails to nourish the region's industrialized base and, in the face of huge advances made elsewhere, Southern Africa's competitiveness falls further and further behind. This overall pattern of weak development potential is fostered by the region's overall demographical profile skewed towards a youth which is increasingly poorly trained.

The necessity for economic restructuring is aggravated by the adoption, throughout the region, of Structural Adjustment Programmes (SAP). In the main, these have been the result of economic strictures from the International Monetary Fund and the World Bank. In some cases—South Africa throughout its transition is the best example—these have been followed upon government policy. The marriage of SAPs to the demands for multi-party democracy throughout the region have put already weak states under even greater political pressure, as Zambia so graphically demonstrates. In this case, both the demands of structural adjustment and the thrust towards multi-partyism was little more than a rearrangement of existing elites. Like many other countries in Southern Africa, Zambia's road to functioning democracy and economic prosperity promises to be much longer than the simplistic formulae offered by the international financial institutions. The country's poor terms of trade and the depressed prices in international commodities plus the ravages of a devastating regional drought have made life difficult for all Zambia's people.

The tragedy is manifold; while elites can comfortably rearrange themselves, real hardship is visited on the lower end of the social strata with, almost inevitably, women and children suffering most acutely. The much hoped-for salvation from civil society has not assisted the poorest and most vulnerable in Zambia nor, as things now stand, will they be positioned to do so.

Here, the theory of multi-partyism and its practise are at odds. There are no easy panaceas for Southern Africa's acute security problems. Take, for instance, the view that the universities will be the possible cornerstone of a democratic renaissance. Outside of South Africa, the region's universities are weak institutions which face, as universities all over the world, a triad of demands—"declining real resources; greater number of academically under-prepared students; the need to prepare an elite capable of leading the country into an internationally competitive economy."[10] The endemic weakness of civil society is deeply rooted throughout the states of Southern Africa. The challenge is to find ways to strengthen it.

Ironically, as elsewhere in the world, it is only in pockets where civil society has taken root; serious questions are raised over the acceptability of particular "kinds" of civil society. Take, as an instructive case, the debate over Islam—a debate which, in Southern Africa certainly, is still in its dormancy. The region's Moslems have shown very little of the virulence which has marked strains of Islam in the Middle East in particular. And yet, neither analysts nor activists are encouraged to believe that Islam is an integral part of a wider agglomeration of civil society which is, to use a dictionary definition to make the point, "spontaneous, customary and not dependent on the law."[11]

But the hand of Islam on the future course of events in Southern Africa is uncertain. The tension in Tanzania over the future of Zanzibar's union with the mainland, which ostensibly turns on the capacity of Zanzibar to pursue a foreign policy independent of Tanganyika, may be the spark which will ignite the flame of militant Islam in the region. If it is drawn closer to the state in any country in the region, it is no longer independent of the law. When this happens, does Islam cease to be part of civil society? The conceptual challenge is, therefore, both to demarcate and understand the social phenomenon around which policies are to be constructed.

The near-epistemological question closes in many ways the circle; the ending of the Cold War has generated great confusion, because it has overturned so many accepted values and ways of approaching scholarship. And yet there are deep ructions underway in Southern Africa, as this chapter has suggested. These will not stand still as analysts and activists adjust their theoretical lenses. We shall not and cannot immediately know the full effects of these because the region, as the rest of the world, is caught between two historical moments. The eyes of analysts and of activists catch sight of the habitual and miss, because of their unfamiliarity, the new issues which will dog the region's path to prosperity, or disaster. This we may call the Updike Syndrome for the lines that stand at the head of this chapter.

Journal articles are last year's news, and books—like this collection—often ancient history. What we know about the ending of the Cold War, we are learning in news-magazines. We are sure of nothing; only that the world is in the throes of a profound reordering—a reordering, perhaps, of its very purpose. The changes which have accompanied the ending of the

Cold War must teach Southern Africans that the future is not what it once promised.

As they regroup, the region's people may come to learn that their search for security started not in prehistory; nor with the arrival of white settlers; nor with mining capital; nor with the formation in 1912 of the ANC; nor with the sentencing of Nelson Mandela to 27 years imprisonment; nor with the collapse of Portuguese colonialism; nor with the victory of Robert Mugabe's ZAPU in the former Rhodesia; nor with the election of F.W. de Klerk as South Africa's President. Southern Africa's history—its people may one day discover—began with the collapse of the Berlin Wall.

Notes

1. These thoughts are drawn from Peter Vale, "Riding the South African Roller-coaster," *New Zealand International Review*, Vol. 17, No. 4 (July/August 1992), pp. 9-12.

2. Kamal S. Shehadi, *Ethnic Self-determination and the Break-up of States*, Adelphi Papers 283 (London: The International Institute for Strategic Studies, 1993), p. 3.

3. *Ibid.*, pp. 5-6.

4. See, for instance, Stephen I. Griffiths, *Nationalism and Ethnic Conflict: Threats to European Security*, Research Report, No. 5 (Stockholm: Stockholm International Peace Research Institute, 1993), p. 13.

5. Frederick van Zyl Slabbert, "Five Ways to Make it in a New SA," *IDASA Annual Report*, 1993, p. 6.

6. See "No Sudden Shifts," *The Sunday Tribune* (Durban), 30 January 1994.

7. See, for example, J. K. Celliers, *To Sell or Die: The Future of the South African Defence Industry*, ISSUP Bulletin, No. 1 (Pretoria: University of Pretoria, 1994).

8. *The Bonn Declaration*, European Parliamentarians Conference: Building Global Human Security, Bonn, 17-18 September 1993 (mimeo.), p. 1.

9. *Human Development Report 1993* (New York: United Nations Development Programme, 1993), p. 1.

10. Robert Klitgaard, "Universities Must 'Begin at the End,' " *Democracy-in-Action*, Vol. 8, No. 1, 1994, p. 16.

11. Roger Scrunton, *A Dictionary of Political Thought* (London: Pan Books in association with Macmillan Press, 1982), p. 66.

2

Regional Economic Co-operation and the Development Challenge in Southern Africa

Robert Davies

Southern Africa entered the 1990s as a region plagued by economic stagnation and growing immiseration for many of its peoples. Statistical evidence indicates that:

- Rates of growth of real Gross Domestic Product (GDP) fell over the course of the decade 1980-1990 to levels below population growth in South Africa and eight of the ten member countries of the Southern African Development Community (SADC) (Table 2.1 in the appendix to this chapter);
- The daily calorie intake per person, which rose in all countries in the region between 1965 and 1980, fell in at least seven SADC member countries between 1980 and 1989 (Table 2.2);
- Only two countries (South Africa and Botswana) made even the lower half of the "medium human development" category of the UNDP's Human Development Index for 1990. Occupying 85th and 104th places in a list of 173 countries, these were both ranked well below countries like Mauritius, Seychelles, Colombia, Syria and Suriname. The remaining nine SADC member countries were in the "low human development" category, occupying places between 117

(Swaziland) and 160 (Angola). Moreover, in the case of South Africa and five SADC member countries, the ranking in terms of the Human Development Index was below that in terms of Gross National Product (Table 2.3).

There is clearly no single factor that accounts for the poor economic performance reflected in such figures. Changes in the world economy in the period since the mid-1970s had a major impact on all countries dependent on primary product exports, including those in Southern Africa. Inappropriate policies and strategies in the face of these changes and poor governance also contributed to the particularly disastrous impact which these changes had on the whole of Sub-Saharan Africa—although it should be noted that there is by no means unanimity over precisely what is understood by "inappropriate policies" or "poor governance." However, whatever the impacting factors which Southern Africa had in common with the rest of the continent or indeed the rest of "the South," there was also an additional factor: the socio-economic crisis confronting the region in the 1990s was a product, too, of violent conflict deriving from the application of a particular security doctrine by South Africa in the 1980s.

Pretoria's security doctrine and conduct in the Southern African region in the 1980s have been documented elsewhere and need not be discussed in any detail here.[1] Prompted by the changing balance of forces in the region after the collapse of the Portuguese African empire and the gathering liberation struggle inside South Africa itself, Pretoria responded to what it perceived as a "total onslaught" by launching a "total strategy" to reassert its hegemony in the region. Unable to entice the rest of the region into a Constellation of Southern African States, South Africa came to rely increasingly on escalating aggression directed against other neighbouring states. This involved at various times conventional military incursions, economic sanctions and other forms of hostile pressure. But the most significant and persistent feature of the strategy was the application of the technique of covert or contra warfare. Rebel movements were sponsored or supported and actual or potential social contradictions in target states were deliberately exacerbated in the belief that by weakening what were seen as adversaries, the embattled apartheid state would strengthen its own security.

The United Nations Economic Commission for Africa (ECA) has estimated that 1.5 million people died between 1980 and 1988 in Angola and Mozambique alone as a direct or indirect result of Pretoria-sponsored wars. While these two countries bore the brunt of this assault, all SADC member states were affected to some degree and the ECA estimates that economic and military aggression cost the then nine SADC member states the equivalent of 62.45 billion US dollars.[2]

In addition to causing considerable direct damage, the climate of conflict and hostility in the 1980s also had a number of less immediately evident socio-economic effects. Large numbers of people were displaced by wars in Angola and Mozambique, and a refugee movement was spawned which rapidly spread across the sub-continent. There were over a million Mozambican refugees in other SADC countries at the beginning of the 1990s, while a further 200,000 to 300,000 had secured some limited protection in the South African "homelands" of kaNgwane and Gazankulu. 300,000 Angolans had sought refuge in Zaire, 100,000 in Zambia and 40,000 in Namibia in the period before the signing of the 1991 Bicesse ceasefire accord (i.e., before the impact of the resumption of fighting after the September 1992 elections).[3] Military expenditure also rose appreciably across the region and in the most extreme cases—Angola and Mozambique—came to account for over 40% of total state expenditure by the end of the 1980s.

At the level of the regional economy, the period following the mid-1970s also saw patterns of economic interaction modified to the disadvantage of SADC member-states. In particular, South Africa reduced its involvement in two important relationships in which it had historically been involved as a buyer and thus as a provider of revenue to other countries—migrant labour and transport. In the case of the former, the proportion of "foreign" workers in the South African mine labour force (the largest employer of foreign migrant workers) declined from over 60% in 1975 to around 40% by the mid-1980s. The absolute numbers of nationals from SADC member countries employed in the mines declined from over 220,000 in 1975 to around 165,000 by 1991.[4] In transport, the period saw both a decline in South Africa's use of facilities in other regional states and an attempt by South African Transport Services (SATS) to divert traffic from landlocked countries which had historically used the services of other regional states. South African traffic through Maputo was cut to around 15% of pre-independence levels, while regional traffic passing through South African ports increased to a maximum of one-and-a-half times the level of 1981-1982 by 1984-1985.

Once again, the reasons for these changes were complex. Some factors derived from trends in accumulation in South Africa. Workers' struggles in the mining industry, growing unemployment and the need to increase labour productivity to maintain profitability under conditions of declining average grades of ore combined to promote greater mechanisation of labour processes. This led to an overall reduction in demand for unskilled labour and a policy of giving greater priority to internal South African sources of labour. In the transport sector, the need to recoup investments made in containerisation of South African ports in the 1970s provided a strong impulse to seek new customers for South African transport facilities.

These were not the only factors, however. An essential component of Pretoria's "total strategy" envisaged manipulating economic relations for strategic purposes. Both migrant labour and transport services were subjected to considerable political manipulation as part of Pretoria's response to the changing regional balance of forces. The effects of the cutback in labour recruitment were not spread evenly among supplier states. Mozambique—seen as a major adversary—was made to bear a disproportional burden, with the numbers of Mozambicans employed in the mines falling in two years from a maximum of 118,000 in 1975 to a minimum of around 40,000. Mozambique was also the only supplier state to be subjected to a specific ban. Imposed in October 1986, this prevented (until it was lifted in October 1988) both the recruitment of Mozambican novices and the renewal of contracts by certain categories of already contracted mineworkers. Political manipulation was even greater in the case of transport services. While "economic measures" (particularly "special contract rates" which offered substantial discounts) played some role in bringing about a transfer of regional traffic flows to the South African network, the major factor was undoubtedly the sabotage of facilities in Mozambique and Angola by South African-backed surrogate forces.

The socio-economic landscape of Southern Africa has, in short, been deeply scarred by a security doctrine premised on the notion that security in one country (apartheid South Africa) would be enhanced by engendering insecurity elsewhere. Not only did this doctrine fail to achieve its apparent intended objective, but it has now become evident that its effects are continuing to rebound negatively on security throughout the entire region, including on the major author of this insecurity, South Africa itself.

One stark example of this is the escalating mass migration of people across the subcontinent. This is no longer confined to movements of people fleeing from wars. Unemployment, stagnation and lack of economic opportunity have led to a significant increase in clandestine "economic migration" from the most to the less impoverished parts of the sub-continent. There are now movements of Angolans to Namibia, of Zambians to Zimbabwe and Botswana and, increasingly, of persons from all over the region and wider continent to South Africa. As far as the movement into South Africa is concerned, no reliable figures are available for anything other than deportations. According to official sources, 61,345 "illegal aliens" were deported from South Africa in 1991—47,074 being Mozambicans and 7,174 Zimbabweans.[5] By the end of 1992, the rate of deportations had risen to over 6,000 a month, bringing the total for the year to over 80,000.[6] These figures are clearly only the tip of the iceberg. Many thousands more succeed in entering South Africa, despite having to run the gauntlet of electric fences, military patrols and the like. Unofficial estimates put the total number of citizens of neighbouring countries in South Africa at anything up to two million, meaning that clandestine or illegal migration to South Africa already involves many more people than legal migration to the mines.

Another consequence both of insecurity and economic stagnation has been the proliferation of arms and drugs smuggling. The AK-47 and the mandrax tablet are now among the most common items in the region's "unrecorded trade," probably contributing in some measure to evening up the acute imbalance in recorded trade in the region.

Under such circumstances, the challenge facing Southern Africa can be simply put: the vicious cycle of poverty and insecurity into which the region was plunged in the 1980s needs to be transformed into a virtuous circle of growth, development and security.[7] Southern Africa needs peace and security in order to create a climate conducive to sustained economic growth and development. But it needs simultaneously to find immediate solutions to a number of urgent development problems if it is to improve the security climate and bring about a much needed transfer of resources from bloated military and security budgets.

The Development Challenge

Development is a notoriously slippery concept. It is generally recognized as referring to an improvement of the human condition in all its aspects—economic, social, educational, intellectual and security. The UNDP's Human Development Index represents an important attempt to conceptualize and measure development, essentially by refining conventional GDP per capita measurements to take account of income distribution, levels of nutrition, literacy and education. Development is then a broader concept than economic growth. Economic growth refers to an increase in the output of goods and services. While growth is a necessary condition for development in countries characterized by poverty and underdevelopment, it is not sufficient. It is quite possible for there to be growth without development, or for there to be great disparities between the rate of growth and its impact on development. As UNDP puts it, "The issue is not only how much economic growth but what kind of growth."[8]

Southern Africa clearly needs to be placed on a development-oriented growth path if it is to address the socio-economic causes of future potential security problems and create the climate of peace and security essential for sustained economic growth. Within a comparatively short space of time, the region needs to find programmes and policies that will significantly increase employment, raise living standards and address urgent problems of housing, education and health. Unless there are pronounced improvements in all these areas across the subcontinent, insecurity in the form of violence, large scale migration, and drugs and arms smuggling must be expected to continue and possibly even to increase. This would, in turn, rebound negatively on the "investment climate" and hence the prospects for economic growth.

Southern Africa needs to achieve all this, moreover, in a changed and changing global context. Technological developments have decisively changed the terms of trade against traditional raw materials. With autarchy no real option and conventional import substitution industrialization programmes looking increasingly unable to generate sufficient growth, all the countries of the region face the challenge of finding new ways to engage more effectively with the world economy—at a time when the "rules of the game" are being changed in a highly uneven and partisan way by the countries of the industrialized North.

All of this, in turn, needs to be viewed against the background of the impact of at least the first generation of Structural Adjustment Programmes (SAPs). Since the mid-1980s, most of the present SADC member countries have found themselves obliged to implement IMF and World Bank approved Structural Adjustment Programmes. These have sought to promote macro-stability through a standard package of sharp currency devaluations, state budget cuts and the withdrawal of subsidies. They have also sought to reduce the role of the state in the economy, "free" markets from what have been seen as distortions created by policy interventions and enlarge the space for private sector entrepreneurship. While credited in a number of cases with contributing to some measure of economic growth, the implementation of SAPs has invariably been accompanied by a widening of social differentials, pressure on the living standards, particularly of the urban poor, and cuts in social expenditure. The Final Report of the United Nations Programme of Action for African Economic Recovery and Development is extremely instructive in this regard. Published in 1991, it concluded that Africa was in a worse state in 1991 than it had been five years earlier, despite the provision of some 128 billion US dollars to support SAPs. According to this report, real per capita income continued to fall by an annual average of 0.7%, while rates of illiteracy, mortality and debt all continued to rise. Expenditure on education fell from a continental average of 6% of government spending in 1985 to only 5% in 1990, partly as a consequence of the overall failure to promote sufficient growth and partly as a direct result of "the adjustment policies of cost-recovery and containment." Health spending likewise fell by a full percent. 30 million more people were unemployed in 1990 than in 1985, and "on average real wages declined by over 30% in the 1980s, in some countries the decline being as steep as 75-80%." The latter, concluded the report, "was partly due to structural adjustment policy measures aimed at reducing the government wage bill and correcting perceived rural-urban distortions."[9]

The Potential Role of Regional Co-operation

What, then, could regional economic co-operation contribute towards meeting the development challenge facing Southern Africa? Two realities of current regional economic relations are immediately pertinent in this regard.

The first is that Southern Africa is already a region in much more than a mere geographic sense of that term. As Immanuel Wallerstein and Sergio Vieira have argued, Southern Africa has been a "social construct" since the third quarter of the nineteenth century.[10] During the period of colonial rule a distinct regional political economy was forged with identifiable structures, patterns of relations and institutions. South Africa and most of the present SADC member states were drawn into it (although in very different ways), and participation in the regional economy came to be of major importance to the domestic economies of several countries. Access to sources of labour, markets and resources in neighbouring countries all contributed significantly to the accumulation process in South Africa. Lesotho, Mozambique, Malawi, Botswana and Swaziland all became dependent for a substantial part of their foreign exchange earnings on transfers from citizens working in South Africa. Traffic passing through Mozambique's ports provided that country with another major portion of its convertible currency earnings. Customs revenue, allocated to the BLNS countries under the Southern African Customs Union (SACU) agreement, came to account for a sizable portion of these countries' total state revenue—over 50% in the most extreme case of Lesotho. Although these relations came under strain during the period of conflict in the 1980s, the essential regionality of Southern Africa has remained intact. The programmes and policies of the SADCC, as it then was, while aiming to reduce ties of dependence on South Africa, were premised on strengthening co-operation among member states, and the degree to which ties with South Africa were actually reduced was in fact modest.

The second important reality, already implicit in the above description of patterns of participation, is that the Southern African regional economy is characterized by great unevennesses and by acute imbalances and disparities. Essentially, the principal poles of accumulation came to be located in South Africa (and to a lesser extent in Zimbabwe), while the other territories became incorporated in subsidiary roles as labour reserves, markets for South African commodities, suppliers of certain services (such as transport) or providers of cheap and convenient resources (like water, electricity and some raw materials). South Africa's visible exports to the rest of the region exceed imports by a factor of more than 5:1. This is not only a product of the stronger productive base of the South African economy; protective tariffs and non-tariff barriers of various kinds have kept goods produced in regional states out of the South African market—even goods produced in other SACU member countries enjoying a hypothetical right of unrestricted access to the South African market.[11]

The acute imbalances and inequities in the existing regional economy have been seen as a barrier to development in SADC member countries. The original founding declaration of SADCC identified incorporation "by metropolitan powers, colonial rulers and large corporations into the colonial and sub-colonial structures centering in general on the Republic of South Africa" as antithetical to "the development of national economies as balanced units...[and] the welfare of the people of Southern Africa."[12] Moreover, as we have already seen, these relations were subjected to further distortions to the detriment of SADC member countries during the period of conflict and destabilization in the 1980s. The net effect is that relations between South Africa and the other countries of Southern Africa are now not only inequitable but are becoming increasingly unsustainable in the old moulds. The current pattern of trade, for example, has been described as selling overpriced goods for hard currency.[13] The gap between the prices of increasingly uncompetitive South African goods and those of comparable goods from elsewhere has widened, while invisible earnings from the provision of services to South Africa (including migrant labour remittances, revenue from transport services and sales of hydropower) have all declined.

Expected political change in South Africa has led to a growing consensus that the forging of closer economic relations between the countries of Southern Africa, including a "post-apartheid" South Africa, could potentially contribute significantly to growth and development. Certainly, several areas in which closer relations could be of benefit can readily be identified. Increased trade with the rest of the region could be of considerable significance for South Africa's manufacturing industries. Although that country's exports to African countries (other than members of the Southern African Customs Union) made up only 8.8% of its total exports in 1992, over 70% of these exports consisted of products in seven categories comprising largely manufactured goods (foodstuffs and beverages; chemical products; plastics and rubber products; articles of base metals; machinery and appliances; vehicles and related and miscellaneous manufactured goods). In some of these cases, exports were a sizeable portion in the category concerned—26.8% of exports of foodstuffs and beverages; 25.5% of chemical products; 45.7% of plastics and rubber products; 10.8% of products of base minerals; 43% of machinery and appliances; 24% of vehicles and 33.3% of miscellaneous manufactures.[14] An increase in this trade could thus provide an important boost to South African manufactured exports.

Other countries, too, could benefit from expanding their exports to South Africa. At present, only Zimbabwe and some of the BLNS countries, foremost among them Swaziland, have more than a token presence in the South African market. Zimbabwean exports have, moreover, declined sharply in recent months—by over 20% from 586 million rand in the four months January-April 1992 to 463 million rand in the corresponding period of 1993.[15] This is at least partly due to the delay in reaching agreement on a new bilateral trade agreement, itself a reflection of a strong underlying protectionist stance towards potential imports from the region. If this were to change, however, agricultural and industrial producers in several neighbouring countries could receive an important boost.

Co-operation in regional construction, infrastructural and resource development projects could also be of considerable benefit. Projects would be of immediate benefit to the countries in which they are located, and the construction process could offer important business to contracting firms. In several cases, notably that of potential water and hydropower projects in several SADC member states, these will not be economically viable unless they can count on exports to South Africa. At the same time, South Africa would benefit in environmental terms by importing hydropower and could well become absolutely dependent on water imports from other countries in the years ahead.[16]

Beyond this, closer regional economic co-operation could establish a firmer basis for more effective participation in the world economy. Southern Africa remains an extremely small player in global terms. Table 2.4 shows that the combined GDP of South Africa and SADC member countries was a little over half a percent of world GDP—roughly equal to that of a country like Finland. All of the individual countries of Southern Africa confront the objective necessity to restructure their economies in the face of a changing global economy, and in particular to reduce their dependence on primary product exports by becoming more significant exporters of manufactured goods. They face the challenge, moreover, of having to do this in a global situation characterized not only by huge disparaties of economic power, but also by the existence of structured disadvantages for less developed countries.

It has been argued that, under these circumstances, a more integrated Southern African regional economy would benefit all the countries and peoples of Southern Africa in at least the following ways:

- by allowing certain economies of scale which will facilitate restructuring at a higher level of productivity;
- by creating a climate conducive to raising levels of investment and encouraging investment in new forms of production;
- by helping to create the kind of competitive environment likely to facilitate innovation;
- by encouraging a rationalization of investments in infrastructure and creating economies of scale which make infrastructural projects economically viable;
- by helping to strengthen the bargaining position of the countries of the region in an asymmetrical world;
- by promoting the freer movement of human resources and thereby increasing output and productivity.[17]

These considerations are generally accepted throughout the region. What is more contentious is the approach to be adopted in attempting to realize such potential benefits which has been underscored by the political changes in South Africa and that country's impending acceptance as a full and legitimate partner by the rest of the region. This has brought to the fore such critical questions as: will the region be able to formulate a realistic development-orientated growth programme, and what role will a democratic South Africa play in the region?

Any examination of the state of the South African economy should rapidly dispel notions of that country emerging as either the saviour or benefactor of the region. As indicated earlier, the South African economy remains enmeshed in the deepest recession since the end of World War II, which has highlighted deep structural problems of the post-war growth path. Moreover, a democratic government will have to address appalling problems of poverty, inequality and social deprivation, in many cases on a par with those encountered elsewhere in the region. On the other hand, both South Africa and other countries stand to benefit from closer ties within the region. The potential benefits from expanded trade and co-operation have already been mentioned. South Africa will also be negatively affected by insecurity generated by economic stagnation in neighbouring countries, and the current pattern of relations—selling overpriced goods for hard currency—provides no basis on which to build a long-term expanding relationship.

Within South Africa, at least three approaches appear to have emerged, each involving some tradeoffs between potential benefits and costs.[18] The first could be described as *neo-mercantilism*. It would involve South Africa acting to promote its own partisan and immediately evident interests, while remaining resistant to the needs and demands of the rest of the region, and indifferent to the longer-term implications of reproducing or exacerbating existing imbalances or inequities. Its main policy thrust would involve one-sidedly seeking to "penetrate African markets" and gain access to profitable contracts or ventures in neighbouring countries, while being resistant or lukewarm to admitting additional imports from, or addressing other concerns of, the rest of the region. It would imply standing aloof from regional organizations, other than those controlled by South Africa, and might also involve "playing hardball" in bilateral negotiations, e.g., over the allocation of SACU revenue or the migrant labour issue. This in many ways describes the nightmare of the rest of the region. One of the factors underlying the current thrust towards bilateral relations with the authorities in South Africa is a belief that pressures from a domestic constituency for jobs and funds could lead the democratic government to adopt just such an insular approach.

From a broader South as well as Southern African standpoint, the danger inherent in such a path is that it could have a number of "boomerang" effects, which might not immediately be felt but which could well rebound on South Africa later. A failure to address the concerns of the region about unbalanced trade could, for instance, provoke retaliatory action that might significantly undercut the potential contribution of regional and continental trade to growth and development. Importers even in long established regional markets for South African goods could turn to suppliers from outside the region. This could be hastened if a democratic South Africa were seen to be interested merely in promoting one-way trade. The experience of Zimbabwe in SADC markets could also be cited as relevant in this regard. The adoption by Zimbabwe of a restrictionist attitude towards imports from Botswana in the late 1980s not only sharply undercut Zimbabwe's exports to that country but also fuelled a negative reputation which had an impact on sales to other "traditional" markets like Zambia and Malawi. And after all, a "neo-mercantilist" approach would be the path least compatible with promoting a new non-militaristic and co-operative approach to regional security.

A second possible approach could be described as *hegemonistic bilateralism*. This would, in principle, be compatible with a greater degree of sensitivity to some of the immediate needs and demands of the rest of the region, but would tend to be rather lukewarm about making commitments to a regional programme or regional organizations. Such an approach would clearly be better than "neo-mercantilism" and would be quite compatible with some accommodation, on a bilateral basis, of some of the needs and demands of other countries. The problem with such an approach is that it is likely to fall short of the needs of regional reconstruction and development. It would also send out wrong signals to regional partners and may well fuel hegemonistic behaviour. The reluctance to become part of organizations established by the rest of the region would not only send out a signal that a democratic South Africa intended unilaterally to set the terms of a regional programme, it would also mean not becoming involved in structures and forums which have an essential role to play in institutional reform and development. It might also mean that in practise South African-based organizations came to have priority, despite the fact that there are serious problems with conceiving of these as vehicles for a broader regional programme. Such an approach could, moreover, face a new government with having to make *ad hoc* decisions about a succession of bilateral issues and problems. These would, of course, also arise under other possible paths, but in this case would do so outside of the framework of a multilateral regional programme.

The third option would be to become *a full and active partner* in a regional programme, in other words a good regional citizen. This is the path most consistent with the objective needs of regional reconstruction. It would, however, pose the greatest challenge in terms of policy development. Such a path would imply

- a willingness not just to enter into discussions with neighbouring states, but also to become a full and active partner in formulating a regional programme that will imply some process of negotiating or re-negotiating a series of concrete relations in various sectors;
- becoming a member of organizations established by the rest of the region, while recognising the need for institutional reform and development;
- contributing to the development of an agreed mutually beneficial programme which would, as argued earlier, need to be seen as combining, in an appropriate and realistic way, elements of co-operation, coordination and integration, rather than being a simplistic polarized choice between co-operation or integration;
- recognizing that any such programme would, in the Southern African context, necessarily have to include significant counter-polarization measures of various sorts, have a strong developmental focus and seek to involve a range of key constituencies in the process of formulation and execution.

At the very least, a programme of regional economic co-operation which is both development-oriented and capable of laying a firm foundation for new forms of security co-operation and disarmament would need to incorporate measures aimed at promoting the following:

- greater real access to the South African market for products from neighbouring countries, particularly those currently excluded by a range of tariff and non-tariff barriers;
- a boost in the earnings of neighbouring states from the provision of services to South Africa, such as water, hydropower and transport;
- some guarantees about the position of migrant workers from the region;
- a more balanced and rational use of the region's transport infrastructure, through addressing the causes of the current distorted overconcentration of regional traffic through the ports and railway system of South Africa;
- a more balanced location of industries and a more equitable distribution of investment;
- more equitable arrangements in a range of existing relations and institutions, including such "thorny issues" as revenue sharing under the Southern African Customs Union agreement.

The Prospects

The installation of a representative government in South Africa has removed one major barrier to the development of the kind of equitable and mutually beneficial programme of regional economic co-operation that is needed to promote both security and sustained economic growth in Southern Africa. Several others will, however, remain. They include:

First, the fact that the focus of existing policy is overwhelmingly at national level with little real priority assigned in practice to regional programmes. This is true also of structural adjustment programmes. Although "outward-oriented," these have, at least up to now, given little priority to regional issues in an apparant belief that "unilateral trade reform" and promoting a greater integration with the world economy at large holds out greater benefits than even a successful regional programme.

Second, the possibility that South Africa as the most powerful state in the region and the one with most to gain, in the short run, from existing patterns of relations could focus on the pursuit of short-term partisan interests. This could be the result of deliberate policy or a "default option," arising from a failure to develop an appropriate regional policy.

Third, and partly linked to the above, is the problem of weak regional institutions. The current reality is one in which formal commitments by governments to regional organizations and programmes are often contradicted in practice. This is manifest both in the low priority accorded to regional co-operation in national economic programmes and in the greater emphasis on bilateralism in regional trade and other relations. Decisions taken by regional organizations have all too often not been implemented as agreed. The record of non-implementation by PTA member states of PTA agreements on tariff reductions and the saga of SADC(C) member states flouting decisions taken at SADC(C) summits not to raise the level of bilateral relations with South Africa are examples of this. While heads of state or government have regularly attended summits of both PTA and SADC(C), day-by-day responsibility for regional affairs has in practice been delegated to relatively junior officials in increasingly fragile state structures. Regional organizations, too, have been notoriously short of resources and dependent on donor support. The present situation could, in short, be summed up as one of weak commitments by weak states to weak regional organizations.

Moreover, despite various claims to the contrary, South African-based organizations (namely SACU and the Common Monetary Area) offer no serious alternative in this respect. They were, in a very specific situation, run by one country in its own interests. The situation was exacerbated by the policies of the South African authorities in the recent "pre-post-apartheid" period. Driven by a desire to promote short-term economic and politico-diplomatic interests, they sought to encourage bilateral dealing with individual states. The expectation (often belied in practice) that this will lead to some special favour or concession, or that any kind of closer relationship with South Africa is the key to promoting growth or investment, can be recognized as a factor further weakening the commitment to regional organizations and decisions by several regional states.

All of these factors must be regarded as barriers to achieving the kind of programme of mutually beneficial co-operation, coordination and integration repeatedly identified as essential to promote growth, development and security in the Southern African region. If they can be overcome, the region has a chance to establish the base for the kind of mutually reinforcing processes of regional economic and security co-operation which could lead to disarmament and release resources for development. If not, regional security co-operation will remain a pipe-dream.

Notes

1. Joseph Hanlon, *Beggar Your Neighbours: Apartheid Power in Southern Africa* (London: James Currey, 1986); David Martin and Phyllis Johnson (eds), *Destructive Engagement* (Harare: Zimbabwe Publishing House, 1986).
2. *South African Destabilization: The Economic Costs of Frontline Resistance to Apartheid* (New York: UN Economic Commission for Africa, 1989).
3. David Sogge, *Sustainable Peace: Angola's Recovery* (Harare: Southern African Research and Documentation Centre, 1992), p. 13.
4. *Annual Report 1991* (Johannesburg: Chamber of Mines, 1991).
5. *The Star* (Johannesburg), 5 May 1992.
6. *The Cape Times* (Cape Town), 15 February 1993.
7. Thomas Ohlson and Stephen John Stedman, *Trick or Treat? The End of Bipolarity and Conflict Resolution in Southern Africa*, Southern African Perspectives: A Working Paper Series, No. 11 (Bellville: Centre for Southern African Studies, UWC, 1992).
8. *Human Development Report 1993* (New York: United Nations Development Programme by Oxford University Press, 1993), p. 2.
9. *Economic Crisis in Africa: Final Review of the Implementation of UN-PAAERD*, extracts reproduced in Backgrounder, No. 5 (Bellville: Centre for Southern African Studies, UWC, 1991), paras. 231-42.
10. Immanuel Wallerstein and Sergio Vieira, "Historical Development of the Region in the Context of the Evolving World System," in: Sergio Vieira, William Martin and Immanuel Wallerstein (eds), *How Fast the Wind? Southern Africa 1975-2000* (Trenton, NJ: Africa World Press, 1992).
11. See Hanlon, *op. cit.*, in note 1; Umesh Kumar, "Economic Dominance and Dependence: The Case of the Southern African Customs Union," in: Oliver Saasa (ed.), *Joining the Future: Economic Integration and Co-operation in Africa* (Nairobi: Africa Centre for Technology Studies, 1991).
12. *Southern Africa: Toward Economic Liberation*, SADCC, 1980.
13. Reginald Herbold Green, *How to Add Ten and One: Some Reflections on Attaining Creative Economic Interaction Between Southern Africa and the "New" South Africa*, paper presented to Africa Leadership Forum Conference on "The Challenges of Post-Apartheid South Africa to Southern Africa in Particular and Africa in General," Windhoek, 1991.
14. Robert Davies, Dot Keet and Mfundo Nkuhlu, *Reconstructing Economic Relations with the Southern African Region: Issues and Options for a Democratic South Africa*, Working Paper Series (Bellville: Macro-Economic Research Group (MERG), University of the Western Cape, 1993).
15. Republic of South Africa, Monthly Abstract of Trade Statistics: Foreign Trade Statistics of the Common Customs Area of Botswana, Lesotho, South Africa and Swaziland, released by the Commissioner for Customs and Excise of the Republic of South Africa, January-April 1993, Pretoria, 1993.
16. See Davies et al., *op. cit.*, in note 14.
17. *Towards Economic Integration*, Theme Document for SADCC Consultative Meeting, Maputo, 29-31 January 1992.
18. See Davies et al., *op. cit.*, in note 14.

Appendix

Table 2.1: Average Annual Growth Rates in Real Gross Domestic Product and Population (Percent)—South Africa and SADC Countries

	GDP		Population	
	1965-80	*1980-90*	*1965-80*	*1980-90*
South Africa	3.7	1.3	2.4	2.4
SADC Countries				
Angola	n.a.	-0.5	2.8	2.6
Botswana	13.9	11.3	3.6	3.3
Lesotho	6.8	3.1	2.3	2.7
Malawi	5.5	2.9	2.9	3.4
Mozambique	n.a.	-0.7	2.5	2.6
Namibia	n.a.	0.4	2.4	3.0
Tanzania	3.9	2.8	2.9	3.1
Zambia	2.0	0.8	3.0	3.7
Zimbabwe	5.0	2.9	3.1	3.4

[Swaziland—figures not given]

Source: *World Development Report 1992* (Washington: World Bank by Oxford University Press, 1992), Tables 2 and 26.

Table 2.2: Daily Calorie Intake Per Person—South Africa and SADC Countries

	1965	1980	1988
South Africa	2,623	n.a.	3,035
Angola	1,897	2,177	1,725
Botswana	2,019	2,152	2,269
Lesotho	2,065	2,400	2,307
Malawi	2,244	2,406	2,009
Mozambique	1,979	1,810	1,632
Namibia	1,882	n.a.	1,889
Swaziland	2,100	2,483	2,578 (1986)
Tanzania	1,832	2,310	2,151
Zambia	2,042	n.a.	2,026
Zimbabwe	2,105	2,137	2,232
High Income Countries (Avg.)	3,083	n.a.	3,398

Source: Sub-Saharan Africa: From Crisis to Sustainable Growth (Washington, D. C.: World Bank, 1990), Table 33; *World Development Report 1991* (Washington, D. C.: Oxford University Press for World Bank, 1991), Table 28.

Table 2.3: South Africa and SADC Member Countries: Human Development Index (HDI), 1990

HDI Category & Rank	Life Expectancy at Birth (years)	Adult Literacy (%)	Human Development Index (max. 1.0)	GNP Rank	HDI-GNP Rank*
Medium HD Category					
85. South Africa	61.7	70.0	0.673	57	28
104. Botswana	59.8	3.6	0.552	69	35
Low HD Category					
117. Swaziland	56.8	72.0	0.458	99	18
120. Lesotho	57.3	78.0	0.431	123	-3
121. Zimbabwe	59.6	66.9	0.398	117	4
130. Zambia	54.4	72.8	0.314	134	-4
135. Namibia	57.5	40.0	0.289	98	37
138. Tanzania	54.0	65.0	0.270	172	-34
153. Malawi	48.1	47.0	0.168	162	-9
157. Mozambique	47.5	32.9	0.154	173	-16
160. Angola	45.5	41.7	0.143	126	34

* A negative sign shows that HDI rank is higher than GNP rank, a positive the opposite.

Source: *Human Development Report* (New York: UN Development Programme, 1993), pp. 136-7.

Table 2.4: Southern Africa Combined GDP in Comparison with Other Countries and World GDP (1989)

	GDP (US-$ mn)	% of World GDP
SADCC countries	27,210	0.14
South Africa	80,370	0.40
SADCC & South Africa	107,580	0.54
Nigeria	28,920	0.15
Hungary	29,060	0.15
Finland	100,860	0.51
Iran	150,250	0.75
Brazil	319,150	1.60
World	19,981,540	

Source: World Development Report (Washington: World Bank, 1991).

3

Time to Decide: Rethinking the Institutional Framework of Regional Co-operation in Southern Africa

Peter Meyns

Southern Africa is undergoing profound changes, and 1994 was a particularly important year in this process. The crucial dates, of course, were 26-28 April when the first non-racial elections were held in South Africa, leading to the formation of a constituent assembly and a transitional executive, encompassing the major political parties voted into the assembly and led by the ANC chairman, Nelson Mandela. At this juncture, South Africa has crossed the threshold to finally join the community of African states. This historic moment also has a significant impact on the future development of regional co-operation in Southern Africa. The era of institutional confrontation, best characterized by the more or less simultaneous establishment of the Constellation of Southern African States (CONSAS) and the Southern African Development Coordination Conference (SADCC) in 1979-1980, has now served its political purpose and can give way to new forms of all-encompassing co-operation between the countries of the region.

The issues related to the incorporation of South Africa into Southern Africa and beyond have received increased attention in academic work, at least since de Klerk announced the beginning of the end of apartheid early in 1990.[1] Inevitably, the existing African regional organizations also had to start thinking seriously about their future relations with a democratic South Africa, just as South Africa began to consider its own post-apartheid interests and options in Africa. What has emerged in this debate is that Southern African countries face more than just the issue of how to incorporate South Africa into a framework of regional co-operation. They also face a situation of stiff competition between existing institutions, notably the Southern African Development Community (SADC) and the Common Market for Eastern and Southern Africa (COMESA), both of which are eager to welcome a democratic South Africa. It is against this background that this contribution looks at the institutional framework of regional co-operation in post-apartheid Southern Africa.

The Changing Global and Regional Environment

There was always a strong international dimension to developments in Southern Africa. Current changes in the region, while fundamentally driven by internal factors, have also been influenced by the changing global environment since the late 1980s. The exact impact of the end of the East-West conflict on the Third World and North-South relations is, however, a subject which continues to give rise to controversial debates. Hope and despair take turns in coming to the fore. Currently, given the abhorrent pictures and reports which reach us daily from Bosnia in former Yugoslavia and from Rwanda or other parts of the world, the feeling of despair prevails, and it appears to many that since the end of the Cold War the world has been besieged by countless conflicts endangering peace. Clearly, these local conflicts are related to the old bipolar world order in that they reflect issues and problems which were contained under the dominant East-West dimension of world politics but surfaced suddenly and in some cases violently when the lid which had structured international relations for over forty years was lifted.[2] Should these conflicts prove to be a transitional phenomenon, the end of the Cold War may yet give way to a more peaceful world in due time.

Using a global perspective, Dieter Senghaas has argued that the "security dilemma" which dominated concerns for world peace during the Cold War era has now been replaced by the "development dilemma."[3] This is not to say that security issues are no longer significant, but failure to solve pressing developmental problems, he suggests, will become the principal threat to peace, particularly in the South, and a major source of local conflicts. Claudia Schmid, looking more specifically at regional conflicts in the South, sees few reasons to argue that the end of the East-West conflict provided opportunities for their peaceful solution. On the contrary, she speaks of a new situation in which a multitude of factors come together to form a complicated web of relations conducive to local conflicts. That this is so, she adds, only goes to show that the East-West conflict was never the main cause of regional conflicts, as some analysts used to suggest, and that the roots of these conflicts have always been essentially local.[4]

It cannot be denied, however, that regional conflicts were often related to the East-West conflict. In some cases the end of the Cold War unleashed new forces of conflict, while in others driving forces of longstanding conflicts were weakened. Schmid acknowledges the need to look at each conflict in its own right, and with regard to Southern Africa it is my view that the latter description is more accurate. On that basis I suggested in an earlier contribution that after the decade of liberation and the decade of destabilization (the 1970s and 1980s respectively) the 1990s might become the decade of peace and reform for Southern Africa.[5] The post-electoral transition in South Africa will be a crucial test for my assessment (and hope). But the independence of Namibia, following the December 1988 New York peace agreements, as well as the July 1991 Bicesse agreement on Angola and the October 1992 Rome agreement on Mozambique were already signs of a new departure in the region. The collapse of the peace process and renewed warfare in Angola, following the September 1992 elections, and the seemingly unending trail of violence in South Africa show, on the other hand, how fragile the various reform situations are. Warnings against undue euphoria are, therefore, equally well founded.[6]

Transitional phases from one order to another defy prediction. They are inevitably characterized by contradictory and often turbulent processes of change which give rise alternately to the feelings of hope and despair mentioned above and can, indeed, delay considerably the peaceful outcome people are waiting for so anxiously. Economic co-operation in Southern Africa is one, albeit an important, element of a new regional order. Ending armed conflicts and creating conditions of peaceful political and economic development are obviously tasks of immediate concern, but finding solutions for, and taking initial steps towards, comprehensive regional co-operation should not be delayed. Indeed, the endeavour has already begun, though in a rather confused way. Future regional co-operation will necessarily differ from the institutional structures which emerged in the 1980s. These were characterized by the political antagonism between OAU member states and African liberation movements on the one hand and the apartheid regime in South Africa on the other, though the relations of interdependence and economic dependence on South Africa persisted throughout this period.[7] Once the dismantling of apartheid began in February 1990, the issue of co-operation after the end of confrontation arose. The aim will be to establish all-embracing structures of co-operation to replace present conflicting ones. The task at hand is "how to add ten and one"—a simple sum, it would seem, but in reality a tricky one.[8]

Whatever the future structure of the region may be, it will have to face the changing international economic environment which is emerging after the end of the East-West conflict. Within the context of the global economy a tendency towards regionalization in the North is becoming apparent, viz. North America (NAFTA), Europe (EU/EEA), Japan and the Pacific, which is likely to push less developed regions in the South to the fringes of the world economy. In Africa, the pressure of marginalization was already manifest during the 1980s. Since the end of the Cold War, the West's interest in Third World countries has diminished further, as the political reasons for providing support to certain states because of the East-West conflict ceased to exist, and the problems of economic transformation and recovery in Eastern Europe came to the fore.

In order to survive under the increasingly difficult conditions of the global economy, one option for the South is to strengthen its own regional ties of co-operation. By and large, experiences of economic co-operation in various parts of Africa during the past 30 years cannot be said to have been very successful. However, of all parts of the continent Southern Africa would seem to have probably the most favourable set of conditions. Even though the region was in a state of crisis at the beginning of the 1990s, it has an undeniable economic potential based essentially on its natural resources. Apart from that it has a comparatively good infrastructure and is also endowed with a greater amount of qualified manpower than other parts of the continent. It is a fact, of course, that this potential exists together with South Africa, and not without it. The region as a whole could become an attractive economic partner for the industrial nations.

The Point of Departure—Regional Inequalities

The continuity of economic interdependence within the region which has characterized South African-Southern African relations for the past century will also be the point of departure for post-apartheid relations. Given the imbalances and biases of these relations in favour of South Africa, it will not be easy to find an arrangement which satisfies the

Table 3.1: SADC Countries and South Africa—Basic Indicators 1991

	Population (million)	Area (1000 sq km)	GNP (US $ bn)	GNP/cap. (US $)
Angola	10.3	1,247	6.0	583
Botswana	1.3	582	3.3	2538
Lesotho	1.8	30	1.1	611
Malawi	8.8	118	2.0	227
Mozambique	16.1	802	1.2	75
Namibia	1.8	824	2.1	1167
Swaziland	0.8	17	0.9	1125
Tanzania	25.3	945	2.4	95
Zambia	8.4	753	3.4	405
Zimbabwe	10.1	391	6.2	614
SADC	84.7	5,708	28.6	338
South Africa	36.8	1,221	91.0	2473

Source: Southern African Political Economy Monthly, 6-10 July 1993, p. 27.

interests of all sides involved. In the past, the political isolation of the apartheid regime was the principal issue; in the post-apartheid era, the economic weight of South Africa will become the main problem. Table 3.1 shows that South Africa's GNP is nearly three times as large as that of all SADC countries combined. The difference between the two is even more clear-cut when GNP per capita is compared. On a general conceptual level two alternative options for future relations of regional co-operation were pinpointed in the basic document submitted to the 1992 Annual Consultative Conference by the SADCC (as it then still was) secretariat. The question is, it was argued, "whether it will be South Africa that joins SADCC, or SADCC that joins South Africa."[9]

After it assumed power in 1989, the de Klerk government stressed its interest in closer ties of regional co-operation on numerous occasions, without limiting its focus to Southern Africa alone. Pursuing his "new diplomacy" in various African countries, de Klerk spoke about his concept of regionalization in Africa, involving four centres, Egypt in North Africa, Nigeria in West Africa, Kenya in East Africa and South Africa in Southern Africa. Each of these centres was described as the "locomotive of growth" in its region. In this perspective, South Africa is seen to be drawing the other countries in the region more closely into its orbit. South Africa as the "regional powerhouse" is at the same time an offer and a challenge to the SADC countries.[10] The ANC as the leader of the new South African government hastened to contradict the "locomotive concept" even before assuming power. Instead, ANC Vice-President Walter Sisulu speaking at the SADC Summit in Windhoek in 1992 stressed South Africa's responsibility to overcome existing inequalities in co-operation with its neighbours. This position had been spelt out in greater detail in an ANC discussion document on economic policy issued in 1991. On regional co-operation it was stated:

> A future democratic government should actively seek to promote greater regional co-operation along new lines which would not be exploitative and which will correct imbalances in current relationships. The new state must be prepared to enter into negotiations with its neighbours to promote a dynamic and mutually beneficial form of co-operation and development. While all of us stand to benefit from such an arrangement, it should be recognised that creating a new non-exploitative form of regional co-operation will require prioritising the interests of the most impoverished of our neighbours in certain areas, according to the principles of affirmative action.[11]

As far as the SADC countries are concerned, it should not be overlooked that because of their economic weakness and/or their dependence on South Africa one or two of its member states are attracted by the locomotive concept. Lesotho, for instance, depends on sending migrant labour to South Africa more than any other SADC country. Economic problems in the mining industry lead to reduced employment and, in turn, repercussions on migrant labour from Lesotho. In order to be able to continue sending workers to South African mines after the end of apartheid, some people in Lesotho have even considered whether their country should not seek incorporation into the South African state. What Lesotho would hope to achieve at the very least is a special agreement ensuring free access of labour to the South African market.[12] There are other countries in the region, for example Mozambique and Zambia, which also hope to receive incentives for their own development by attracting investments from South Africa and—in the case of Mozambique—a more intensive use of available transport facilities.

It is quite another question whether post-apartheid South Africa will be able to meet its suffering neighbours' expectations. Its economy was already in a severe crisis in the 1980s, and in the 1990s the transformation of apartheid society will entail costs of redistribution which will place a heavy burden on the country's financial means. South Africa will be doing its best to attract foreign investment into the country. In this situation, the ANC-led government will also be more concerned about the needs and expectations of its own population than the wellbeing of neighbouring countries. Thus, it is the new South Africa's internal problems which will direct the policy of the government towards exploiting the opportunities offered by the regional market in the country's national interest.

Time to Decide

The countries of Southern Africa would be well advised not to presume that a post-apartheid government will adopt a selfless and altruistic regional policy. Their aim should be to achieve self-reliance and pursue regional co-operation simultaneously. In the basic document submitted to the 1992 Annual Consultative Conference SADCC declared that it would welcome co-operation with a democratic South Africa, but that "the current dominance of South Africa over the rest of the region would continue to be both undesirable and unacceptable."[13] The aim is that South Africa should join SADC after the dismantling of apartheid on the basis of equality and equal rights. However, moving against established economic relationships and vested interests will not be an easy matter.

Competing Institutions

At the beginning of the 1990s, as the region was moving towards the post-apartheid era, several institutions of economic co-operation existed in Southern Africa, with overlapping memberships as shown in Table 3.2.

There are two lines of division between these organizations. The principal distinction is the one between African initiatives (SADC, COMESA) and groups centred on South Africa (SACU, CMA). The second line of division can be identified between the two African regional co-operation initiatives as a result of the different circumstances which gave rise to their establishment.

Table 3.2: Membership in Southern African Regional Co-operation Institutions (1993)

	SADC	FLS	PTA/COMESA*	SACU	CMA
Angola	X	X	X		
Botswana	X	X		X	
Lesotho	X		X	X	X
Malawi	X		X		
Mozambique	X	X	X		
Namibia	X	X	X	X	X
Swaziland	X		X	X	X
Tanzania	X	X	X		
Zambia	X	X	X		
Zimbabwe	X	X	X		
South Africa				X	X

* PTA/COMESA has a total number of 22 member states, those not mentioned in the table coming from Eastern Africa.

SADCC/SADC

The Southern African Development Coordination Conference (SADCC) was founded in 1980. In 1992 it transformed itself into the Southern African Development Community (SADC). By 1993, all ten members had ratified the new treaty. The establishment of SADCC was closely related to the opposition against apartheid in South Africa. The idea initially came from British and EEC partners of the African states in the region, who wanted to coordinate their aid to countries in the frontline against apartheid.[14] It was taken up by the group of Frontline States (FLS), who convened the preparatory conference in Arusha in 1979 which led to the foundation of SADCC one year later.[15] SADCC's membership in 1980 included Angola, Botswana, Lesotho, Malawi, Mozambique, Swaziland, Tanzania, Zambia and Zimbabwe and grew to ten in 1990 when Namibia joined after achieving independence. SADCC's aim of eventually encompassing the whole of Southern Africa was reflected from the beginning in the invitations it extended to those liberation movements in Namibia (SWAPO) and South Africa (ANC and PAC) supported by the OAU to attend its summit meetings and annual consultative conferences as observers. After the reform process started in South Africa in early 1990, SADCC invited the ANC and PAC to participate in all its activities at all levels.[16] At this stage, the Executive Secretary of SADCC Simba Makoni even referred to them as "full members of the SADCC."[17] When SADCC formalized its structures and adopted the SADC treaty in 1992, the liberation movements could not, of course, become members. However, referring to the imminent end of "the inhuman system of apartheid," the signatories of the "Windhoek Declaration" expressed their conviction that it would be "only a matter of time before a new South Africa is welcome to join the family of free and majority-ruled States of the region."[18]

In pursuing its aims, SADCC opted for a loose inter-governmental form of organization and operated on the basis of sectoral areas of cooperation which were coordinated by different member states. Where necessary, a technical secretariat was set up, as in the case of the "transport and communications" sector.[19] In the first decade of its existence, however, SADCC was only very partially successful in fulfilling its aim of reducing its members' dependence, particularly on South Africa. SADCC put the main focus of its efforts on the transport sector where the implementation of its projects, especially those in Mozambique, bore some resemblance to the labour of Sisyphus as a result of South African destabilization. Nevertheless, keeping the Beira Corridor open during the 1980s was a noteworthy success. From 1986 to 1990, the total port throughput in Beira even increased from 1.3 million tons to 1.83 million tons per year.[20] Another high priority sector, regional food security, was coordinated by

Zimbabwe but showed serious flaws when it was put to the test. The severe drought in large parts of the region in 1991-1992 was not prognosticated by the early warning system, nor was its impact alleviated by the supposedly available reserve stocks. Admittedly, this was from all accounts the most severe drought the region had experienced this century, but decisions regarding grain storage and maize price policy had also been taken in Zimbabwe, which made the situation worse.

Notwithstanding such setbacks, the overall performance of SADCC in the face of South Africa's aggressive regional policy deserves praise not only in respect of the effective mobilization of international donor support, but also for creating an atmosphere of solidarity among Southern African countries which bridged political and ideological differences. SADCC's loose inter-governmental form of organization had for many years been seen as its strength because it left member countries' sovereignty untouched and thereby facilitated the co-operation of states with different ideological beliefs and development strategies. Frequent discrepancies between national interests and regional proclamations, however, increasingly lent support to the argument that SADCC needed to assume a degree of supra-nationality in order to be able to operate more effectively as an autonomous policy-making body.[21] In 1989 the SADCC summit meeting decided to formalize the organization's structures.[22] The 1992 treaty, establishing SADC, was the first step on this new path.

From SADCC's coordination of development projects SADC plans to move forward to institutionalized "development integration." This involves formulating "policies aimed at the progressive elimination of obstacles to the free movement of capital and labour, goods and services,"[23] but at the same time applying a certain degree of socio-economic coordination and planning. By regulating the free play of market forces in this way, the "development integration" approach aims to facilitate a more balanced and equitable co-operation among member states.[24] The range of areas across which SADC member states have committed themselves to coordinating, rationalizing and harmonizing "their overall macro-economic and sectoral policies and strategies" is quite ambitious. The list of areas of co-operation now encompasses:

a) food security, land and agriculture;
b) infrastructure and services;
c) industry, trade, investment and finance;
d) human resources development, science and technology;
e) natural resources and environment;
f) social welfare, information and culture; and
g) politics, diplomacy, international relations, peace and security.[25]

By projecting an intensification of co-operation between its member states, SADC became more similar to the PTA, to which we now turn.

PTA/COMESA

The Preferential Trade Area for Eastern and Southern African States (PTA) was inaugurated in 1982 as one regional section of the ECA and OAU plan for establishing a pan-African economic community. In 1993 PTA member states adopted a new treaty, transforming their institution into the Common Market for Eastern and Southern Africa (COMESA). The aim of working towards economic co-operation among all countries in Africa had been initiated in 1980, when the OAU Summit adopted the "Lagos Plan of Action." Little progress was made in the 1980s, but in 1991 the OAU Heads of State or Government signed the "Treaty Establishing the African Economic Community," also referred to as the Abuja Treaty, reiterating their commitment to closer economic co-operation at continental level. It was agreed in these two documents that regional economic communities were an important building block for the ultimate aim of continental co-operation.

When PTA adopted the COMESA Treaty in November 1993, it had twenty-two member states, of which four had only become members in that year, i.e., Namibia, Madagascar, Seychelles and Eritrea which had just achieved its independence. The other eighteen members were: Angola, Burundi, Comoros, Djibouti, Ethiopia, Kenya, Lesotho, Malawi, Mauritius, Mozambique, Rwanda, Somalia, Sudan, Swaziland, Tanzania, Uganda, Zambia and Zimbabwe. These twenty-two countries automatically qualify for COMESA membership. In addition to them, the treaty lists two further countries as potential members, namely Botswana and post-apartheid South Africa.[26] Of the ten member states of SADC nine are also members of PTA and likely to join COMESA. Only Botswana has persistently refused to become a member of PTA. One or two other SADC members, Mozambique for instance, are said to have joined PTA and COMESA for principally political reasons, i.e., in the interests of African solidarity.[27]

Contrary to SADCC whose approach was production-oriented, PTA was based on the neo-classical free trade model of integration, a preferential trade area being the first step in the well-known sequence of integration advancing to a free-trade area, a customs union, a common market and, finally, an economic community (or an economic union as in Western Europe). The principal aim is to promote trade between member states through trade liberalization, the underlying philosophy being that the intensification of trade relations will also promote economic growth and development.

PTA was conceived from the beginning to advance step by step up the stages of integration ladder. Therefore, contrary to the foundation of SADC which was for SADCC members a transition to a more formalized structure of co-operation, the adoption of the COMESA Treaty was a step forward in the process of integration which started in 1982. From its inception, PTA was a more highly institutionalized body than SADCC. It established a Clearing House for intra-regional trade, geared to overcome foreign exchange shortages as a hindrance to trade between member countries, and introduced a Unit of Account of the PTA (UAPTA) on the basis of which intra-regional monetary transactions are calculated. The Clearing House was set up in 1984 in Harare and expanded its transactions in the first five years after which business went down again.[28] Though it did reduce the use of foreign exchange in intra-regional trade, remaining balances had to be cleared in hard currency every two months. Net importers were, therefore, regularly under pressure. The need to earn foreign exchange kept other traders away from the PTA Clearing House. Travellers' cheques issued on the basis of the UAPTA also had a hard time, as they were not generally accepted by banks within the region.[29] The increase of overall intra-regional trade fell behind expectations. The General-Secretary of the PTA Bingu wa Mutharika was able to note an increase of 8% p.a. between 1985 and 1991.[30] In terms of the share of intra-PTA trade to total external trade of PTA members, however, there was a reduction from 7.7% in 1980 to 6.6% in 1988 according to a recent OECD study.[31] Furthermore, regional trade is dominated by a few countries, notably Kenya and Zimbabwe.

PTA/COMESA spokespeople have always been at pains to make clear that their organization "is not merely a trade oriented institution" but one "whose mandate is to promote economic and social development."[32] This is reiterated by the COMESA Treaty which says in Article 3:

> The aims and objectives of the Common Market shall be:
> a) to attain sustainable growth and development of the Member States by promoting a more balanced and harmonious development of its production and marketing structures;
> b) to promote joint development in all fields of economic activity and the joint adoption of macro-economic policies and programmes to raise the standard of living of its peoples and to foster closer relations among its Member States;
> c) to co-operate in the creation of an enabling environment for foreign, cross-border and domestic investment including the joint promotion of research and adaptation of science and technology for development;

d) to co-operate in the promotion of peace, security and stability among the Member States in order to enhance economic development in the region;

e) to co-operate in strengthening the relations between the Common Market and the rest of the world and the adoption of common positions in international fora; and

f) to contribute towards the establishment, progress and the realisation of the objectives of the African Economic Community.[33]

This list of objectives to be pursued by COMESA leaves no doubt as to the fact that there are significant overlaps between COMESA and SADC not only in respect of membership in Southern Africa but also in terms of the areas of co-operation and development both organizations intend to embark upon.

SACU and CMA

The Southern African Customs Union (SACU) and the Common Monetary Area (CMA) are closely related and can be dealt with together, as they both reflect co-operation initiatives centred on South Africa. SACU has a history which goes back into the colonial era when South Africa pursued —albeit unsuccessfully—a policy of incorporation with regard to the British "High Commission Territories," as they were then. In its present form, SACU was established in 1969, after the BLS states, Botswana, Lesotho and Swaziland, had become independent and a new treaty was signed. CMA was established in 1974 as the Rand Monetary Area (RMA) and changed its name in 1986. SACU originally had four member states, South Africa and the BLS countries. Under South African occupation, Namibia had been incorporated into SACU arrangements. Only after achieving independence in 1990 did Namibia become a formal member. When the Rand Monetary Area was set up in 1974 to institutionalize monetary and financial co-operation among SACU members on the basis of the South African rand, Botswana did not join.[34] In 1992 Namibia also joined the CMA, increasing its membership to four countries.

SACU is an expression of the long-standing close economic ties of the countries most dependent on, and involved with, South Africa. The customs union treaty guarantees them a share of the joint customs revenue which is somewhat higher than their external trade's contribution to overall customs revenue. This gives them a secure source of revenue for their respective national budgets. Membership in the customs union also gives them duty-free access to the goods supply on the South African market. The other side of the arrangement is that South African products are often expensive compared to similar products available on the world market and that South Africa monopolizes the location of industrial investments.

SACU's approach to regional co-operation is based on neo-classical integration theory, similar to PTA/COMESA. Overlapping membership between these two institutions, therefore, raises certain difficulties, notably in respect of the PTA most-favoured-nation treatment clause and the SACU rule that members may not "enter into concessionary agreements with outside countries unless their partners agree."[35] To allow Lesotho and Swaziland, and later Namibia, to become members, PTA had to adopt a special protocol which waived the application of certain clauses in the PTA Treaty by these countries for a certain number of years, as Botswana and South Africa were not, for instance, prepared to grant preferential treatment to their imports from PTA countries. Granting a waiver for a limited period of five years was meant to give SACU members of PTA time to decide in favour of one side or the other. In effect, however, because Lesotho in particular could not be expected to leave SACU, the waiver was extended when it expired. When the COMESA Treaty was signed it also included a special "Protocol relating to the unique situation of Lesotho, Namibia and Swaziland," again limited to five years.

Overlapping membership between SADCC and SACU, on the other hand, did not pose any difficulties. The loose form of organization adopted by SADCC did not preclude membership in other institutions, and all four BLNS states, therefore, immediately joined SADCC. Indeed, Botswana has provided the seat and has held the chairmanship of SADCC since its inception. The transformation of SADCC into a more formalized institution encompassing economic integration, as envisaged by the SADC treaty of 1992, will in due course change the situation. And South Africa's entry into the post-apartheid era will in any case place regional co-operation on a new footing.

The question still remains, however, what role, if any, SACU and CMA can be expected to play in Southern Africa after apartheid. The assessments of SACU could not be wider apart. The BLNS states complain about the delays (about two years) in revenue transfers. South Africa is unhappy with the revenue sharing formula which it feels is too strongly biased in favour of the BLNS states. The nature of SACU as a "captive market" for unduly expensive South African products is seen as a severe disadvantage for the BLNS countries. Against this background, Reginald Green characterizes SACU as being "terminally ill."[36] Jan Isaksen suggests that the balance of costs and benefits might end in a "draw."[37] Gavin Maasdorp sees SACU and CMA as "institutions which have been functioning tolerably well for a long period." There is "no merit," he argues, "in breaking up these two groupings," all the more so as "SACU is increasingly being seen as a possible building block for Southern African integration."[38] To support this view he mentions three other SADC members, namely Malawi, Mozambique and Zambia, which have indicated an interest in joining SACU.[39]

Conflicting Interests

It has become clear that the degree of institutional overlap between various regional organizations in Southern Africa is quite substantial. They have existed side by side for a number of years, but as South Africa approached the end of the apartheid era and closer co-operation with the rest of the region was considered, the harmonization and rationalization of regional institutions increasingly appeared necessary. The fact that the existing institutional arrangements also reflect conflicting interests within the region makes the task all the more urgent.

PTA/COMESA Versus SADC

Looking to the future, the main conflicting line between existing regional organizations no doubt runs between SADC and PTA/COMESA. Both were established at the beginning of the 1980s. Having emerged under different circumstances and being characterized by different forms of organization and modes of operation, they seemed to complement each other quite well during the first decade of their existence. However, when the process of change was initiated in South Africa in 1990 and SADCC began to modify its outlook to focus more strongly on regional integration (including a post-apartheid South Africa) rather than concentrating principally on reducing its members' infrastructural dependence on South Africa, the two organizations entered into competition with each other. When they transformed their organization to become the SADC in 1992, the SADCC member states declared, as PTA/COMESA also did, that they viewed their efforts at regional integration in Southern Africa as part of the continental effort to establish an African economic community.[40] It was clear then that SADC and PTA/COMESA were pursuing similar aims, albeit by partially different means.

At this point in time, there was broad agreement among analysts that the SADC-PTA/COMESA relationship needed to be reviewed. Lloyd Ching'ambo, for instance, argued: "Whatever the merits of having either SADC or the PTA, it is clear that the region has to settle the issue of regional multiplicity."[41] Similarly, Ibbo Mandaza suggested that in the interests of the goal of regional co-operation and integration "it appeared essentially anomalous—and even counterproductive to that goal—to have the two organizations exist side by side while pursuing much the same objectives."[42] Maasdorp, in his turn, deplores "the lack of clarity regarding the future relations between SADC and the PTA: increasingly, these two organisations seem to be duplicating one another's functions, and this is a vexing issue in attempting to delineate a future path for the region to take."[43]

Though SADCC and PTA maintained an image of complementarity prior to the current phase of preparing for the post-apartheid era, their institutional relations could not be described as good. On the contrary, as Mandaza has pointed out, a rivalry existed between them from the beginning. While PTA was being prepared under the auspices of the Economic Commission for Africa in the 1970s, a few British and EEC officials, keen to coordinate their countries' support for the beleaguered states of Southern Africa, came up with the idea of setting up SADCC. According to Mandaza, "the protagonists of the PTA viewed the SADCC idea as a direct threat to an initiative that was essentially 'home-grown' on the continent." For them SADCC "was a counter-offensive designed at best to hegemonise an African initiative."[44] After failing to convince the ECA to adopt their idea, the SADCC initiators turned to the Frontline States who went on to establish SADCC. ECA in its turn proceeded with the foundation of the PTA. Against this background, the two organizations tended to operate as if the other one did not exist. Communication between their respective secretariats was minimal. Their executive secretaries were hardly on speaking terms. Indeed, PTA's first Secretary-General Bax Nomvete looked upon SADCC as a neo-colonial organization.

Within SADCC the attitude towards PTA was not uniform. Zambia, for instance, was chosen to host the PTA headquarters and subsequently came to be regarded as a firm supporter of PTA. On the other hand, one SADCC member state, i.e., Botswana, has persistently refused to join PTA. Other SADCC members, particularly those closely associated with the Frontline States such as Mozambique and Angola, were also initially reluctant to join PTA. Even within each SADC country it is not unusual to encounter different attitudes to regional co-operation in different sections of the bureaucracy. Given PTA's prime focus on trade promotion, the ministry of trade and commerce would tend to deal with, and be in favour of, PTA/COMESA, while SADC's concern with project coordination would usually be dealt with by the planning authority which would, therefore, also be likely to support SADC. Because of the more highly politicized nature of SADC, the foreign ministry could also be expected to take a greater interest in its existence.

Among SADC members, PTA/COMESA has often been described as "an unwieldy organization with little common ground among its disparate members."[45] Mozambique's President Joaquim Chissano was quoted as saying

> I would be happy if I could be proved to be mistaken if I say that my country is only vaguely known by many of the PTA member countries which are not SADC members, and has very little if any economic, trade and cultural contacts with such countries.[46]

Responding to a question on the geographical diversity of the countries covered by the PTA, the PTA Secretary-General Bingu wa Mutharika replied rather unconvincingly that he did not see it that way, "because all countries in PTA and SADC are not divided by any geographical barrier. They lie in the same geographical set up, one next to the other until you reach Ethiopia, Sudan or Djibouti. Therefore, a single trading bloc is quite feasible in my view."[47]

When the need to clarify relations between SADCC and PTA began to impose itself in the early 1990s, the fact that nine of ten SADCC members were also PTA members led to a confusing sequence of events. On PTA's annual summit meeting in Lusaka in January 1992 the assembled heads of state or government "resolved that PTA and SADCC be merged into a single Common Market for Eastern and Southern Africa, within the context of the Abuja Treaty for the African Economic Community."[48] As PTA covers a geographically more comprehensive area, it was thought SADCC would be incorporated into PTA and die a natural death. However, only a few days later SADCC held its Annual Consultative Conference with its co-operation partners in Maputo and tabled a "basic document" putting forward the plan to transform itself into an economic community. The short-term need to "minimise duplication and conflicts arising from overlapping memberships" was acknowledged, but it was clearly stated that at the highest point of integration "it will not be practicable for countries to belong to more than one regional community."[49]

The expectation that this future regional institution would grow out of SADCC was underlined when the organization held its annual summit meeting in Windhoek in August 1992 and—notwithstanding the decisions taken by PTA in January in the presence of eight SADCC members, six of which were represented by their heads of state—took the decision to implement the plan outlined in the "basic document" and transformed itself into the Southern African Development Community (SADC). Having been challenged by PTA and facing what some had referred to as a "struggle for survival," SADCC/SADC had now staked its own claim. There was little doubt that the haste with which SADC was formed, leaving no time to expose the draft treaty to a wider public debate in the member countries, was determined by the aim to pre-empt PTA.[50] Unavoidably, the impression arose of a degree of animosity between the two organizations leading one group of analysts to comment:

> The adoption of contradictory resolutions by two regional organisations with overlapping memberships, certainly points to some considerable confusion and raises questions about the degree of commitment of member states to either.[51]

The animosity between SADC and PTA/COMESA was strongly reflected in the two executive secretaries, each committed to the wellbeing of his organization. Prior to the 1993 PTA Summit Bingu wa Mutharika went on record as saying: "For us the merger is on. We do not care what SADC says. The goal will be achieved because eight out of 10 members of SADC are also members of the PTA." SADC's Executive Secretary Simba Makoni immediately issued a dementi saying that the two would work together in areas of common interest and that there could be no question of a merger.[52]

At the PTA Summit in 1993, Zambia again argued in favour of a merger, but this time there was no unanimity. PTA did proceed to adopt the "Treaty Establishing the Common Market for Eastern and Southern Africa" (COMESA) later in 1993, in accordance with a decision taken in 1992. At the founding conference in Kampala in November, there was a flurry of excitement when Zimbabwe initially refused to sign the treaty, allegedly to demonstrate its dissatisfaction with the continuing uncertainty regarding the future regional institutional structure.[53] By this time, however, the heads of state of Eastern and Southern Africa, members of PTA/COMESA and SADC alike, had already decided to raise the decision on the future institutional framework of regional co-operation in Southern Africa to the political level to avoid further embarrassment. The summit meetings of both organizations agreed in late 1992 and early 1993 to commission a group of consultants from the region to prepare a report on the matter. The consultants' brief was to study "the harmonization, coordination and rationalization" of SADC and PTA/COMESA in view of "the elimination of duplication and overlapping in the activities" and "the integration of activities of the two organizations where required in the interests of cost-effectiveness and improved services to member countries."[54]

The Role of Donors

The somewhat belated arrangement between SADC and PTA/COMESA to tackle the future of their relationship in the region also has to do with the role of international donors. In his address to the SADC Annual Consultative Meeting in January 1993 Zimbabwe's President Mugabe explicitly mentioned their concern about the existence of the two organizations and their overlapping mandates.[55] Having contributed quite significantly to the dichotomy between the two and to the more prominent role SADCC played in Southern Africa in the 1980s, the donors had now modified their position. As the reform process got underway in South Africa, the SADC projects they had been funding to reduce the region's infrastructure dependence on the apartheid regime became less urgent.[56] Donors quickly began to reconsider their regional policy. They envisage closer co-operation between South Africa and the rest of the region and, what is more, an important role for South Africa as an intermediary for their co-operation with the whole of Southern Africa.

One institution that attracted their attention in this context was the Development Bank of South Africa (DBSA). This bank was established in the 1980s as part of the Constellation of Southern African States (CONSAS), the regional co-operation initiative the apartheid regime launched in 1979 in pursuance of its destabilization policy. CONSAS was stillborn as it never got beyond incorporating the TVBC homelands and did not manage to attract a single SADCC state. DBSA, however, did expand to become an effective regional development bank in the course of the 1980s. For the World Bank and other development agencies it appeared to be a suitable partner to channel development funds to countries in the larger Southern African region.[57]

In line with their rediscovered interest in South African institutions, some donors hastened their clients in the region to set up links of their own in South Africa, at a time when the SADCC executive secretary still felt that premature relations with South Africa might weaken the reform process towards a democratic post-apartheid state.[58] Streamlining regional co-operation institutions was clearly in the interest of the donors' new approach to Southern African development. However, they kept a low profile on the issue of how to reorganize co-operation structures so as not to be seen to be biased too strongly in favour of South Africa.

South Africa's Future Relations with Southern Africa

After years of confrontation it was not surprising that the form of future co-operation with South Africa was contentious. Among the countries in the Southern African region the perceptions of future relations with South Africa range from fear of enhanced economic domination to hope for developmental benefits. SADC cleared the way for the membership of a democratic South Africa, but did not discard its rhetoric against South African regional hegemony and in favour of equitable and mutually beneficial co-operation. SADC's Executive Secretary

Simba Makoni, who terminated his ten years in office in 1994, was particularly articulate in this respect, saying on one occasion after the 1993 Summit Meeting:

> SADC harbours no expectations, nor desire that a democratic South Africa will play the role of 'engine or locomotive of growth in the region,' nor do we entertain any notions of that country becoming a 'donor' to the rest of us.[59]

He has hardly been unaware that a number of SADC member countries, not only SACU members but one or two others as well, were eager to forge closer links with South Africa. Zambia, for instance, whose President Frederick Chiluba declared a few months after he had been voted into office:

> Highly developed countries have upgraded their links—including Japan—while we are waiting on the sideline, once again being marginalized. Yet we have a more vital interest in what happens in South Africa than any others. The scale and magnitude of the South African economy is such that it can destroy as much as uplift.[60]

Chiluba was addressing the Summit Meeting of PTA, whose Secretary-General Bingu wa Mutharika was said to be rather more receptive to South African overtures than Makoni.[61] However, Chiluba's proposal to forge closer ties with South Africa without delay was rejected at this meeting in early 1992 by Ugandan President Museveni, who wanted to keep the de Klerk government under pressure until the reform process in South Africa was irreversible.[62]

The possibility that South Africa would keep its distance from SADC because it was perceived in parts of the civil service and business circles as an anti-South African organization, as one observer suggested,[63] seems rather backward-looking. After all, South Africa, represented by the liberation movements ANC and PAC, had been involved with SADCC from the very beginning. As soon as he embarked on the process of dismantling apartheid, de Klerk did engage in active diplomacy throughout Africa, aimed at reestablishing relations frozen as a result of the sanctions campaign and seeking new business openings.[64] But his government did not seem to be in a hurry to join either SADC or PTA/COMESA. After all, South Africa's trade relations with the Southern African countries in particular had remained close notwithstanding sanctions, and from an economic viewpoint it did not appear to be absolutely necessary to join the existing regional co-operation bodies in order to win new markets.[65]

In institutional terms, the future of SACU will have to be taken into consideration when deciding on South Africa's relations with PTA/COMESA or SADC. Certain sections of the de Klerk government seemed to give some thought to the idea of dissolving SACU in order to join PTA/COMESA.[66] Maasdorp, arguing from a strictly economic point of view which he finds supported by the opinion of businesspeople throughout the region, challenges this position by observing that "(i)t is seldom wise to discard systems which are working" and that SACU represents the highest level of integration achieved in the region so far. "If the region is to build on its strengths," he adds, "the obvious starting point is to examine the only form of existent economic integration, i.e., the SACU (and, with it, the CMA)."[67] His approach could be referred to as a "five plus six" approach, in contrast to the "ten plus one" approach to South Africa's future relations with Southern Africa proposed by Green.

An alternative stand is adopted by Rob Davies, Dot Keet and Mfundo Nkuhlu. They take a political viewpoint and suggest that a democratic South Africa should join both PTA/COMESA and SADC. They sidestep the issue of increasing overlaps between these two organizations, although they are fully aware of it, and also fail to discuss the implications for SACU of South African membership in PTA/COMESA. Their principal concern is to avoid laying down conditionalities prior to membership and to ensure that a democratic South Africa is "seen to be willing to participate as an equal partner in a regional programme."[68] In the words of an African consultant, this would be "an African solution," i.e., a solution which avoids conflicts as far as possible.

Options for a Future Institutional Framework of Regional Co-operation in Southern Africa

When Uganda's President Museveni, PTA/COMESA chairman from 1993 to 1994, was asked whether he favoured a SADC-PTA/COMESA merger he gave a diplomatic answer:

> We are not hooked on a merger. All we want is rationalization. We have appointed a committee of consultants to look into this matter. If they recommend that it will be a duplication of efforts or there is a need for rationalization or a merger or that the two organizations can live side by side, then we will go for whichever. All we want is efficiency.[69]

What then are the conceivable options for a future institutional framework of regional co-operation in Southern Africa? The following five come to mind.[70]

A Merger Between SADC and PTA/COMESA. This option would involve the creation of a single entity within the geographical area outlined by the COMESA Treaty. COMESA would, in effect, become the only regional co-operation body in the whole area. SADC would be incorporated into COMESA and cease to exist. SACU and CMA would also have to dissolve; alternatively, SACU/CMA might be incorporated initially under a special agreement while COMESA advances in stages to the level of integration the SACU countries have already attained.[71]

The rationale behind this approach is familiar from the theory of integration and usually hinges on the two phrases "size of market" and "economies of scale." That is how PTA Secretary-General Bingu wa Mutharika looks at it, arguing that the merger between PTA/COMESA and SADC "was intended to consolidate the two institutions into a stronger economic grouping capable of mobilizing a larger market and of adequately addressing the problems of balkanization, international hegemony and marginalization of black Africa."[72] A commentator in Zambia put it a little more blandly when he said that there is merit in the nine SADCC member states "merging with PTA to rationalize trade. There is greatness in numbers, the bigger the group, the better for Africa."[73] However, this rationale—so convincing in theory—has all too often been found wanting in practice because of the lack of complementarity of market production in most developing countries.

The Establishment of Two Regional Co-operation Bodies, One in East and One in Southern Africa. This option would involve splitting PTA/COMESA into two halves and merging the southern half with SADC. SACU/CMA would have to be dealt with as suggested above. Dividing the PTA/COMESA area in this way is in line with the Abuja "Treaty Establishing the African Economic Community" which explicitly identifies five sub-regions in Africa, namely North, West, Central, East and Southern Africa, as building blocks for the continental community.[74] It should be remembered that when PTA was being planned in the 1970s, Zimbabwe was still under white minority rule which fostered interest in creating new links for Southern African states in East Africa, viz. the Tanzania-Zambia-Railway (TAZARA). After Zimbabwe's independence and with South Africa entering the post-apartheid era, Southern Africa has become a sub-region which includes the whole geographical area and, therefore, would seem to merit a separate regional co-operation body.

The difficulty with this option is how precisely to divide the PTA/COMESA area as it is now. Should Tanzania remain with Southern Africa (as a SADC member) or "return" to East Africa? Mandaza suggests, on the contrary, that the southern region should expand to include Kenya, Uganda, Rwanda, Zaire, and even Djibouti (!), making it, so to speak, the "new SADC of Eastern and Southern Africa."[75] Maasdorp, in his turn, would not include East Africa but could see some of the Indian Ocean islands joining the Southern African region.[76]

The Maintenance of the Status Quo. Though conceivable, this option would surely offer an unsatisfactory perspective for the future, as it would involve carrying on as before. The duplication of efforts, created as both PTA/COMESA and SADC have endeavoured to expand their activities to cover "all fields of economic activity" (COMESA Treaty), would persist. Should the heads of state be unable to agree on anything else, donors as well as private businesspeople would certainly oppose this option.

The Harmonization of Relations Between PTA/COMESA and SADC. This option would ensure the continuing existence of both organizations, but it would also require modifications in their respective range of activities so as to eliminate duplication of efforts. Presumably, this is what former SADC Executive Secretary Simba Makoni had in mind when he referred to "SADC's development thrust and PTA's expertise in trade promotion."[77] If a division of labour along these lines were to be agreed, SADC would need to retreat from some of the tasks it had assumed under its Windhoek Treaty and concentrate again (as in SADCC days) on regional infrastructural development, while COMESA would focus on trade liberalization. SACU/CMA would need to dissolve or negotiate a future modus vivendi with COMESA, as suggested above.

Smaller Groups Within the Larger Institutional Framework. This could be referred to as the ECOWAS option, because it is similar to the regional cooperation setup which operates under the Economic Community of West African States, also initiated by the ECA.[78] It allows for the existence of smaller groups within the broader framework of ECOWAS in West Africa and PTA/COMESA in Eastern and Southern Africa. Admittedly, this option looks very much like the ultimate "African solution."

Nevertheless, in an area as large and diverse as the one covered by PTA/COMESA, there are also considerations in its favour. The principal one is that smaller groups of countries can come together to pursue specific interests which they have in common and form appropriate organizations. Eastern and Southern Africa have several such distinctive groupings, and SADC is one of them. Others are the Indian Ocean Commission, the East African Community which collapsed in 1977 but which Kenya, Tanzania and Uganda agreed in 1993 to revive in a new form,[79] or the Intergovernmental Authority on Drought and Development in the Horn of Africa. This option also gives room to smaller groups which have already established a higher level of integration, such as SACU and CMA. According to the concept proposed by Maasdorp,[80] it can allow for smaller groups to advance towards economic integration at a pace suitable to their specific conditions, while simultaneously cooperating with the other members of the larger body, the PTA/COMESA, to achieve the longer-term aim of forming a common market and an economic community together.

It is generally agreed that Southern Africa is an African region with distinctive features of its own, as is true of other parts of the PTA/COMESA area. Therefore, it makes sense to allow countries in this region to establish their own structures. With the demise of apartheid in South Africa the group of Frontline States which made an important contribution since the mid-1970s to further the cause of liberation in Southern Africa can be said to have fulfilled its role. But new tasks of ensuring a durable structure of peace and security in co-operation with a democratic South Africa (dealt with in detail elsewhere in this volume) need to be tackled, and SADC, given its more comprehensive regional membership, can provide the required framework. The need for some form of security-based co-operation in post-apartheid Southern Africa lends additional legitimacy to the continued existence of SADC.

The adoption of this option would have to be seen as a new departure, otherwise it might simply turn out to be the maintenance of the status quo under the guise of change. The existing groups within the PTA/COMESA area need to be carefully scrutinized and if necessary modified in their aims and purposes or even dissolved, in order to streamline the whole institutional structure of regional co-operation and to achieve the efficiency so strongly stressed by Museveni. To characterize this approach as the ECOWAS option, however, also reflects the difficulties—experienced in West Africa—inevitably involved in the process of its implementation.

Time to Decide: A Partly Speculative Conclusion

The heads of state and government of the whole SADC and PTA/COMESA area have set their sights on determining the future of their regional co-operation organizations. The regional consultants commissioned to advise them on the matter submitted their report in April 1994, after which a Joint Committee of Ministers, three from PTA/COMESA and three from SADC, was due to consider the consultants' recommendations. When the heads of state and government receive the committee's report and recommendations, it is for them to decide. The heads of state and government themselves, rather than the consultants, are the crucial actors. The future of co-operation in the region will be the result of a political decision. It can only depend on the political will of the countries involved and the consensus which they can achieve. In drawing conclusions from the preceding analysis of the institutional framework of regional co-operation in Southern Africa, therefore, we will have to consider what is desirable and what is feasible.

It seems to me that the desirable option is the establishment of two separate regional co-operation bodies, one of which would cover the

Southern African region. There can be little doubt that the PTA/COMESA area is too large and unwieldy. Countries in the Horn of Africa and in Southern Africa have very little in common. As long as white minority rule persisted in Southern Africa, linking Eastern and Southern Africa within the framework of PTA gave the Frontline States in Southern Africa some much-needed backing. The situation today is a different one. The region can now look to its future as an entity and needs to focus principally on the new challenge of incorporating South Africa.

Should Southern Africa be identical to SADC plus South Africa? Tanzania might consider re-joining Eastern Africa, particularly if the East African Community is revived. In the post-Nyerere era its commitment to Southern Africa has not been as strong as it was before. Zaire, on the other hand, has been seeking admittance to SADC (as well as to PTA/ COMESA) for years, unsuccessfully so far because of its ongoing differences with Angola. The Indian Ocean island states of Madagascar and Mauritius might also be considered for membership as they are geographically closer to Southern than to Eastern Africa. However, there is much to be said for keeping SADC essentially as it is, plus South Africa of course, which has been represented from the beginning by ANC and PAC. SADC has achieved a degree of mutual understanding and political cohesion as well as common experience in development co-operation, but now needs to focus more strongly on advancing economic integration. Botswana, the only SADC member not to have joined PTA/COMESA, is likely to be a strong advocate of this option, possibly alongside with the other BLNS states and with non-SACU SADC members like Mozambique which are seeking closer relations with South Africa. Whether this option is feasible, however, depends essentially on the possibility of achieving a consensus on the division of PTA/COMESA into two institutions. This is unlikely.

The feasible option, therefore, is likely to be the one retaining smaller groups within the larger institutional framework. This would allow all existing institutions to continue to exist, while reorganizing the aims and purposes of individual groups so as to minimize duplication. It would be in line with the time-honoured tendency of bureaucratic institutions to perpetuate their own existence, while at the same time facilitating an African solution of avoiding undesirable conflicts among states with overlapping regional affiliations. As long as the smaller groups and the perceived regional interests of which they are an expression are given sufficient room to manoeuvre, this option could nevertheless stengthen those initiatives which do have some meaning for the countries involved in contrast to the oversized dimension of the PTA/COMESA area, for whose peoples and countries growing together in any meaningful way is still a remote prospect indeed.

Notes

1. See, for instance, Bertil Odén (ed.), *Southern Africa After Apartheid: Regional Integration and External Resources* (Uppsala: The Scandinavian Institute of African Studies, 1993); Gavin Maasdorp, Alan Whiteside (eds), *Towards a Post-Apartheid Future: Political and Economic Relations in Southern Africa* (London: Macmillan, 1992); Anthoni van Nieuwkerk, Gary van Staden (eds), *Southern Africa at the Crossroads: Prospects for the Political Economy of the Region* (Johannesburg: South African Institute of International Affairs, 1991).

2. See Ernst-Otto Czempiel, *Weltpolitik im Umbruch: Das internationale System nach dem Ende des Ost-West-Konflikts* (Munich: Beck, 1993).

3. Dieter Senghaas, *Friedensprojekt Europa* (Frankfurt: Suhrkamp, 1992).

4. Claudia Schmid, "Regionalkonflikte im Süden nach dem Ende des Ost-West-Konflikts: alte Probleme und neue Trends," *Nord-Süd aktuell*, Vol. 6, No. 4, 1992.

5. Peter Meyns, "The New World Order and Southern Africa in the 1990s," in: van Nieuwkerk, van Staden, *op.cit.*, in note 1.

6. See T. Ohlson, S. J. Stedman, *Trick or Treat? The End of Bipolarity and Conflict Resolution in Southern Africa*, Southern African Perspectives, No. 11 (Bellville: Centre for Southern African Studies, University of the Western Cape, 1991); Rob Davies, "After the Euphoria: What is Happening to the Southern African Dream?" *Work in Progress*, No. 87, March 1993.

7. See J. Blumenfeld, *Economic Interdependence in Southern Africa* (London: Royal Institute of International Affairs, 1991); R. T. Libby, *The Politics of Economic Power in Southern Africa: From Conflict to Co-operation* (London: Pinter, 1991); J. Hanlon, *Beggar Your Neighbours: Apartheid Power in Southern Africa* (London: Catholic Institute of International Relations, James Currey, 1986).

8. R. H. Green, "The Economic Implications of Post-Apartheid: How to Add Ten and One," in: F. G. N. Mosha (ed.), *The Challenges of Post-Apartheid South Africa* (Windhoek: Africa Leadership Forum, 1991).

9. "SADCC: Towards Economic Integration," Basic Document, SADCC Annual Consultative Conference (Maputo: mimeo., 1992), p. 20.

10. Rob Davies, "South Africa and the SADCC: Regional Economic Co-operation After Apartheid," in: G. Moss, I. Obery (eds), *South African Review 6* (Johannesburg: Ravan, 1992).

11. Cited in: Arne Tostensen, "What Role for SADC(C) in the Post-Apartheid Era," in: Odén, *op. cit.*, in note 1, p. 151.

12. See S. Santho, M. Sejanamane (eds), *Southern Africa After Apartheid: Prospects for the Inner Periphery in the 1990s* (Harare: SAPES, 1991).

13. SADCC, *op. cit.*, in note 9, p. 20.

14. Ibbo Mandaza, "The Bases of the PTA-SADC Dispute," *SAPEM*, Vol. 6, No. 5, March 1993.

15. Amon J. Nsekela, (ed.), *Southern Africa: Toward Economic Liberation* (London: Rex Collings, 1981).
16. *Post-Apartheid Regional Co-operation*. Conference Report, Gaborone 27-29 April 1992 (Amsterdam: African-European Institute, AWEPAA: 1992), p. 25. The reference is to a discussion contribution by Lt. Gen. Mompati Merafhe from Botswana.
17. "Simba Makoni—Interview with the Executive Secretary of SADCC," *SAPEM*, Vol. 5, No. 2, November 1991, p. 6.
18. "SADCC/SADC—Towards the Southern African Development Community: A Declaration by the Heads of State or Government of Southern African States (The Windhoek Declaration)," reproduced in: *SAPEM*, Vol. 5, No. 11, August 1992, p. 26.
19. See J. Hanlon, *SADCC in the 1990s: Development on the Frontline*, Special Report, No. 1158 (London: Economist Intelligence Unit, 1989).
20. Oliver S. Saasa, "The Effectiveness of Regional Transport Networks in Southern Africa: Some Post-Apartheid Perspectives," in: Odén, *op. cit.*, in note 1, p. 132.
21. Lloyd Ching'ambo, "SADC: The Rebirth of SADCC," *SAPEM*, Vol. 5, No. 11, August 1992, p. 23.
22. Makoni, *op. cit.*, in note 17, p. 5.
23. "Treaty of the Southern African Development Community (SADC)," reproduced in: *SAPEM*, Vol. 5, No. 11, August 1992, p. 33.
24. See Rob Davies, *Integration or Co-operation in a Post-Apartheid Southern Africa: Some Reflections on an Emerging Debate*, Southern African Perspectives, No. 18 (Bellville: Centre for Southern African Studies, University of the Western Cape, 1992).
25. "Treaty of the SADC," *op. cit.*, in note 23, p. 35.
26. "Treaty Establishing the Common Market for Eastern and Southern Africa," not published (1993), p. 4.
27. Personal communication in Mozambique.
28. Gavin Maasdorp, Alan Whiteside, *Rethinking Economic Co-operation in Southern Africa: Trade and Investment*, Occasional Papers on International Co-operation (Johannesburg: Konrad-Adenauer-Stiftung, 1993), pp. 24-7.
29. "UAPTA Cheques Fail to Take off," *African Business*, December 1993, p. 7.
30. "Bingu wa Mutharika—Interview with the PTA Secretary-General," *SAPEM*, Vol. 6, No. 7, April 1993, p. 12.
31. "OECD, Regional Integration and Developing Countries," cited in: "Lofty Ambitions of COMESA," *New African*, January 1994, pp. 23-24.
32. Bingu wa Mutharika, *op. cit.*, in note 30, p. 12.
33. COMESA Treaty, *op. cit.*, in note 26, p. 10.
34. Gavin Maasdorp, *Economic Co-operation in Southern Africa: Prospects for Regional Integration*, Conflict Studies, No. 253 (London: RISCT, 1992), p. 6.
35. *Ibid.*, p. 19.
36. Green, *op. cit.*, in note 8, p. 94.

37. Jan Isaksen, "Prospects for SACU After Apartheid," in: Odén, *op. cit.*, in note 1, p. 187.
38. Maasdorp, *Economic Co-operation...*, *op. cit.*, in note 34, pp. 26-5; see also Maasdorp and Whiteside, *Rethinking Economic Co-operation...*, *op. cit.*, in note 28.
39. Maasdorp, *op. cit.*, in note 34, p. 24.
40. SADCC/SADC, *op. cit.*, in note 18, p. 26.
41. Ching'ambo, *op. cit.*, in note 21, p. 24.
42. Mandaza, *op. cit.*, in note 14, p. 40.
43. Maasdorp and Whiteside, *op. cit.*, in note 28, p. 40.
44. Mandaza, *op. cit.*, in note 14, p. 41.
45. "The Last Signature Is Coming," *Africa South & East*, December 1993-January 1994, p. 27.
46. Cited in: F. Goncalves, "Thinking of SADC," *SAPEM*, Vol. 6, No. 12, September 1993, p. 24.
47. Bingu wa Mutharika, *op. cit.*, in note 30, p. 13.
48. "PTA—Final Communiqué of the Tenth Meeting of the Authority of the Preferential Trade Area for Eastern and Southern African States" (Lusaka 1992), p. 9.
49. SADCC: Towards Economic Integration..., *op. cit.*, in note 9, p. 36.
50. See Ching'ambo, *op. cit.*, in note 21; Ibbo Mandaza, "SADC: An Economic Agenda or a mere Political Expression?" *SAPEM*, Vol. 5, No. 11, August 1992.
51. Rob Davies, Dot Keet, Mfundo Nkuhlu, *Reconstructing Economic Relations with the Southern African Region: Issues and Options for a Democratic South Africa*, Occasional Paper Series (Bellville: Macro-Economic Research Group, MERG, University of the Western Cape, 1993), p. 57.
52. Cited in: "Merger in Tatters?" *West Africa*, 1-7 March 1993, p. 333.
53. "Treaty Transforms PTA into Common Market," *African Business*, December 1993, p. 7; "Regional Tariff Reduction Convinces Harare to Sign Accord," *Southscan*, 26 November 1993; "The Last Signature Is Coming," *Africa South & East*, December 1993-January 1994, p. 27.
54. "Terms of Reference for the Joint Study on Harmonization, Coordination and Rationalization of the Activities of the PTA and the SADC" (mimeo), n.p. n.d. (1993).
55. His speech is cited in: Mandaza, *op. cit.*, in note 14, p. 43.
56. Maasdorp, *op. cit.*, in note 34, p. 16.
57. See Peter Vale, "South Africa's New Diplomacy," in: Moss, Obery, *op. cit.*, in note 10.
58. See "Editorial: Whither SADCC?" *SAPEM*, Vol. 5, No. 2, November 1991, p. 2, and the interview with SADCC Executive Secretary Simba Makoni in the same issue of *SAPEM*.
59. Cited in: Goncalves, *op. cit.*, in note 46, p. 24.
60. Frederick Chiluba, *Marching Towards a Common Market* (Opening Statement by Mr. F.J.T. Chiluba, President of the Republic of Zambia, on the Occasion of the Opening Ceremony of the 10th PTA Summit at Mulungushi Conference Centre), Lusaka, Zambia, 30 January 1992 (mimeo.), p. 8.

61. See Mandaza, *op. cit.*, in note 50, p. 19.

62. "PTA Summit Meeting in Lusaka: Differences Over Attitude to South Africa Voiced," *Facts and Reports*, Vol. 22, 1992, Item D 112; *Sunday Express* (Lusaka), 2 February 1992.

63. "The Last Signature Is Coming," *Africa South & East*, December 1993-January 1994, p. 27.

64. André du Pisani,"Ventures into the Interior: Continuity and Change in South Africa's Regional Policy (1948-1991)," in: van Nieuwkerk, van Staden, *op. cit.*, in note 1.

65. Maasdorp, *op. cit.*, in note 34, pp. 15, 18-19.

66. Maasdorp and Whiteside, *op. cit.*, in note 28, p. 41.

67. *Ibid.*, pp. 40-1.

68. Davies, Keet, Nkuhlu, *op. cit.*, in note 51, p. 58.

69. "Interview with President Yoweri Museveni," *The Courier*, No. 141, September-October 1993, p. 26.

70. In summarizing these options I have benefited from discussions with Gilbert Mudenda, one of the regional consultants mentioned by Museveni, in January 1994.

71. Maasdorp, *op. cit.*, in note 34, pp. 20-6.

72. Bingu wa Mutharika, *op. cit.*, in note 30, p. 13.

73. *Daily Express* (Lusaka), 31 January 1992.

74. "Treaty Establishing the African Economic Community," reproduced in: Gino J. Naldi (ed.), *Documents of the Organization of African Unity* (London/New York: Cassel, 1992), p. 204.

75. Mandaza, *op. cit.*, in note 14, pp. 40, 43.

76. Maasdorp and Whiteside, *op. cit.*, in note 28, p. 47.

77. Cited in: "Merger in Tatters?" *West Africa*, 1-7 March 1993, p. 333.

78. S. K. B. Asante, *The Political Economy of Regionalism in Africa: The Case of the Economic Community of West African States* (Westport: Greenwood, 1985).

79. "Interview with Ali Hassan Mwinyi, President of Tanzania," *Executive* (Nairobi), August 1993, p. 28.

80. Maasdorp and Whiteside, *op. cit.*, in note 28, pp. 47-51.

4

Organizing Collective Security: African Experiences

Ivor Richard Fung

There is a misleading tendency to believe that any international security arrangement, including even conflict management efforts, peace-keeping operations and other multilateral military institutions, constitutes collective security. Africa, a crisis-ridden continent, has been a laboratory for diverse security arrangements carried out under subregional organizations, the Organization of African Unity (OAU) and the United Nations. Not all of these arrangements, in which two or more states participate, necessarily constitute collective security following the conventional understanding of the term. Generally, collective security is predicated on a treaty that encourages member states to resolve their differences peacefully, and by the same token authorizes them to adopt collective coercive measures, including the use of force against a recalcitrant member.

Drawing examples from existing arrangements, this chapter sets out to clarify, in the first part, the concept and modern practice of collective security in general. Part two will analyze the various attempts that have been undertaken in Africa. The international environment has changed drastically over the past few years both in the configuration and in the behaviour of states towards one another, a development that has had a considerable impact on the nature and sources of conflicts. The need to re-adapt or re-invent national and international military and security institutions on the continent has thus become an inescapable reality. The third part of the chapter will, in this regard, focus on the emerging challenges and prospects for collective security in Africa in the coming decades.

The Concept and Practice of Collective Security

Until about 1919 the predominant and most popular approaches to international security included, most importantly, the world government theory and the balance of power systems. The world government theory postulates a single supreme authority at the world level with coercive powers that can enable the settlement of disputes between the nations of the world. It is based on the assumption that only universal power will bring universal peace.[1] A study of world government must be based on imagination, since such a government has never existed, not even experimentally. The balance of power, on the contrary, has existed in many different situations.[2] It has consisted in the distribution of power among states in such a way that each state will be too weak to wage war successfully on any of the others. It has functioned as a kind of deterrence, whereby the potential aggressor is deterred by the potential combined power of all the other states in the system.

With the birth of the League of Nations in 1919 following the First World War, the old proposal for something in-between world government and the balance of power, "whereby states would give up some but not all of their authority" or sovereign rights, gained considerable momentum as "collective security."[3] By forming a collective security system, states demonstrate that they have attained a reasonable degree of maturity, communication and interdependence and a "sense of shared social values" that transcend their perception of each other as enemies. Thus, as Karl Deutsch put it, they come to form a "security community."[4]

Though the term "collective security" is often loosely used, it connotes in its technical meaning a number of states joined together by a treaty with the explicit commitments to renounce the use or the threat of force in their relations and to "gang up" on the member state that resorts to aggression. Security problems of a purely domestic nature, such as violations of basic human and minority rights, ethnic uprisings and other political upheavals, are usually not taken into account in a traditional collective security system. Paradoxically, however, it is the domestic conflicts with attendant transborder security problems that have most often threatened international peace and security, particularly in recent decades.

Collective Security and Collective Defence

In a collective security system, threats from outside the system are usually not taken into account. A collective security system is different from a collective defence system such as the North Atlantic Treaty Organization (NATO), the defunct Warsaw Pact or the Frontline States Alliance, which were designed to counter attacks from without and with specific enemies in mind. NATO was created primarily to check aggression from the Soviet bloc and to deter the expansion of communism into Western Europe. The formation of the Warsaw Pact came as a logical response to NATO, with the additional mission of consolidating Soviet influence in Eastern Europe. The Republic of South Africa and the destabilizing policies of apartheid constituted the main motive for the creation of the Frontline States Alliance. Thus the underlying characteristic of all collective defence systems is the pledge of all member states to gang up against a common enemy in the event of an attack. Usually, the enemy is predefined and is the motive for the formation of the system. In a collective security system, on the other hand, it is presumed that "any member of the system might, at any time, behave in such an aberrant manner that corrective measures would be necessary."[5]

While a collective security system may endure much longer, a collective defence system simply becomes obsolete and irrelevant when the predefined enemy disappears. The end of the Cold War, the dissolution of the Soviet Union together with the collapse of the bipolar international order as well as the ongoing auspicious democratic changes and the gradual erosion of apartheid in South Africa have together ushered in a new political configuration of the international system.

Though these developments have profoundly affected the existence of post-World War II defence alliances, they have not diminished the possibility for conflicts to erupt. As a matter of fact, international security has become even more elusive now than in the past, owing to the emergence of several deadly ethnic conflicts in almost every part of the globe, most notably in Europe and in Africa. This state of affairs has lent impetus to rethinking the roles of military and security institutions and their modes of operation at the domestic and international levels. In other words, how can collective security or collective defence systems be utilized in domestic conflict situations? The Yugoslav conflagration has pushed Europeans to the wall, not only demonstrating that tribal wars can occur even in the heart of so-called civilization, but also putting to the test the effectiveness of one pillar of the post-World War II European security architecture: the Conference on Security and Co-operation in Europe (CSCE).

In the cases of NATO and the Frontline States Alliance cited above, Europeans and Southern Africans are in search of new security systems that can best respond to their respective security realities today. In both cases, the role of the former enemy (the states of the former communist bloc in the case of NATO and the Republic of South Africa in the case of the Frontline States Alliance) is of crucial importance in the establishment of a new security order and enduring structures. NATO has established co-operation links with the former Warsaw Pact states under the auspices of the newly created North Atlantic Co-operation Council. This new "Partnership for Peace," principally propounded by the United States, also encourages bilateral agreements with the former member states of the Warsaw Treaty Organization as well as with neutral and non-aligned countries in Europe so as to increase the capacity of NATO for crisis management, peace-keeping and peace-making as well as for humanitarian relief in case of natural disasters.

The task at hand now is for Europeans and the United States, a custodian of trans-Atlantic security, to redefine the operational objectives of NATO as a viable multilateral conflict management mechanism in Europe whose urgent priority would be to grapple with the many tribal wars Europe is affected by. The European security scene is further characterized by arrangements under the Western European Union (WEU) which in addition to the Common Foreign and Security Policy of the European Union was charged, during the Maastricht Summit meeting, with providing the framework for a common European policy on defence. Thus, Europe's inability to develop a viable security system, as proposed by Hans-Dietrich Genscher, at that time foreign minister of Germany, has led to the emergence of a multidimensional security system based on a network of closely related and even complementary institutions. In the view of some people, this European security network draws inspiration from co-operative security.[6]

With the demise of apartheid in South Africa and the positive political will shown by South African statesmen for subregional co-operation, individual researchers, research institutions in the field of peace and relevant non-governmental organizations are galvanizing efforts to design a new security order in Southern Africa. The means used comprise publications, conferences and private consultations among policy-makers. There seems to be emerging consensus on the vital need to revise the mandate, structure and composition of the Frontline States Alliance and to examine the effective ways and means of establishing an inter-state committee for defence and security questions in the subregion which would complement, in the security field, the efforts of a revamped Southern African Development Community (SADC).[7]

There is no doubt that an apartheid-free and democratic South Africa, with the demonstrated military prowess and technology of the apartheid regime, will play a key role in the orientation of subregional security; but there are still many questions at this embryonic stage of institution-building for security. What will be the relationship between such a committee and the FLS? Considering developments in other parts of Africa, where security institutions are embedded in development-oriented arrangements, is SADC going to reinforce its security provisions to the extent of housing the said committee? Will the committee have the structure of a collective security mechanism or that of a collective conflict management system?

Collective Security and Collective Conflict Management

Generally, collective conflict management consists of multilateral efforts by relevant intergovernmental organizations such as the United Nations, the OAU, the OAS, the Arab League and ASEAN to prevent and contain inter-state or domestic disputes. In a sense, collective conflict management entails conflict resolution measures taken before or during the escalation of a conflict with the objective of re-establishing a peaceful order. Modern mechanisms of conflict resolution include peace-making and peace-keeping operations.

Peace-making is a set of diplomatic actions usually effectuated at an early stage of a conflict through mediation, "good offices" or arbitration with the purpose of preventing and containing escalation by creating peaceful conditions for mutual understanding and reconciliation of the parties to the conflict. Peace-making is often carried out by a respected, non-controversial individual. Such an individual may represent an international institution. Reporting on the *Time* magazine nomination of its 1993 Men of the Year (Yitzhak Rabin and Yasser Arafat for their role in the reconciliation process between Israel and the PLO, Nelson Mandela and F. W. de Klerk for their contribution to the democratic opening and de-apartheization of South Africa), Lance Morrow states:

> Peace-making, like war-making or courtship, depends upon exquisitely balanced, mysterious and usually unpredictable combinations of context, timing, luck, leadership, mood, personal needs, outside help and spending money—all of these factors swirling around in a kind of Brownian motion.[8]

Although in bilateral contexts statesmen and celebrities are known to have successfully performed the role of peacemakers, their actions cannot be classified as collective conflict management actions for the simple reason that such peacemakers are not mandated by an international organization or the international community. Chapter VI of the United Nations Charter deals with collective peace-making measures, most of which have been elaborated upon by Secretary-General Boutros-Ghali in his report to the Security Council entitled "An Agenda for Peace." The line between peace-making and peace-keeping is becoming increasingly blurred, especially as the former measures have sometimes been deployed simultaneously with the latter in large-scale conflicts.

Peace-keeping in its traditional sense involves the deployment of an international neutral force to keep the peace between warring parties in an inter-state conflict once a cease-fire has been agreed. The prior consent of the parties is a determinant factor for the deployment. The concept of peace-keeping has recently evolved to include deployment in civil conflict situations, the monitoring and supervision of elections, political administration, civilian participation and delivery of humanitarian and relief assistance. But still a great deal of confusion exists as to what peace-keeping actually comprises.

Current developments in South Africa's peace and democratization process are signalling another kind of peace-keeping force at the domestic level, which will be made up of civilian and military representatives of the country's major political factions with the task of maintaining peace and security during the transition period. The idea of an interpositional neutral international force has been rejected by the factions concerned. In this sense, the domestic peace-keeping force in South Africa has, in some ways, proved an innovative element in the ever broadening concept of peace-keeping. In view of the strong demand for impartiality on the part of the peace-keeping force, analysts and observers were eager to see the contribution of this South African experiment, the success of which attested to the country's political maturity.

The relationship between collective security and collective conflict management may be that the deployment of the latter signifies the non-existence or the failure of the former in the prevention of a conflict. Collective conflict management has so far been the most widely known and relatively successful security effort, deployed by almost all contemporary political organizations either at the subregional, regional or universal level. In the case of the United Nations, for instance, between 1945 and 1985, 159 disputes were dealt with and the management success score was about 23%.[9] In addition, between 1945 and 1993 the world organization mounted about twenty-eight peace-keeping and truce supervision missions, many with legally expanded and unprecedented mandates and scopes.

Global and Regional Collective Security

At the global level, the outbreak of the Second World War blatantly demonstrated the failure of the collective security system of the League of Nations. The United Nations has done no better, at least up to now. Its collective security system as enunciated in article 2 of the charter has been overburdened with more than 160 disputes brought to the organization. Apart from Operation Desert Storm, the enforcement action in Iraq following its August 1990 invasion of Kuwait, the United Nations has registered little or no major success in this field. It has been argued that both in the Iraq case and in the Korean war in 1950, the United Nations was used as an instrument to achieve the foreign policy aims of the United States and other Western powers. These were situations of "subcontracts," some observers have criticized.[10] It cannot, however, be gainsaid that there was a breach of the peace in both situations that required the action of the world organization in order for it to justify its existence. The ways in which the United Nations responded to the crises, even though by proxy, as some critics would say, reflected the political realities prevailing in the international system. It should be borne in mind also that the United Nations does not have standing logistical means and personnel that can be deployed independently when the need arises. So the UN depends on contributions from member states (chapter VII of the charter) and on the political harmony which they may demonstrate in the implementation of an operation.

While the experiences of the League and the UN suggest that collective security (as opposed to collective conflict management) hardly works at the global level, it might succeed in regions where differences between states are not so great, thanks to geographical contiguity and cultural affinities. This approach to peace can be called "regional collective security."[11] In principle, regional collective security may function better when it is conceived and operated within the framework of a politico-economic arrangement, where member states have other (economic) values at stake and have felt the necessity of preserving them through the maintenance of a secure and peaceful environment.[12] So far, no regional organizations have been set up solely for a collective security purpose. Today, most collective security systems are designed within the framework of economic communities. Modern politico-economic arrangements, especially at the subregional or regional level, constitute confidence- and security-building measures. Within these arrangements, development imperatives require that the more Hobbesian characteristics of the realist views which consider security in purely military terms be attenuated by a system-centred perspective which also takes cognizance of economic demands among states.[13]

The role of regional organizations in security management as a whole is very significant. The Organization of American States (OAS), the Arab League and the Organization of African Unity (OAU) have offered various conflict management opportunities, and have sometimes been successful in the peaceful settlement of disputes brought to them in their respective regions. Between 1945 and 1990 the OAS and the Arab League dealt with thirty-four and thirty-one disputes respectively, and achieved management success percentages of 32% for the OAS and 22.5% for the Arab League. About thirty disputes were brought to the OAU between 1963 and 1990 and the management success percentage of about 39% (including management assistance from the International Court of Justice in some cases) was realized.[14]

Regional Collective Security Experience in Africa

A discussion of collective security in Africa is by and large a discussion of collective conflict management efforts undertaken by the OAU, the Economic Community of West African States (ECOWAS), the Accord de Non-Agression et d'Assistance en Matière de Défense (ANAD). Other economic and development-oriented organizations such as the Arab Maghreb Union (AMU), the Economic Community of Central African States (ECCAS, with particular reference to its United Nations Standing Advisory Committee on Security Questions in Central Africa) and the Southern African Development Community (SADC) have arrangements and security provisions in their respective charters that have not yet been put to the test.

The Organization of African Unity (OAU)

In the preamble to the OAU Charter, security concerns are construed as a medium through which the attainment of the organization's goals of the unity, prosperity, justice and dignity of the African people can be enhanced. Two mechanisms for security matters have been conceived in the charter: the Commission for Mediation, Conciliation and Arbitration and the Defence Commission. In June 1993, the OAU adopted an ambitious mechanism for conflict prevention, management and resolution, tacitly admitting thereby the incapacity of its earlier security mechanisms to deal with increasing regional insecurity.

The Commission on Mediation, Conciliation and Arbitration. The establishment of the Commission on Mediation, Conciliation and Arbitration (CMCA) came as a practical response to OAU's member states' concern expressed in article 19 of the OAU Charter regarding continental security.

By that article, member states pledged to "settle all disputes among themselves by peaceful means." The CMCA was formally institutionalized by a separate protocol approved by the OAU's supreme organ, the Assembly of Heads of State and Government, meeting in Cairo in July 1964. At that meeting, the composition of the CMCA was set at twenty-one members, including the bureau of one president and two vice-presidents. The conditions of service of the CMCA were also worked out and included the following:

According to article 12 of the protocol, "the Commission shall have jurisdiction over disputes between states only." This caution was obviously in keeping with the sacrosanct principle of non-interference in the internal affairs of states, provided for in article 3 of the charter. This limitation, however, was to constitute one of the constraints that would handicap the work of the commission, since about three quarters of the disputes that beset the continent are internal, sometimes with serious transborder spillovers. Article 19 of the protocol specifies that "in case of a dispute between member states, the parties may agree to resort to any one of these modes of settlement: mediation, conciliation and arbitration." Mediation and conciliation are understood as political mechanisms for dispute settlement, and arbitration as a legal instrument invested with an arbitral tribunal.

In spite of the many crises, disputes and armed conflicts that have occurred in Africa since the establishment of the CMCA, the twenty-one members have never met, let alone taken any mediation, conciliation or arbitration action in an attempt to fulfill the commission's mandate and justify its thirty years of existence. This inactivity has been attributed by a cross-section of critics to the absence of a legal and operational framework for the commission. The propensity of member states to devise political mediation on an ad hoc basis has been perceived as an additional drawback. This preference for ad hoc arrangements is often explained by the fact that, in the event of a dispute, not only would the recommendations of an institutionalized mechanism, such as the CMCA, carry some legal weight, they would also have to be public and morally, if not legally, binding upon the parties to the conflict, and in order to be credible, they would have to set some punitive measures or reparations for the aggressor.

This appears to be the hitch which results in the chronic reluctance of African leaders to respect African security instruments. As James Jonah puts it, the problem with resorting to ad hoc arrangements is that,

> in the past few years, this practice has evolved into a situation where the current Chairman of the OAU has been utilized as the focal point for the resolution of a number of African disputes. While this is a welcome development, the arrangements remain inchoate; that is to say, there is no

precise idea as to what are the responsibilities of the Chairman of the Assembly of Heads of State and Government of the OAU... The practice has been complicated by the lack of clarity in the respective roles of the Chairman and the Secretary-General of the Organization.[15]

However, moribundity is not unique to the Commission for Mediation, Conciliation and Arbitration. The same story can be told of the OAU Defence Commission.

The Defence Commission. The Defence Commission is one of the three specialized commissions established by the Assembly of Heads of State and Government pursuant to the provisions of article 20 of the OAU Charter. It came into existence as a compromise solution between the conflicting positions of the Casablanca "progressive" group of states, which, during the lengthy and heated debates that led to the creation of the OAU, advocated a Joint African High Command that would defend the continent in case of external aggression, and the Monrovia "moderate" group of states, which saw in this proposal a step towards a radical and precipitate implementation of the political unity of the continent. The Monrovia Group stood for the division of the continent into independent and sovereign states on the basis of colonial borders, and it viewed continental unity only in terms of the common aspirations of all the sovereign states acting in concert. In any case, the OAU in its structure and objectives is a concrete victory for the Monrovia Group. Accordingly, the Defence Commission is no more than a security mechanism, with the loose mission of resolving African conflict peacefully.

However, the tragedy is that the commission, just like the CMCA, has in its thirty years of existence not succeeded in resolving any of the more than fourty internecine and inter-state armed conflicts that have occurred on the continent. In fact, the only achievement of the commission, if that can be called achievement, is to have met nine times at ordinary sessions during which it, *inter alia*, adopted the recommendation on the setting up of a military bureau within the Department of Political Affairs in the Secretariat of the OAU. As of today, that bureau is made up of only one military officer. The bureau and the commission were instrumental in the formulation of Decision AHG/DEC/113(XVI) Rev. 1, by which the Assembly of Heads of State and Government expressed its wish to establish an OAU defence force. The commission has also met once in thirty years in extraordinary session in an attempt to discuss South Africa's aggression against newly independent Angola in 1975.

The Defence Commission has had a number of high-sounding intentions, none of which has been translated into concrete action, including: the creation of a defence and peace-keeping organization; unified military training; the establishment of regional defence units; an inter-African military academy whose objectives would include military training and standardization of military equipment and the armed forces; an OAU defence force; and the creation of an African peace corps. It can be argued that the failure to attain consensus, a fundamental requirement in decisions on multilateral military and sensitive political matters, coupled with member states' basic lack of faith and political will in the continental organization, has largely contributed to the Defence Commission's moribund functioning. But the interesting thing is that this difficulty has not shattered the hopes of some concerned Africans who still remain devoted to the search for workable solutions to the continent's daunting security problems. The recent adoption in June 1993 in Cairo of OAU Declaration AHG/DECL.3 (XXIX) on the establishment of a mechanism for conflict prevention, management and resolution cannot be interpreted otherwise.

The OAU Mechanism for Conflict Prevention, Management and Resolution. In the words of the declaration, the establishment of such a mechanism constitutes "an opportunity to bring to the processes of dealing with conflicts in our continent a new institutional dynamism, enabling speedy action to prevent or manage and ultimately resolve conflicts when and where they occur." The mechanism, which will work on the basis of the consent and the co-operation of the parties to a conflict, will be guided by "the objectives and principles of the OAU Charter; in particular, the sovereign equality of member states, the respect of the sovereignty and territorial integrity of member states, their inalienable right to independent existence, the peaceful settlement of disputes as well as the inviolability of borders inherited from colonialism." The mechanism treats peace-keeping as an ultimate conflict resolution instrument, one that should be deployed only after the complete exhaustion of preventive diplomacy and peace-making which can forestall the occurrence or escalation of conflicts. Peace-building operations are envisaged in order to consolidate peace processes and prevent a relapse into conflict. In this respect, the declaration states that "civilian and military missions of observation and monitoring of limited scope and duration may be mounted and deployed." In the event that conflicts escalate, the mechanism makes provision for the OAU to resort to the United Nations and to seek member states' practical contributions to and effective participation in United Nations peace-keeping operations in Africa.

The declaration stipulates that the seat of the mechanism shall be Addis Abeba, the headquarters of the OAU, and that the mechanism will be built around a central organ which shall function at the level of heads of state as well as that of ministers and ambassadors accredited to the OAU or duly authorized representatives. The members of the central organ will be members of the Bureau of the OAU Assembly of Heads of State and Government elected annually. The OAU Secretariat shall constitute the operational arm of the mechanism.

If a parallel can be drawn between the mechanism and the United Nations' structures in matters of peace-keeping, it may be said that the central organ plays the political role of the security council in determining the prospects of applying the mechanism in a conflict. Unlike in the Charter of the OAU and its related security mechanisms evoked earlier, the role of the OAU Secretary-General in the work of the mechanism is more than just administrative. Like the UN Secretary-General, who acts under the authority of the security council, the OAU Secretary-General shall, "under the authority of the Central Organ and in consultations with the parties involved in the conflict, deploy efforts and take all appropriate initiatives to prevent, manage and resolve conflicts." He will rely in the execution of these tasks on the human and material resources of the secretariat.

The broadened role of the OAU Secretary-General in the work of the mechanism is an auspicious development that may enhance possibilities of success for the OAU in conflict resolution. This may be true particularly in the light of the well-known criticism that the OAU peace-keeping sham in Chad was largely attributable to the OAU's unclear methods of work. For instance, in addition to the enormous logistical problems, the OAU did not establish adequate arrangements for reporting during its peace-keeping adventure in Chad:

> In contrast with the well-tried and tested experience of the United Nations [in this field], there is no clear-cut procedure for the commander of the forces to make regular reports to the Secretary-General of the OAU. Even when reports are filed with the Secretary-General of the OAU, he does not know what he should do with the reports.[16]

Unlike earlier mechanisms whose creation was initiated by member states, it should be borne in mind that the mechanism is largely the conception of Secretary-General Ahmed Salim, who has toiled against powerful currents for its realization. The fact that the central organ held its organizational meeting in December 1993, barely six months after the establishment of the mechanism, is being held as a sign of seriousness, particularly for an organization that has an established reputation of nonchalance, procrastination and other characteristics of failure.

However, at the very heart of this hope and early euphoria stands the financial threat that may paralyze the mechanism which, like many existing structures, is expected to function on the basis of "a special fund governed by the relevant OAU financial Rules and Regulations which will be established for the purpose of providing financial resources to support exclusively the OAU operational activities on conflict management and resolution." The said fund will be made up of financial appropriations from the regular budget of the OAU, voluntary contributions from member states and from other sources within and outside Africa, as appropriate. With the present financial and economic difficulties faced by almost all African states, a situation that does not show signs of improvement in the near future, together with ever dwindling contributions to the regular budget of the OAU as well as the increasing precariousness of voluntary contributions, it may be unrealistic to expect much success from the mechanism, even in the next decade. Little attention is being paid to African problems today, as the continent continues to be marginalized in international affairs. The international community is increasingly becoming weary of Africa's multiple problems and its demonstrated inability to keep its house in order. External donors will have to choose between contributing to the United Nations for the management of African conflict and to the OAU mechanism. The limits of the UN in conflict management are at least already known. So the mechanism will have to prove that it can do better than the UN in order to attract foreign contributions. Fundraising has become a herculean task nowadays, and African subregional organizations have been finding it difficult to attract foreign funds for their projects. Even the ECOWAS has been lobbying hard to enlist foreign support for its peace-keeping operation in Liberia.

The Economic Community of West African States (ECOWAS)

As its name indicates, ECOWAS is an economic- and development-oriented organization made up of sixteen countries in West Africa (Benin, Burkina Faso, Cape Verde, Cote d'Ivoire, Gambia, Ghana, Guinea, Guinea Bissau, Liberia, Mali, Mauritania, Niger, Nigeria, Senegal, Sierra Leone and Togo). It has two security-related mechanisms known as: (1) Protocol on Non-Aggression, and (2) Protocol relating to Mutual Assistance on Defence.

The ECOWAS Protocol on Non-Aggression. The Protocol on Non-Aggression came into effect following its signature on 22 April 1978 in Lagos. It is based on the affirmation that ECOWAS "cannot attain its development objectives save in an atmosphere of peace and harmonious understanding among the member states of the Community." Basically, the protocol appears as a classical non-aggression pact that appeals to member states to refrain in their relations with one another, from "the threat or use of force or aggression or from employing any other means inconsistent with the Charters of the United Nations and the Organization of African Unity against the territorial integrity or political independence of other member states." It is a pledge to member states to resort to all peaceful means in the settlement of disputes arising among themselves. In the spirit of article 5, "any disputes which cannot be settled peacefully among member states shall be referred to a committee of the Authority [the supreme organ of ECOWAS]. In the event of failure of the aforementioned committee, the disputes shall finally go to the Authority."

The Protocol on Non-Aggression does not explicitly say what the authority should do with a dispute when it is finally brought to it. In addition to the lack of coercive provisions, this lacuna reveals the protocol to be ultimately a soft structure, the success of which depends on the good faith and the rare mutual trust among member states. World history is littered with violations of non-aggression pacts of this nature. The drafters of the ECOWAS protocol were certainly conscious of the inherent weakness in non-aggression pacts as viable security instruments in a human society of conflicting interests which sometimes lead to war. To this end, therefore, they added another protocol to the ECOWAS Treaty with a more aggressive and constraining character when they met in Freetown in 1981 to sign the Protocol on Mutual Assistance on Defence.

The ECOWAS Protocol on Mutual Assistance on Defence. In contrast to the Protocol on Non-Aggression, the Protocol on Mutual Assistance commits ECOWAS to take collective military action against an aggressor. The implementation of the protocol is entrusted to three institutions: the Authority, which decides on the expediency of military action; the Defence Council, which has the responsibility of examining the situation, the strategy to be adopted and the means of intervention to be used; and the Defence Commission, charged with the responsibility of examining the technical aspects of defence matters.

The preamble to this protocol underlines member states' awareness of "the fact that external defence of their states depends entirely on each sovereign state, and that such a defence will be more effective with the coordination and pooling together of the means of mutual assistance provided by respective member states within the framework of this Protocol." Article 2 sets out the basis and principle for intervention in the following manner: "Member states declare and accept that any armed threat or aggression directed against any member state shall constitute a threat or aggression against the entire Community"; article 3 attempts very ambiguously to specify the nature of intervention: "Member states resolve to give mutual aid and assistance for defence against any armed threat or aggression." The mode of intervention is spelled out in article 17: "When there is a conflict between two member states of the Community, the Authority shall meet urgently and take appropriate action for mediation. If need be, the Authority shall decide only to interpose the AAFC [Allied Armed Forces of the Community] between the troops engaged in the conflict." Though never tested, the provisions of article 17 of the protocol have been invoked in several situations, including the

Mali-Burkina Faso clash over the Agacher strip in 1985 and the Senegal-Mauritania border dispute in 1989.

Internal conflict situations are dealt with by article 18, which states that (1) "in the case where an internal conflict in a member state of the Community is actively maintained and sustained from outside, the provisions of article 6, 9 and 16 of this Protocol shall apply";[17] (2) "Community forces shall not intervene if the conflict remains purely internal." This is a rather ambigous wording. Thus, paragraph 1 of article 18 is often considered, though with some controversy, as constituting the basis for the establishment of the ECOWAS Monitoring Group (ECOMOG) in Liberia in 1990. It is certainly difficult to delineate a "purely internal conflict," since all insurgent groups receive military and logistical assistance from outside in almost all African internal armed conflicts. In addition, the transborder ethnic configuration of African states together with the flow of refugees across national boundaries in times of war make it difficult for neighbouring states to stay uninvolved, in one way or another, in a conflict.

The merit of the Protocol of Mutual Assistance on Defence has been recognized by the international community through the ECOMOG, which in spite of the legal irregularities surrounding its formation and its political and organizational setbacks underscored the importance of subregional organizations in conflict management. As a legal instrument, the protocol combines aspects of a traditional collective security system and a collective defence system in accordance with our working definitions, as stated at the beginning of this chapter. In practice, however, the implementation of the protocol has fallen short of the requirements of these two security systems. This is because the ongoing ECOMOG undertaking in Liberia, perceived as ECOWAS' most ambitious achievement, is more of a collective conflict management effort bordering upon peace-keeping or even peace-enforcement than a collective security or a collective defence action.

The Accord de Non-Agression et d'Assistance en Matière de Défense (ANAD)

The initiative for the creation of the ANAD came from the six member states of the Communauté Economique des Etats de l'Afrique de l'Ouest (CEAO) and Togo on 9 June 1977 in Abidjan, where the organization is now headquartered.[18] The ANAD has a dual role as a conflict management mechanism and a semi-collective defence system.

The ANAD as a Non-offensive Conflict Management Mechanism. The constiutional objective of the ANAD was to intervene in the process of preserving peace and security in the countries concerned by way of conflict prevention and conflict resolution. Like many other security arrangements on the continent, the ANAD calls on its member states to resolve their differences peacefully and to refrain from using force or threatening to use force in their relations. In addition, it forbids member states from resorting to the use or the threat of force even on a non-member country. In the words of its secretary-general, the ultimate objective of the ANAD is thus *urbi et orbi*, since it is in essence useful for the subregion, for Africa and for the world as a whole.[19] This ideal of peace is reinforced by the prohibition it lays down for member states on harbouring foreign opposition leaders and subversive persons of other countries on their territories.

The ANAD carries out conflict resolution functions by putting in place a commission made up of two representatives per member country who may use mediation, conciliation or arbitration in the settlement process as appropriate. The choice of arbitration, however, is accompanied by the commitment of the parties to the conflict to accept the decision of the arbitral tribunal as binding. The Conference of Heads of State and Government of the ANAD is also charged with the responsibility of finding peaceful solutions to any existing conflict among the members. Should a conflict break out between two member states in spite of all preventive efforts, the mechanism provides for the interposition of a peace-keeping force between the parties. This is the method that was used when the ANAD intervened in the armed clash that followed the border dispute between Mali and Burkina Faso in 1985.

The ANAD as a Collective Defence Mechanism. Although the ANAD does not, of course, have belligerent and expansionist aims, it does have a defensive doctrine which enables it to deal with an invading aggressor. Two protocols (the Additional Protocol on Defence Matters and the Amendment to the Additional Protocol on Defence Matters) concretized the member states' desire to assist each other in defence matters on the basis of equality and the respect of mutual interests. The ANAD thus possesses legal instruments for collective defence in case of an external aggression. Thus, though there is no explicitly predefined or even an implied enemy, as would be the case in a traditional collective defence system,[20] the ANAD appears as a collective defence system. As such, an attack on an ANAD member state is treated as an attack on the system as a whole, and it is to be responded to in the following manner:

- diplomatic measures: direct collective pressure; intervention of third parties; recourse to international bodies, such as the ECOWAS, the OAU, the United Nations;

- coercive measures not involving the use of armed forces: suspension or severance of trade and technical relations; freezing or seizure of property; various boycotts; suspension or severance of diplomatic relations;
- the use of armed forces, the *ultima ratio regum*: member states would contribute troops and military equipment as warranted by the magnitude of the attack and form a unified force under one command.

The use of armed forces by the ANAD against an outside enemy has not occurred, nor has any of the preceding coercive measures been taken. These are traditional sanctions also provided for in the Covenant of the League of Nations and currently used by the United Nations in many and varied situations. The rationale behind sanctions is to bring the aggressor or the recalcitrant nation to comply with the prevailing order and accepted norms in the community without the use of armed force, which would otherwise result in human casualties and material damage of considerable proportions, affecting in particular the innocent civilian populations. In addition to addressing purely strategic and military threats, the mandate of the ANAD also involves the protection of the civilian population in case of natural disasters, such as epidemics, floods, earthquakes, famine and fires. Such efforts are classified under the defence of the economies and the welfare of member countries.

Unlike the OAU's moribund security mechanisms, the ANAD is a relatively functional mechanism that has proven its worth within its sphere of jurisdiction. Its contribution to the settlement of the Mali-Burkina border dispute has been registered as a major achievement. An occasion for the ANAD to demonstrate its collective defence capabilities has not yet emerged, since all major conflicts in the area have been domestic. Thus, the most important function of the ANAD has been to serve as a confidence-building mechanism, contributing to the creation of a sense of common belonging and harmony among its members. Nevertheless, the existence of the ANAD, like that of its mother organization, the CEAO, has contributed to continued suspicion and mistrust within the ECOWAS, the larger framework to which all ANAD's members belong. Many ECOWAS members, especially the anglophones, have reportedly called for the dissolution of the ANAD as a means of reinforcing the security arrangements of the ECOWAS—the Protocol of Non-Aggression and the Protocol for Mutual Assistance on Defence.

Other Security Arrangements in Africa

As stated earlier, most economic and development-oriented organizations in Africa see security as an unquantifiable requirement and as a basis for any meaningful development projects. The Preferential Trade Area (PTA) and the Southern African Development Community (SADC) have recognized this fact by inserting into their respective treaties clauses that directly or indirectly call for member states to make efforts to maintain a peace and security climate that would enhance economic opportunities. But these are simple expressions of wishes and good intentions that are not binding and would only be workable in a climate of confidence and trust.

On the other hand, the Arab Maghreb Union (AMU), a political organization made up of Algeria, Libya, Morocco and Tunisia, is predicated on the historical, religious and linguistic affinities that unite its members. Contrary to the PTA and the SADC, the Arab Maghreb Union has adopted a stronger tone that has little to do with confidence and trust among member states in matters of defence and security. In this field, as a matter of fact, member states strive to preserve their independence vis-à-vis one another. The four member states seem, however, to have created among themselves a security haven against an external aggression by article 14 which states that "any aggression directed against one of the member states shall be considered as an aggression against the other member states." In contrast to a traditional collective security system by which a threat that would call for collective action emanates from within the system, the treaty of the AMU puts emphasis on the external element, as can be seen in article 15:

> Member states pledge not to permit on their territory any activity or organization liable to threaten the security, the territorial integrity or the political system of any of them. They also pledge to abstain from joining any alliance or military or political block directed against the political independence or territorial integrity of the other member states.

However, as in other cases, the AMU security provisions have not yet been employed, in spite of manifest frictions among the union's members as regards their individual defence relations with non-member and extra-African countries. Most probably, the provisions have not been used because the driving force behind the creation of the union itself—external threat and aggression—has not yet occurred. In any event, the many differences among the AMU members make it difficult to foresee any collective military action against external aggression. Libya, for instance, with its ever-recurrent problems with the West and the USA in particular, has had no particularly meaningful support from the union.

A panorama of African security arrangements would certainly be incomplete without the inclusion of the fledgling United Nations Standing Advisory Committee on Security Questions in Central Africa. The Standing Advisory Committee was established on 28 May 1992 by the UN Secretary-General at the request of the 11 member states of the Economic Community of Central African States (ECCAS), pursuant to General Assembly resolution 46/37B of 6 December 1991.[21] Its establishment was perceived as a means to reinforce security in that subregion given the fact that security was not a great concern in the largely economic- and development-inspired treaty of the ECCAS.

The Standing Advisory Committee cannot be treated as a collective security system. It is a mechanism that ultimately strives to bring about peace by providing an appropriate forum and conditions for discussing political and technical ways and means that would facilitate the preservation of durable and meaningful security, including confidence-building measures in Central Africa. It is not legally binding and has no coercive powers. Its legal basis is the United Nations resolution, cited above, and the treaty of the ECCAS within which it should be operating.[22] The institutional objective of the committee is "to develop confidence-building measures and to encourage arms limitation and development in the Central African subregion."[23] The deliberations of the committee take place at different levels, including meetings of experts (high-level military and civilian officials), ministerial meetings and talks between the heads of states of the ECCAS as appropriate.

The committee is looked upon as a novel undertaking for the UN and the subregion; it is believed to be a unique endeavour of much promise in the field of security in this area, due in particular to its comprehensive programme of work. This programme includes the recent adoption of a non-aggression pact and current efforts towards an agreement on a balanced reduction of military forces, equipment and budgets in the subregion as well as the establishment of a standing inter-state general staff for crisis management and peace-keeping. Other tasks of the committee comprise education and training in the fields of preventive diplomacy, peace-building, peace-making and peace-keeping, including compliance and verification methods.

Contrary to the other African collective conflict management mechanisms that have been discussed earlier in this chapter, the Standing Advisory Committee on Security Questions in Central Africa is indeed seen to be a unique institution not only because of its United Nations sponsorship, but also because it is a pragmatic measure that brings to bear both military and civilian viewpoints in addressing defence and security questions.

Recent deliberations in the committee's experts and ministerial meetings indicate a long-term intention to form a common army in the subregion and a clear desire on the part of the member states to co-operate closely with and to draw from the experience and resources of the United Nations to advance the security interests of the subregion, especially in the present post-Cold War era.[24] It has been reported that

> the adoption of the non-aggression pact between the countries of the subregion and the Committee's decision to mandate its officers to play a more active political role and to undertake visits of solidarity and sympathy to countries engaged in conflicts, among other initiatives, mark the beginning of major achievements in the field of preventive diplomacy and confidence-building, which have already shifted the Committee's work into higher gear after only a year of existence.[25]

The solidarity and sympathy visits of the committee's officers to countries involved in conflicts can be seen as a measure signalling the evolving role of the committee in domestic conflict.

Clearly, all the mechanisms we have reviewed above, either within the framework of the Organization of African Unity or within the structures of subregional economic organizations, distance themselves from the traditional concept of collective security. The United Nations Standing Advisory Committee on Security Questions in Central Africa, as a security mechanism, is even further remote from this concept and seems to signal a new trend in the building of security institutions on the continent. In this new trend, conflict prevention and conflict management are gaining momentum as practical mechanisms that can address the many security concerns inherent in nation-building, particularly at a time when the foundation of the continent's security is being shaken by the salutary wind of democracy. These developments inevitably raise the question of the applicability of the traditional security concept in Africa.

The Prospects for Collective Security in Africa

Though there may be variations in the theory and practice, the very existence of the idea of collective security ultimately signifies international society's rejection of aggression as morally acceptable in international affairs. In an African international system where conflict endures, the relevance of collective security, conceived of as legally mandatory coercion by a group of states against any government that transgresses the peace, cannot be gainsaid. The concept needs, however, to be re-examined in the face of changes in African politics and the growing number of threats to the continent's security.

African Security Realities Versus Collective Security

The past few years have witnessed the collapse of the bipolar international system and the end of the Cold War which helped sustain many African armed conflicts, particularly in Angola, in Mozambique, in Ethiopia-Somalia and also the endemic South African low-intensity warfare. Now peace processes are underway in these places, but emerging ethnic and other civil tensions—ironically relating to democratization in many countries—are seriously threatening to tear apart the very security fabric of the entire continent. In addition to Angola, Burundi, Liberia, Rwanda, Somalia and the Sudan which, by late 1994, could still be treated as countries in a state of war, in Algeria, Cameroon, Chad, Congo, Kenya, South Africa, Togo and Zaire in particular, security has remained mortgaged to the political and economic stalemates that have paralyzed the functioning of the state machineries in these countries and have found expression in continuous and pervasive violence.

The gravity of the situation is such that several million Africans have been affected and several tens of thousands have died from this new form of instability and insecurity in the past two years, mainly from governmental repression and individual and organized group raids. Frequent attacks with bombs and other explosives, never before seen on the continent, have gained momentum in recent times and have taken a considerable toll in human life. This state of affairs has prompted opposition groups in the countries concerned to call for external assistance and collective mechanisms, such as peace-keeping operations, that would restore stability and address the plight of the victimized populations. In essence, the call can be interpreted as a humanitarian plea, albeit with political undertones that border upon interference in the domestic affairs of states, a concern which traditional collective security does not address.

The principles of "non-interference" and "sovereignty," so boldly inscribed in most African international treaties, should be critically reviewed for collective security to be given a chance in situations where states have voluntarily come together, ceding part of their sovereignty by adhering to a treaty in order to enhance their various national interests. More than ever before, domestic conflicts with their attendant transborder implications, such as the flow of refugees, the sensitiveness of ethnic minority questions and the risk of weapons proliferation, pose security problems at subregional and regional levels at a time when the recent ease in territorial disputes and related inter-state incidents that provided the original incentives for the formation of collective security systems would seem to indicate that sanity is being restored.

Indeed, the end of the Cold War together with the decrease of the influence of external powers in African affairs and the growing commonality in economic hardships and political upheavals are initiating an era of increased communication and maturity rather than the erstwhile antagonistic competition among African leaders. This auspicious moment when the continent seems to rely mainly on itself for its own salvation constitutes a golden opportunity to devise durable security mechanisms at domestic and inter-state levels: increased democratization, at least in the long run, can bring about stability. At the same time, the formation of common subregional armies and inter-state general staffs, already under discussion in some circles in Africa, would strengthen the process of integration that has been initiated by the various subregional organizations and would go a long way towards facilitating the collective management of domestic crises without undue fear of interference.

The existing structures of collective security and collective management systems are not equipped, at least legally, and were not created to deal with domestic threats to security, though the porous nature of African states makes it easy for the domestic disorders in a given state rapidly to become a concern for the neighbours. Beyond the political consideration of non-interference, there is a compelling humanitarian urge in situations of armed conflicts to which neighbours and non-neighbours cannot remain indifferent and which can, in fact, provide a legitimate base for intervention. In 1979, Tanzania explained its internationally applauded armed intervention in Uganda, which led to the ousting of the sanguinary Idi Amin, as, *inter alia*, a humanitarian measure to halt the killings and the systematic violations of human rights in that country. Furthermore, peace-keeping and humanitarian operations have been deployed in Liberia and in Somalia by the ECOWAS and the United Nations respectively without the unanimous approval of the parties to the conflicts in these countries.[26]

While lawyers are at work codifying the emerging concepts of interference and inserting them into the legitimate concerns of modern collective security, the concept of security itself has broadened from its strategic and military focus to include concerns, such as environmental degradation which, more than any war, threatens the existence of more than 100 million Africans every year,[27] diseases such as AIDS which exact high human tolls, and poverty which, in addition to the physical threat that it constitutes, also debases the dignity of the African person. The question therefore arises: should the non-military threats to human security be an object of collective security? The question has attracted many responses; some in favour of extending the domain of collective security to the non-military field, and others against such an extensive use of collective security, fearing it would only obfuscate the already elusive concept.

Actually, there is no reason for collective security to be concerned with non-military threats, which can best be managed through the establishment of regimes specifically constructed for this purpose. Efforts to fight the non-military threats under such regimes may help to mellow strategic and economic competition and would more easily call forth the cooperation of states than would a system designed to deal with military threats which most often exacerbate political sensitivity.[28] Daniel Deudney, a strong supporter of ecological management, has argued that while

> the degradation of the natural environment upon which human well-being depends is a challenge of far-reaching significance for human societies everywhere ... this challenge has little to do with the national-security-from-violence problem that continues to plague human political life.[29]

The implications of ecological insecurity for human society cannot be overemphasized, particularly in Africa where any meaningful development has so far largely involved the exploitation of the environment in one way or another. It is encouraging that African states and the OAU have begun to devise relevant policies in this field independent of the challenges of traditional collective security.

Challenges to Collective Security in Africa

In Africa, the major challenges to collective security at the subregional or regional levels include, most importantly, the lack of collective political will on the part of member states and the scarcity of resources, the existence of parallel military arrangements between individual states and foreign powers as well as the weaknesses inherent in collective security itself, such as its inability to provide means to deal with ancillary effects of its use, i.e., measures to bring under control the human and material damage caused by the deployment of collective security. In addition, there is little provision in the practice of collective security for the enhancement of post-conflict reconciliation and peace consolidation that would forestall an early relapse into conflict.

The collective political will and consensus of the member states of a collective security system is an essential requirement that can facilitate the deployment and success of an operation staged in the name of that system. Unfortunately, this has not always happened in the few collective security operations taking place in Africa. The ongoing ECOWAS operation in Liberia is a case in point. The very establishment of the ECOMOG was beset with fundamental legal and political differences that threatened to tear the entire endeavour apart and has since then contributed to a straining of relations among a cross-section of the member states. The legal provisions of the relevant ECOWAS Protocols, as noted above, that provided the foundation for the operation have been a matter of serious controversy and conflicting interpretations among the members; so much so that there have been two major camps: one, the minority, believing in the legality of the deployment and the other, possibly because of the interests of its individual leaders or nations in the Liberian conflict, arguing that the conflict was purely internal and therefore offered no legal basis for ECOWAS intervention. A similar disagreement had arisen within the framework of the OAU regarding its peace-keeping involvement in Chad.

The two cases have revealed an additional political challenge to collective security, notably power ranking among states. Nigeria, which has always taken the lead in providing political and logistic solutions to the bottlenecks arising in the course of the two operations, has reportedly been portrayed as an hegemonic power. This perception has very often created mistrust and suspicion, which have then hindered genuine co-operation among member states to the detriment of the operations.

Political problems have constituted disincentives for African states to cultivate trust in their collective security arrangements and contribute logistically to their functioning. Peace-keeping is an expensive conflict resolution mechanism that requires adequate personnel and logistical resources in order for it to succeed. The legendary sham of the OAU operation in Chad has largely been attributed to its failure to fulfill this requirement. It failed partly because it did not gather consensus, was branded partial and lacked the necessary moral force that could have conferred upon it an acceptable degree of respectability, even among the member states. African states must have faith in and respect their own institutions.

This may not come about very easily or very soon, particularly in the security field where the legacy of colonialism has bestowed defence and security co-operation pacts with former colonial powers upon a great number of African states. As a matter of fact, about thirty-nine military co-operation and security assistance agreements bind African countries with non-African powers, some of whom have also established about thirteen military and telecommunication bases and missile test sites on the continent.[30] The African states concerned have shown greater respect for, and trust in, such arrangements to which they resort more easily than to continental collective security initiatives.[31] These initiatives have scarcely been tested and have also often been bypassed in favour of the United Nations.

Organizing Collective Security

Collective Security in Africa and the United Nations

In his report to the Security Council entitled "Agenda for Peace,"[32] UN Secretary-General Boutros-Ghali calls for member states and regional organizations to initiate peace efforts at regional levels and to provide full support to UN peace-keeping and related missions in accordance with the provisions of Chapter VIII of the United Nations Charter. For

> with new kinds of security challenges regional arrangements or agencies can render assistance of great value. The defusion of tensions between states as well as the peaceful resolution of conflicts are issues that can be suitable for regional action in many cases.[33]

This is what Boutros-Ghali calls in his report "an integrated approach to human security."

The United Nations has been involved in the resolution of African conflicts since as long ago as 1960, when it mounted its first peace-keeping mission in the Congo. Since then it has been present in African conflicts more than any continental security arrangement. It staged the United Nations Mission for the Referendum in Western Sahara (MINURSO); the United Nations Transition Assistance Group in Namibia (UNTAG), concluded in March 1990 with the independence of Namibia; the United Nations Angolan Verification Mission (UNAVEM I and II); the United Nations Observer Mission in South Africa (UNOMSA); the United Nations Operation in Mozambique (ONUMOZ); the United Nations Mission in Rwanda (UNAMIR); the United Nations Observer Mission to Verify the Referendum in Eritrea (UNOVER); the United Nations Observer Mission in Liberia (UNOMIL); and the United Nations Operation in Somalia (UNOSOM). Though they differ in their mandates, all these UN missions share the objective of maintaining peace in Africa. Their differing mandates not only reveal the specific nature of each conflict, but put together, they all show the evolving capacity of the United Nations in resolving conflicts and preserving international order. Thus, the United Nations, through its collective conflict management mechanism, has demonstrated in Africa (with varying degrees of success) its capacity to assist in the re-creation and building of a nation (Namibia, Eritrea), to verify the withdrawal and disarmament of troops (Angola), to monitor the cease-fire and supervise elections (Western Sahara, Rwanda, Angola, Mozambique), to observe negotiations of a political nature that would lead to democratization and the restoration of peace and order (South Africa), and to facilitate the delivery of humanitarian assistance, the restoration of order and peace and the rebuilding of a nation (Somalia).

In some of these missions, the UN has been assisted by African states and has worked in conjunction with the OAU. In contrast with the OAU and other subregional security arrangements, however, UN mechanisms enjoy greater respectability and moral strength, partly owing to the belief by most Africans that these UN mechanisms are more efficient, better equipped and possess a higher degree of impartiality. For Africa to improve its conflict management performance, it would have to cultivate self-confidence and overcome the myth of its own incapacity in this field. After all, some of the UN peace-keeping operations have been successfully led by Africans both in the military and political domains. Thus, there are enough resources and experienced African personnel who can successfully carry out collective conflict management tasks. What is mostly required is the necessary political will. Lieutenant General Emmanuel Erskine, a veteran Ghanaian UN peace-keeper, has suggested the setting-up of a permanent secretariat at the OAU that would coordinate member states' peace-keeping efforts.[34]

The readiness to resort to the United Nations thwarts the development of genuinely African initiatives. The role of the United Nations is being enhanced in an international system that is becoming narrower. Today, many regions look up to the United Nations collective security mechanism whose tasks have been increased fourfold in the past five years. Regional collective security, particularly as it was originally conceived, is bound to become a figment of imagination, in spite of the UN Secretary-General's "integrated approach to human security." The UN capacity is clearly overburdened and its resources have been stretched so thin that many analysts have argued that the world organization has reached an anti-climax in its capacity to resolve world conflicts. Successful as it may be in general, the UN performance in Somalia for instance has sometimes been ridiculous and has remained below the expectations of many Africans.

Conclusions

Collective security following its classical meaning has not been exercised in Africa. Today, the term is increasingly understood as collective conflict management, a field in which Africa has had wide experience at the regional and subregional levels particularly under the auspices of economic and development-oriented organizations and the OAU. But collective conflict management has not always worked on the continent for various reasons, including the lack of political will, the scarcity of resources and the African leaders' lack of respect for and confidence in continental security mechanisms. In this regard, there has been an extensive use of extra-African security arrangements at bilateral and multilateral levels, a habit which does not augur well for the development of genuine African initiatives, on the one hand, and the continent's international image, on the other hand.

The idea of traditional collective security would be difficult to implement in Africa, owing to the acute growth of domestic sources of conflicts which the idea does not address. Instead, peace-making, though with rare success, has gained momentum in recent years. Within this framework, the OAU has made use of ad hoc mechanisms, such as the "good offices" of its secretary-general or its chairman in the settlement of disputes both at domestic and at inter-state levels. Its new mechanism on conflict resolution is expected to be an institutionalized arrangement that would be used in both situations.

An emerging trend in security institution-building puts emphasis on crisis prevention, conflict management and confidence-building among states. This is the character of the United Nations Standing Advisory Committee on Security Questions in Central Africa which was established at the request of the member states of the Economic Community of Central African States (ECCAS). Developments in Southern Africa, with the gradual demise of the apartheid regime, are revealing the need for similar structures that would befit the post-apartheid security realities of Southern Africa.

Notes

1. David Ziegler reflects along the lines of the Italian fourteenth-century poet Dante Alighieri who, in his *Divine Comedy*, "advocated a universal kingdom including all the states of Europe." Ziegler further reports that in his book, *De Monarchia*, which appeared in 1313, Dante purports that "peace is impossible without a single authority that can settle quarrels among those beneath it." See David Ziegler, *War, Peace and International Politics*, 3rd edition (Boston: Little, Brown and Company, 1984), pp. 133-4. See also Inis Claude, Jr., *Power and International Relations* (New York: Random House, 1962), pp. 243-55; and his *Swords into Plowshares*, 4th edition (New York: Random House, 1971), p. 424.

2. Ernst B. Haas, "The Balance of Power: Prescription, Concept or Propaganda?" *World Politics*, Vol. 5, No. 4 (July 1953), pp. 442-77, counted eight different usages of the balance of power.

3. See Ziegler, *op. cit.*, in note 1, p. 185; and Joseph S. Nye, *Peace in Parts* (Boston: Little, Brown and Company, 1971), pp. 3, 129.

4. Karl Deutsch et al., *Political Community and the North Atlantic Area* (Princeton: Princeton University Press, 1957), quoted by Tom Farer "Regional Collective Security Arrangements," in: Tom Weiss (ed.), *Collective Security in a Changing World* (Boulder: Lynne Rienner Publishers, 1993).

5. Mohammed Ayoob, "Squaring the Circle: Collective Security in a System of States," in: Weiss, *ibid*.

6. Jean Klein, "Organisation de la Défense, mais aussi de la Prévention des Conflits," *Le Monde Diplomatique*, No. 477, December 1993, pp. 4, 5.

7. The idea of a defence committee first emerged at an international seminar on "Confidence- and Security-building Measures in Southern Africa," sponsored by the United Nations Regional Centre for Peace and Disarmament in Africa in co-operation with the Namibian government in Windhoek, from 24-26 February 1993. The idea has been elaborated upon at subsequent security conferences in the subregion, notably the May 1993 Midgard (Namibia) Conference on "Security, Co-operation and Development in Southern Africa," where participants urged the establishment of an inter-state defence committee. According to discussions at Midgard, the committee "could draw on the fruitful experience of a similar body which was established in the framework of the FLS. The proposed committee would, however, assume different responsibilities. It ought to consist of senior military officials who meet on a regular basis and ad hoc in contingencies." For more on the committee and other relevant discussions on security in post-apartheid Southern Africa, see the report on the Midgard Conference published by the Peace Research Institute Frankfurt (PRIF Reports, No. 31, 1993).

8. See Lance Morrow, "To Conquer the Past," *Time*, 3 January 1994, p. 35.

9. See Ernst B. Haas, "Collective Conflict Management: Evidence for a New World Order?" in: Weiss, *op. cit.*, in note 4, p. 64.

10. Tom Weiss and Leon Gordenker, "Whither Collective Security? An Unsettled Idea in a Changing World," in: Weiss, *op. cit.*, in note 4, pp. 209-19.

11. Ziegler, *op. cit.*, in note 1, p. 186.

12. This can be interpreted in the framework of integrationist theories of regional organizations where it is argued that development and security can be maximized through confidence-building policies among the member states.

13. Ivor Richard Fung, *Militarism in African States: The Case of Mozambique 1975-1989* (Yaounde: IRIC, 1991), p. 212.

14. Haas, *op. cit.*, in note 9.

15. James Jonah, "The OAU: Peace-Keeping and Conflict Resolution," in: Yassin El-Ayouty (ed.), *The Organization of African Unity: Thirty Years After* (Westport: Praeger, 1994), pp. 4-5.

16. See *ibid.*, p. 7.

17. Article 6 reads as follows: "1. The Authority on the occasion of the annual ordinary meeting of ECOWAS shall examine general problems concerning peace and security of the Community; 2. The Authority may also hold extraordinary sessions on defence matters where circumstances so require; 3. The Authority shall decide on the expediency of military action and entrust its execution to the Force Commander of the Allied Armed Forces of the Community (AAFC); 4. Decisions taken by the Authority shall be immediately enforceable on the member states." Article 9 reads: "In case of armed intervention, the Defence Council assisted by the Defence Commission shall supervise with the authority of the state or states concerned, all measures to be taken by the Force Commander and ensure that all necessary means for the intervention are made available to him. The actions of the Force Commander shall be subject to competent political authority of the member state or states concerned." Article 16 reads: "When an

external armed threat or aggression is directed against a member state of the Community, the Head of State of that country shall send a written request to the current Chairman of the Authority of ECOWAS, with copies to other members. This request shall mean that the Authority is duly notified and that the AAFC are placed under a state of emergency. The Authority shall decide in accordance with the emergency procedure as stipulated in article 6 above."

18 . The Economic Community of West African States (CEAO) is made of six French-speaking countries in West Africa: Burkina Faso (formerly Upper Volta), Cote d'Ivoire, Mali, Mauritania, Niger and Senegal. Togo was the only non-CEAO country that became a founding member of the ANAD.

19 . See General Jean Gomis' address to the "Conference on Confidence-building, Security and Development" within the framework of the Economic Community of Central African States, Lomé, Togo, 15-19 February 1988.

20 . It is often assumed that the ANAD was formed to counter an eventual attack from the anglophone West African block, notably Nigeria, which had maintained conflicting relations with Cote d'Ivoire for subregional leadership, and Ghana which has always constituted a threat to Togo since the 1959 UN-sponsored referendum by which British Togoland chose to be part of Ghana.

21 . ECCAS is made up of the following countries: Angola, Burundi, Cameroon, Central African Republic, Chad, Congo, Equatorial Guinea, Gabon, Rwanda, Sao Tome and Principe and Zaire.

22 . ECCAS member states are examining the inclusion of an additional protocol in the treaty of the ECCAS that would provide legal grounds for the existence of the committee and its various security instruments such as the non-aggression pact within the framework of the community.

23 . See United Nations General Assembly Resolution 46/37B of 6 December 1991 cited above.

24 . The Standing Advisory Committee meets every six months and each meeting consists of two levels: the level of military and civilian experts and the ministers of defence and of foreign affairs.

25 . United Nations, "Review and Implementation of the Concluding Document of the Twelfth Special Session of the General Assembly: Regional Confidence-Building Measures. Report of the Secretary-General," Document No. A/48/412, 11 October, 1993, p. 10.

26 . The deployments took place after the disintegration of the legitimate governments in these countries.

27 . Ivor Richard Fung, "The OAU and Environmental Questions," in: El Ayouty, *op. cit.*, in note 15, p. 106.

28 . Mohammed Ayoob, *op. cit.*, in note 5, p. 49.

29 . Daniel Deudney, "The Case Against Linking Environmental Degradation and National Security," *Millennium: Journal of International Studies*, Vol. 19, No. 3 (Winter 1990), p. 474.

30 . Fung, *op. cit.*, in note 13, p. 61.

31 . Cameroon, for instance, has often turned to France for assistance in its border dispute with Nigeria. This was the case in 1981 when six Nigerian soldiers were allegedly killed in the disputed area and a request for military equipment

was made to France in preparation for an eventual retaliation by Nigeria. On this note see an unpublished paper by Joseph Owona, "Le Désarmement en Afrique." The dispute resurfaced in December 1993 and escalated into a brief exchange of fire in February 1994 with casualties on both sides. The presence of French military advisers and paratroopers from the French military base in the neighbouring Central African Republic was reported in Cameroon in the wake of the fray. Though the Cameroonian authorities have explained their appeal for French military intervention as a legal exercise of their country's sovereignty, the underlying justification is the belief that these extra-African troops are better equipped and more experienced than any subregional or regional arrangement. The example of Cameroon is one of many, especially in French-speaking Africa.

32. Boutros Boutros-Ghali, *An Agenda for Peace* (New York: United Nations, 1992).

33. See *Report of the Secretary-General on the Work of the Organization* (New York: United Nations, 1990), p. 26.

34. General Emmanuel Erskine, "African Military and Peace-Keeping Operations," in: *Confidence and Security-building Measures in Southern Africa*, Disarmament: Topical Papers, No. 14 (New York: United Nations Department of Political Affairs, 1993), pp. 17-25. General Erskine was the first Force Commander of the United Nations Interim Force in Lebanon (UNIFIL).

5

Crisis Prevention and Conflict Management in Southern Africa in the Post-Cold War Era

Willie Breytenbach and Pál Dunay

New eras often give rise to new vocabularies. The increase in the number of violent international conflicts since the end of the East-West conflict has led to the incorporation of many new terms in the area of conflict resolution. Instead of different types of "peaceful dispute settlement," we now speak of "conflict resolution" and "security management," and instead of "enforcement measures," we somewhat euphemistically use the word "peace-making." Most of the pressing conflicts in today's world are not subject to traditional conflict resolution methods, since they are not international. For the most part, they have domestic roots and result from the scarcity of economic resources, from underdevelopment and from deficiencies in political systems. In cases such as these, one cannot apply any of the traditional methods of conflict management. It seems that the international community, ranging from decision-makers to analysts, is inclined to treat all these conflicts as essentially similar. But when we take a closer look, the following questions emerge: 1) Which conflicts will be subject to conflict management or resolution? 2) Which methods can be applied? and 3) Who are the actors in the process?

Before dealing with these questions, it has to be pointed out that conflict "prevention" is the most effective means of conflict "management." If states are able to detect potential conflicts at an early stage and can take the appropriate steps in order to prevent them from breaking out, conflict management, narrowly defined, becomes unnecessary. However, one has to take note of the fact that conflict prevention involves a number of difficulties. On the practical side, conflict prevention depends on two factors: early detection—intelligence and information gathering—and the adoption of adequate countermeasures. However, few members of the international community possess the technical means or extensive human intelligence to detect potential conflicts at a sufficiently early stage. Therefore, the question of the sharing of relevant information after it has been gathered, processed and evaluated arises. Will and should other states become involved in the exercise, thus potentially (pre-)determining decision-making procedures in different parts of the world? And finally, once states share the same version of the facts concerning the conflict potential developing in or originating from another country, there is still room for debate about which countermeasures should be adopted.

But there is a more general point to be made, namely that conflict prevention suffers from an inherent contradiction. If it is successful, it may never become clear whether there was a real conflict and hence whether there was anything to be prevented. This, too, has practical implications. If there were no real conflict, those who claim to have prevented one in fact did nothing but interfere in the affairs of a state without justification. Things may be even worse if interference is justified but not successful. Then it can easily happen that conflict prevention may contribute to escalation.

Finally, it has to be noted that conflict prevention elevates the nonmilitary and internal dimensions to a special position. This is particularly relevant for Africa. Douglas Anglin, among others, refers to the mood of pessimism that is returning to the continent. He alludes to the problems of democratic governance and economic pathology, which he links by observing that there is an "increasing recognition in Africa that democracy is a prerequisite for meaningful development."[1] Thus, securing two basic conditions—stable peace and democratic governance—may be seen as eliminating the most fundamental sources of conflict on the continent.

There is a controversy, however, as to whether democracy (by encouraging "debate, discussion and learning between states and societies") or authoritarianism is more conducive to development, since authoritarian regimes are considered "more likely to be able to withstand societal pressures to abandon costly economic policies. Some argue that Africa's economic crisis is so severe that the risks of the democratic solution are too high and may fatally delay the imposition of needed reform."[2] In light of the fact that it is by and large the same people who simultaneously offer the promises of democracy and the hardships of structural adjustment, this controversy hardly comes as a surprise. It is, however, a universal debate. The widely held view on the continent that "Africa is not ready for democracy,"[3] or pervasive sympathies for the "democratic centralism" once offered by the socialist regimes in Europe to aspiring autocrats in order "to justify their rule on the basis of promoting development, protecting the interests of a particular class, anti-imperialism or other forms of ideology,"[4] have lost much of their clout. In this regard, the end of the Cold War has clearly had an impact.[5] But as long as there is no unequivocal empirical evidence to demonstrate that only democratic countries can perform economically and secure sustained development, the debate will remain inconclusive. And with respect to conflict management, one has to be aware that democracy both increases the potential for conflicts and provides ways of solving them in a civilized way.

Sources and Types of Conflicts in Southern Africa

Conflict prevention and conflict management both require a clear understanding of the possible sources and types of conflict which have become an increasingly pressing concern of the international community. During the Cold War, politicians and analysts by and large paid attention to different conflicts only in their relation to the predominant East-West antagonism, but this situation has changed. The international political agenda is now dominated by a range of conflicts with deep domestic—and in many cases ethnic—roots. This is also true for Africa, and for Southern Africa in particular. In the past, the continent experienced two distinct, though related, "conflict formations": the struggle for "national liberation," for independence from European colonialism, which partly coexisted with and was partly succeeded by the struggle against apartheid. These conflicts and their relationship with the overarching East-West antagonism dominated the agenda on the African continent, though of course there were numerous others on a regional or local level. However, with decolonization completed and apartheid overcome, these two formations have lost their relevance. Therefore, drawing conclusions from the past will hardly provide the necessary sense of direction for the future. Neither of the previously dominant types of conflict will be characteristic of the future political life on the continent.

In all likelihood, conflicts will be more diverse than hitherto. Consequently, it will be more important than ever for conflict management to familiarize itself with the specific conditions within and around individual states and with the root causes of given conflicts. Furthermore, it has to be taken into consideration that the bulk of conflicts will not be inter-state in the traditional sense. In present circumstances, military threats are predominantly domestic and intra-regional only to the extent that inadvertent escalation may be caused by the cross-border activities of armed rebel groups and their supporters.[6] Thus, it is conflicts over distribution and political participation, compounded by ethnic strife, which have already become the major concern of conflict management.[7] As the significance of ethnic conflicts increases, possibly becoming the decisive type of conflict in the coming years, diplomats, mediators and peacemakers will have to operate in largely unknown terrain. This will aggravate a situation which is already complicated enough due to the fact that ethnic and other grassroot conflicts have a tendency to be protracted and difficult to resolve.

The rise of ethnicity, in Africa as elsewhere, could lead to more separatist uprisings following the pattern of Biafra, Shaba or Eritrea. These examples were of the secessionist (or breakaway) type. In other cases, for example in the Ogaden area of Ethiopia, the Somalis who live there have fought for re-incorporation into Somalia. This kind of irredentism is not yet a major issue in Africa, but could happen anywhere as a result of the arbitrarily drawn political boundaries from the time of partition after the Berlin Conference of 1884-1885. With the international doctrine of (ethnic) self-determination, now in the ascendant, the territorial sovereignty of many African states—based on colonial boundaries—is likely to be challenged. As Jeffrey Herbst has put it:

> The norm of sovereignty, which African countries successfully used as a cover to repress those who challenged the existing nation-states, is also now being threatened in a world increasingly concerned with self-determination.[8]

In addition, it has been clear for a long time that the demands made by Southern Africa's sources of conflict exceed the financial, political and intellectual resources at the region's disposal. Under present conditions, where military conflict no longer dominates the agenda, those problems which most directly affect the life of the population have to take priority. Some of them serve as a framework for addressing conflicts effectively, like the elimination of violence and the introduction of a functioning political system. These have been mentioned above. The following is not an exhaustive catalogue of additional sources of conflict in Southern Africa; it will merely touch upon some selected topics and issues which have already become matters of contention and may be relevant to the prospects of regional co-operation and eventual integration:

- droughts, agricultural failure, imposed structural adjustment and the resulting poverty and famine, together with ongoing civil strife, are some of the most salient causes behind the refugee problems in Africa. Malawi has had to deal with the most Mozambican refugees, and currently it is Tanzania and Zaire which are suffering from the enormous influx of refugees from Rwanda. But in future, civil strife and collapsing economies may cause "near uncontrollable" migration of peasants and ordinary economic refugees fleeing to South Africa and perhaps to a post-drought Zimbabwe.[9] Most illegal migrants in South Africa are Mozambican and, to a smaller extent, Zimbabwean;
- foreign fishing fleets are plundering marine resources, which poses serious challenges to famine-stricken and agriculturally depleted African states.[10] On a continent ravaged by cyclical droughts, competition for water is already serious (the conflict between Egypt, Sudan and Ethiopia over the water of the Nile is a case in point), and the future may even see this competition become a cause of war;[11]
- the landlocked states face serious trade and transportation problems, reminiscent of the way South Africa blocked transport routes during the destabilization years;[12]
- access to ports will remain a crucial issue in the quest for increased exports of commodities or manufactured products and for the importation of food and fuel;
- the prevalence of cross-border problems of cattle-rustlers, poaching and car theft rackets call for police and licensing authorities to co-operate on a multilateral basis;
- in the socio-economic fields, various domestic conflicts may arise from the collapse of social services as a result of inadequate health services related to the spread of AIDS, tuberculosis, cholera and malaria. This may lead either to more refugees or to further deterioration of social services;
- the reconstruction of systems comes with its own complexities. In the first place, the structural adjustment programmes could have destructive consequences, for example cuts in bureaucracies (creating an unemployed middle class); the devaluation of African currencies and higher costs of living; debt servicing at the expense of the provision of social services; budget deficits; the commercialization of peasant agriculture emphasizing cash and not food crops; societal inequalities between producers and consumers; higher food prices; higher interest rates, etc. On top of that, the problem of the rehabilitation of war economies in Southern Africa poses a task of a particular magnitude;
- finally, there is the potential for large-scale smuggling in the region (the smuggling of drugs has already become a serious problem,

linking South Africa with Latin America and the Far East, often through Africa) if South Africa were to join COMESA. The South African Customs Union (SACU) would then have to disband, meaning that the member states (Botswana, Lesotho, Swaziland and Namibia) would have to impose tariffs on imports from South Africa, which would entail higher domestic prices in those countries, inevitably leading to smuggling.[13]

Conflict Management and Resolution in Post-Apartheid Southern Africa

The specifics of present-day conflicts in Southern Africa, as briefly mapped out in the preceding section, clearly have repercussions on the methods to be applied in efforts at conflict management. Since their root causes are predominantly non-military and domestic, accompanied by an escalatory potential beyond the respective national borders, traditional methods, such as mediation and peace-keeping or enforcement, may not necessarily be applicable. They certainly need as much qualification as the well-established principle of non-interference in the domestic affairs of nation-states. Similarly, one has to take a fresh look at the potential actors and their respective capabilities for pursuing effective conflict management.

Since the end of bipolarity, the international community has not only had to deal with an increasing number and a large variety of conflicts. For simple practical reasons, it has also displayed a tendency to apply "soft" as opposed to "intrusive" methods of conflict resolution. At the same time, a measure of confusion has emerged, as analysts and decision-makers alike tend to blur the distinction between means of peaceful settlement of disputes and enforcement measures, clearly separated in documents like the UN Charter. Yet, it has to be reiterated that the most fundamental conflicts in Africa, such as those over distribution and political participation, cannot be resolved by international action in the traditional sense. They rather call for wide-ranging international co-operation, for development assistance or for popularizing democratic political values. For this reason, some analysts even advocate not involving states or intergovernmental organizations in conflict resolution at all. Instead, they call for "training programs, monitoring efforts by NGOs and civic education, focusing on tolerance and peace."[14] In any case, conflict management will become more complex, after the dominant conflict formations have been overcome. The diversity of contemporary conflicts will make individual treatment indispensable.

One way of managing conflicts has been the application of traditional methods of dispute settlement, such as mediation between the conflicting parties, irrespective of whether the conflict is international. The readiness to mediate can never be regarded as an interference in the affairs of the parties, which has not surprisingly made the initiation of mediation quite popular for decades. The mediator can be a state, an international organization or an individual acceptable to all parties to the conflict. Opinions vary on whether it is better for the "optimal mediator" to be a neutral with no direct interest in the outcome, or a party with its own interest in the resolution of the conflict. It certainly facilitates mediation if in the framework of subregional institutions or regional organizations ad hoc bodies are readily available to conflicting parties.

Among "soft" measures, peace-keeping, though not provided for in the UN Charter, has gained prominence. It means locating monitors or troops in conflict zones to separate the fighting parties when they have been able to agree upon some temporary settlement, e.g., a cease-fire. Southern Africa has had fairly extensive experience with peace-keeping, and has seen both successes and failures. It seems that there will not be many conflicts in the region where this method, based on the consent of the parties, can safely be applied. Even in Angola, where it was easy to identify the conflicting parties—a necessary though insufficient condition of successful peace-keeping—UN monitors had to withdraw due to the continuing hostilities. Instead, more intrusive measures, such as sanctions, had to be considered, but neither neighbouring countries nor SADC or the international community at large appear ready to employ these in any effective manner. They have not even been able to put the most essential measure in place: a curfew on the channelling of major weapons systems to UNITA.[15]

Peace-keeping is not the only method to have been practised in Southern Africa. This region is the only part of the world where, during the Cold War, the United Nations applied non-military sanctions against individual states—Rhodesia and South Africa, because of their apartheid regimes. Since the end of bipolarity, the world organization has been able to agree more frequently upon enforcement measures. However, experience indicates that neither the readiness nor the resources exist for the regular application of sanctions or more far-reaching measures. As far as readiness is concerned, it may be indicative that the UN Security Council fell short of declaring the spring 1994 massacres in Rwanda to be genocide, which would have made the application of sanctions against the country mandatory.

Given the fact that most contemporary conflicts are domestic in nature, conflict management requires active interference in the domestic affairs of sovereign states. This in turn requires the readiness of states to accept this interference. On the one hand, the traditional absolute respect for state sovereignty has been eroding for quite some time due to economic integration and a wide range of transnational activities. On the other hand, this attitude is more prevalent in regions where trans-border interaction is regarded as a natural phenomenon than in countries where those in power forcefully protect their newly acquired, or re-acquired, independence, as in Africa. One has to keep this fact in mind in order not to make unrealistic proposals. For instance, the idea of granting international organizations, such as the OAU, more competence to interfere in the domestic affairs of its member states for purposes of conflict resolution, may be illusory. It is not just a constitutional affair to amend the charter of this organization, since the OAU was only acceptable to African states on the basis of its current provisions. The primacy of independence over unity, i.e. the absence of any provision for conceding any aspect of state sovereignty to the organization, is not incidental.[16]

It has to be noted, however, that "state sovereignty" has not been entirely unconditional since the end of World War II. Even though the Charter of the United Nations proclaimed that "[n]othing in the...Charter shall authorize the United Nations to intervene in matters which are essentially within the domestic jurisdiction of any state..." (paragraph 7, article 2), at the conference drafting the charter a number of exceptions were established, including not only enforcement measures against an aggressor but also the following: "if the fundamental freedoms of individuals were grievously outraged so as to create conditions which threaten peace or obstruct the application of the charter, then they cease to be the sole concern of each state."[17] In addition, several documents, including agreements on human rights or decisions of the General Assembly on self-determination in support of decolonization, have led to a situation where one can at least speak about a balance between the respect for state sovereignty, on the one hand, and that for human rights and self-determination, on the other. At the beginning of the 1990s, the UN Security Council even went one step further. In resolution 688 of 5 April 1991, it broke new ground in international law by approving the right to interfere on "humanitarian grounds." However, so far the international community has hardly been able to apply these rules, apart from cases of extremely massive and grave violations. Thus, conflicts below the level of massacres on the scale seen in Rwanda may remain unaffected by humanitarian intervention.

It may take decades for the international community to develop the necessary routine for determining in which case intervention in affairs which, fully or partially, belong to the domestic jurisdiction of states is unequivocally considered legitimate. In this regard, ethnic conflicts with deep historical roots and based on widespread animosity between population groups pose particular problems. Attempts to suppress such conflicts normally bring about nothing more than a temporary solution. Furthermore, given the mix of ethnic groups in most countries, there is not much chance of imposing a territorial solution. In principle, the call for border revisions should only be contemplated in cases when "there is a civil war between communal groups with irreconcilable differences or when a central state has agreed to dissolve itself and new international boundaries have to be drawn."[18] One has to add that even in cases of violence territorial changes should only be considered when ethnic groups are territorially separable, so that the revision of borders promises the termination of hostilities. Instead, one should guarantee respect for human rights, while in the short run a variety of measures can be considered which might include the separation of people belonging to different ethnic groups.

This leads to the question of who the most appropriate actors are to employ these measures of conflict management. Once this was the exclusive domain of the superpowers, who had a decisive say in the bipolar system of international relations and regulated or controlled conflicts, either themselves or through proxies. As a consequence, conflict management by other countries or by multilateral institutions remained limited. The global character of the conflict excluded other actors from making any meaningful contribution. They were unable to address the decisive East-West conflict, and this effectively barred institutional or state intervention in any conflict where the superpowers expressed their interests. This was most obvious in the centre of the East-West conflict, in Europe, which became a sanctuary where only the two global powers could "resolve" conflicts in their respective spheres of influence.[19] But it also became true for the other continents, though to a lesser degree. There the dominant conflict between East and West did not necessarily determine but clearly overshadowed and shaped regional relations.

It was inherent in the bipolar order that the political establishments in East and West prevented co-operation in the resolution of conflicts even in cases where settlement would have been in the common interest of mankind.[20] Thus, co-operative conflict prevention, or resolution, by the two superpowers became possible only in the second half of the 1980s when the Soviet Union started to realize that competing with the United States in every corner of the globe according to the simple logic of a zero sum game had proved neither beneficial in political nor affordable in economic terms. Within a relatively short period of time, which came to an end with the dissolution of the Soviet Union, these common endeavours produced tangible results: the visible co-operation in the liberation of Kuwait from Iraqi occupation, the resolution of the conflict in and around Namibia, the (temporary) ending of the Angolan civil war and the cease-fire in Mozambique. These settlements, which came about relatively easily following coordinated US-Soviet pressure on the warring parties, may be indicative of the relevance of external involvement in such protracted conflicts. Others, however, ranging from Angola to Afghanistan, have either turned into purely indigenous confrontations or revealed the local causes which were decisive all along.

It is this type of conflict which has resulted in violent clashes in many parts of the world since the end of the East-West conflict. Whereas in inter-state or domestic conflicts, posing a direct threat to international security, efforts at management or resolution by other states or international organizations may be most effective, this is not necessarily true in the case of purely indigenous conflicts. However, it frequently happens that for one reason or another parties cannot settle disputes on their own, or their efforts require assistance. In such cases, non-governmental actors may be considered with the coordinating and facilitating support of states and intergovernmental organizations. Conflict resolution attempts, either with the participation of states or with the active involvement of non-governmental actors, are not mutually exclusive. However, the combination of methods appropriate to the given conflict has to be carefully selected.

It is a characteristic feature of international relations in the twentieth century that intergovernmental organizations play an increasing role in regulating world affairs. This tendency is valid globally as well as regionally. However, it is necessary to draw attention to the fact that the policies of international institutions are determined by their members. Consequently, members can use and misuse them at the same time. Members can take refuge behind the "will" of organizations when they are reluctant to take certain steps, such as intervention in a conflict or the application of sanctions. Conversely, they may seek the limelight in their national capacity when they deem it appropriate—a gambit particularly favoured by the big powers who dominate these institutions. The conflict in ex-Yugoslavia is a case in point; failures are frequently attributed to the international organizations, whereas any minor success is said to be the achievement of the "good offices" of those powers in whose capitals documents, reflecting the "breakthrough," were signed.

The question of how far states from other continents should get involved in problem-solving in Southern Africa is a pressing and contentious one, and principally concerns the great powers. Its sensitivity lies in the fact that for centuries Africa was a play ground for non-African states, ranging from colonizers to superpowers—and this history is by no means over, as continuing French activities there demonstrate. Thus, too great an external influence could be to the detriment of the region. Too little engagement, however, would leave the African states almost exclusively reliant on their own means, which tend to be considered inadequate to the tasks at hand. Yet the capacity of African countries and their institutions should not be underestimated. It is important to recognize that "mediation within the OAU has been quite successful in resolving low-level squabbles, particularly those involving personal disputes among African leaders."[21] Furthermore, another "important trend of recent years is the growing participation of African militaries in UN and regional peacekeeping efforts," not least within Africa.[22]

Nevertheless, it is undeniable that the increasing number of severe conflicts is outpacing indigenous capabilities for tackling them effectively and for eliminating their root causes. This situation will require external powers to provide assistance, though their activities should in each case be legitimized and supervised by an international authority such as the United Nations. Despite reservations about non-African interference in the affairs of the region, international institutions will have to play a role well into the future, participate in conflict management and channel the necessary assistance from other states. At present, however, one has the impression that in the process of its overall marginalization the international community is paying not too much, but too little, attention to the African continent.

It has also to be emphasized that conflict management by international institutions still tends to overemphasize the institutions' political, mediatory and sanction-enforcing roles, though more often than not the traditional types of conflict either coexist with others, like ethnic tensions or rivalry over resources exacerbated by famine and desertification, or are overshadowed by them, as we have seen in the recent case of Rwanda with temporary mass migration compounded by epidemics. These facts do not make the continuing efforts of international institutions less important, be they regional, continental or global.[23] However, their specific activities have to be supplemented by the endeavours of organizations which can go beyond short-term conflict management to contribute to the eventual elimination of the root causes of the conflict. These include the specialized agencies of the United Nations, such as the UNHCR, the International Organization on Migration, the FAO and the WHO as well as several non-governmental organizations.

The Removal of Inter-bloc Antagonism in Southern Africa

With the end of the East-West conflict, Southern Africa has lost much of the strategic significance it had acquired during the Cold War. Consequently, there is no reason to assume that external powers, and this means in the first place the permanent members of the United Nations

Security Council, will play an active role in managing and resolving regional conflicts. Early hopes and expectations that international institutions would be able to play a decisive role have had to be abandoned. Therefore, the region will have to foster its own capabilities, set up adequate institutions and mechanisms and acquire the necessary means to pursue conflict management on its own. This, however, requires a minimum degree of co-operation, and possibly integration, which until very recently appeared inconceivable.

Until 1988, the Southern African region was characterized by two opposing power blocs: the "majority" bloc (or African liberation alliance) and the "minority" bloc (or colonial-settler alliance);[24] the former consisted of the Frontline States, especially Zambia, Tanzania and a number of liberation movements, notably the Angolan MPLA and Mozambican Frelimo (until 1974); the Zimbabwean ZANU and ZAPU (until 1980); and the Namibian SWAPO (until 1988). South Africa's African National Congress (ANC) and Pan Africanist Congress (PAC) had a special status in this alliance in that they were offered bases and transit facilities as well as observer status in many inter-state bodies and a special place in the OAU's Liberation Committee in Dar es Salaam. The second bloc consisted of South Africa, the Portuguese-controlled administrations of Angola and Mozambique, Rhodesia and Southwest Africa. As they acquired independence (or, in the case of South Africa, became democratic) between 1974 and 1994, these four political entities switched from one bloc to the other, thereby creating the possibility of a single entity in the future.

Reflecting and partly reproducing the global antagonism, these opposing alliances made any thought of collective—or even co-operative—security in the region unrealistic. Despite decolonization, the legacy of two bloc formations was preserved when South Africa "neutralized" at least two members of the opposing bloc by signing a non-aggression pact with Swaziland in 1982 and another with Mozambique in 1984, the Nkomati Accord.[25] In both cases, the signatories undertook not to allow their respective territories to be used for acts of violence, terrorism or aggression against the territorial integrity of the other.[26] The New York Accord of 1988, signalling the independence of Namibia and foreign troop withdrawals from Angola, also stated that the signatories (in this case Angola and South Africa) would not allow their territories to be used for subversion against the other. This meant that the ANC was forced to close its camps in Angola.

The two blocs have, to a large degree, disappeared. These external and domestic changes mean that new objective conditions have appeared which promise, for the first time, the final integration of the two opposing power blocs of the colonial era. However, while states in Southern Africa interact on a variety of levels and for reasons of geographic proximity, common history and culture and political objectives,[27] it goes without saying that not all these countries are of similar importance for the region or internationally. There are also significant differences in their relationships with one another.

What will be the role of the new South Africa in the region? South Africa is clearly the regional hegemon and dwarfs the neighbouring countries in various respects. Even though it is obvious that after the April 1994 elections the previous antagonism has finally come to an end, the new situation must be assessed realistically. South Africa will face a host of (transitional or less transitional) domestic problems, but nevertheless will have to make its voice heard in the conflicts raging in its neighbourhood. It cannot remain neutral in conflicts like the continuing civil war in Angola, since such conflicts have indirect effects on South Africa even if the country tries to remain uninvolved. South Africa has to act in response to such destabilizing events like migration or extensive weapons smuggling. That is why it is unrealistic to suggest that the most developed country of sub-Saharan Africa could focus on other regions of the world, "leaving behind" its underdeveloped neighbourhood.[28]

As long as it remains unclear how the interaction of South Africa and its neighbourhood will develop, it is a primary task to consolidate the grounds of a new relationship. The best way to do this is through sub-regional integration, using the integrative role of a regional hegemon. Even though this may create suspicion or a feeling of inferiority among the smaller partners, this is the most likely pattern for South Africa's future role in the region. An early definition of South Africa's role is of decisive importance, as it is a precondition of integration. Integration is not a panacea, but it does carry the promise that the region will eventually be able to cope with its most urgent problems.

Conclusions

After decades of bipolarity, the world has started to adapt to the realities of a new multilateral system, but it will take decades to learn how this system can function properly and what roles the different actors, states and international institutions will play. As the number of conflicts has increased, following the end of the Cold War and with the termination of its self-regulating effect, it is obvious that the international community will have to pay attention to more diversified conflicts. It is likely that the main actors in international politics will not have sufficient energy to pay attention to, and get actively involved in, the management of several conflicts simultaneously. Consequently, those regions which are not the primary strategic concern of the great powers will have to recognize that the world will pay decreasing attention to their problems. The most important question is whether the support provided to them for self-interested reasons during the last decades will be replaced by support based on co-operation and the recognition of their needs.

More attention will have to be paid to regional conflict management. For Southern Africa this means that the OAU and SADC will have to develop the relevant conflict resolution capacity, since at present these institutions are not equipped to tackle domestically generated conflicts and do not have enforcement mechanisms at their disposal. It also requires a consensus on all, or most, of the remaining questions, such as whether to proceed with regional conflict management, how to define "security," whether to provide peace-keeping and peace-making forces, whether to consider the adoption of the CSCE or another model, whether to link regional structures with SADC or not, and what role South Africa ought to play in this regard. It is also necessary that these institutions adapt to the changing circumstances in the region.

The complexity of Southern Africa's problems makes co-operation between institutions imperative. Those political organizations, the UN and the OAU, which have played an eminent role in conflict resolution in the past have to continue their activity and increase their coordinating role, as many sources of conflict can only gradually be eliminated by steady efforts on the part of specialized agencies and non-governmental organizations. Thus, regional conflict management will remain an integral part of the global endeavours.

Notes

1. Douglas Anglin, "Conflict in Sub-Saharan Africa, 1992-1993," in: *Les Conflits dans le Monde, 1992-1993: Rapport Annuel sur les Conflits Internationaux* (Quebec, 1993), p. 8.

2. Thomas Ohlson and Stephen John Stedman, *The New Is Not Yet Born: Conflict Resolution in Southern Africa* (Washington, D.C.: The Brookings Institution, 1994), pp. 219-21.

3. David L. Peterson has written that "Africans neither want it nor understand it. What Africa really needs is food, stability, and development.... Democracy only gives rise to tribalism and war; it hinders economic development. Africa is still too poor and illiterate for democracy," in: "Debunking Ten Myths About Democracy in Africa," *Washington Quarterly*, Vol. 17, No. 3, 1994, p. 129.

4. Carol Lancaster, "Democratization in Sub-Saharan Africa," *Survival*, Vol. 35, No. 3, 1993, p. 49.

5. Abiodun Alao, *African Conflicts: The Future Without the Cold War*, London Defence Studies, No. 19 (London: King's College, 1993), p. 8.

6. Douglas Anglin, "Conflict in Sub-Saharan Africa, 1991-1992," Unpublished Special Paper [Ottawa: Carleton University, 1992], p. 9.

7. This classification has been introduced by Ohlson and Stedman, *op. cit.*, in note 2, p. 250.

8. Jeffrey Herbst, "The Potential for Conflict in Africa," *Africa Insight*, Vol. 22, No. 2, 1992, p. 105.

9. Peter Vale, "The Case for a Conference for Security and Co-operation in Southern Africa," in: Anthoni Van Nieuwkerk and Gary van Staden (eds), *Southern Africa at the Crossroads: Prospects for the Political Economy of the Region* (Braamfontein: South African Institute of International Affairs, 1991), pp. 148-53.

10. Anglin, 1992, *op.cit.*, in note 6, p. 8.

11. Simon Baynham, "The New World Order: Regional and International Implications for Southern Africa," *Africa Insight*, Vol. 22, No. 4, 1992, p. 93.

12. Anglin, 1992, *op.cit.*, in note 6, p. 5.

13. G.M.E. Leistner, "Post-Apartheid South Africa's Economic Ties with Neighbouring States," *Development Southern Africa*, Vol. 9, No. 2, May 1992, p. 173.

14. Peterson, *op. cit.*, in note 3, p. 140.

15. To control the transfer of small weapons such as the AK-47 would have been impossible anyway.

16. For more details, see Sam G. Amoo, "Role of the OAU: Past, Present and Future," in: David R. Smock (ed.), *Making War and Waging Peace: Foreign Intervention in Africa* (Washington, D. C.: United States Institute of Peace Press, 1993), pp. 242 and 249.

17. United Nations Conference on the International Organization. Selected Documents (i.e., the documents of the 1945 San Francisco conference establishing the United Nations), quoted by Elisabeth Boles, *The West and South Africa: Myths, Interests and Policy Options* (London: Croom Helm, 1988), p. 5.

18. Kamal S. Shehadi, *Ethnic Self-determination and the Break-up of States*, Adelphi Papers, No. 283 (London: The International Institute for Strategic Studies, 1993), p. 72.

19. This certainly does not mean that we regard the roles played by the United States and the Soviet Union in Europe between the late 1940s and the late 1980s as equivalent.

20. It should suffice to mention the events in Cambodia in the second half of the 1970s.

21. I. William Zartman, *Ripe for Resolution: Conflict and Intervention in Africa* (Oxford: Oxford University Press, 1989, second edition), p. 282.

22. Chester A. Crocker, "Strengthening African Peace-making and Peacekeeping," in: Smock (ed.), *op. cit.*, in note 16, p. 266.

23. For the institutions on the African continent, see Ivor Richard Fung's contribution to this volume.

24. Anne-Marie Kriek in her D.Litt. et Phil. dissertation ('*n Analise van die Aard van die Magskonfigurasie in die Suider-Afrikaanse Regionale Stelsel, 1969-1990* (Pretoria: University of South Africa, 1992), p. 286) using the concepts of Cantori and Speigel (L. J. Cantori, S. L. Speigel, *The International Politics of Regions: A Comparative Approach* (Englewood Cliffs: Prentice Hall, 1970)) argues that the

greater region comprised two opposing power blocs, a "black bloc" and a "white bloc," obstructing a collective security regime for the region as a whole.

25. The Nkomati Accord of 1984 between South Africa and Mozambique may be regarded as an expanded version of the non-aggression treaties between South Africa and Ciskei, Venda and Bophuthatswana. The security agreement with Swaziland is less extensive but broader in scope, as it also provides for mutual assistance in combatting terrorism, insurgency and subversion. See M. Hough, W. Booyse and M. van der Merwe (eds), *Current Selected South and Southern African Treaties, Agreements and Declarations* (Pretoria: Institute for Strategic Studies, 1985), p. 1.

26. *Ibid.*, Article Three of the Nkomati Accord.

27. Similarly Solomon N. Nkiwane, *Regional Security and Confidence-building Processes: The Case of Southern Africa in the 1990s*, UNIDIR Research Paper, No.16, 1993, p. 3. Nkiwane uses the term "subordinate international system," which is rather imprecise as it does not make it clear to what this subsystem is subordinated. For this reason, it may be better to use the word *subsystem* instead. There is no doubt that a geographical region with its natural interactions is a subsystem of the international community.

28. This scenario is mentioned by Ohlson and Stedman, *op. cit.*, in note 2, p. 255.

6

Security Dilemmas in Southern Africa: A Case for Confidence-building Measures?

Hans-Joachim Spanger

Measures designed to enhance confidence and security have long been an integral part of regulating inter-state relations and of efforts to control, reduce and eliminate weapons inventories. They include bilateral measures, such as the Hot Line established in 1963 between Washington and Moscow in order to facilitate rapid communication, as well as multilateral measures, such as the 1936 Convention of Montreux regulating naval passage through the Bosporus. In most cases they have been concluded as politically binding agreements, as reflected by the whole array of measures negotiated and agreed upon in the framework of the Conference on Security and Co-operation in Europe (CSCE). They have been part and parcel of arms control agreements, as, for instance, in the case of the provisions on information exchange in the Treaty on Conventional Forces in Europe (CFE), and they have also been adopted as independent measures. And though confidence-building measures have been most prominent on the European continent, they have also had a role to play in other parts of the world, notably in the Sinai disengagement accords concluded from 1974, and the Contadora Draft Act drawn up in 1986 as part of the peace process in Central America.

107

It is a conspicuous fact that confidence-building measures have played no role—or only a very minor one—in Africa up to now. Certain principles, such as sovereign equality, non-interference in internal affairs, respect for territorial integrity and the peaceful settlement of disputes, are laid down in the OAU Charter. But up to now these principles have not been underpinned by any concrete agreements or measures—apart from the setting-up of a Commission of Mediation, Conciliation and Arbitration, which failed to come into operation because the member states were not prepared to submit to the workings of an external mechanism.[1] Only in very recent times, as a response to the ending of the East-West conflict, have more insistent demands been made that confidence-building measures should be agreed in Africa as well—both at the continental and at the subregional level. Thus in 1991, the then Tanzanian Minister for Foreign Affairs Abdu Kinana expressed the view that "with the dismantling of apartheid, the countries of the region should be able to chart a common strategy on confidence-building measures and on security and, finally, to start reducing their military expenditures."[2] Similarly, the "Kampala Document: Towards a Conference on Security, Stability, Development and Co-operation in Africa," issued by the African Leadership Forum in May 1991, besides proposing a whole series of institutional arrangements, stressed the relevance of confidence-building measures.[3] The United Nations in particular has also endeavoured, through a series of expert conferences, to get the idea of confidence-building measures established on the African continent.[4]

Confidence-building measures, commonly characterized as the "junk food of arms control," appear indeed particularly suited to the African continent, given that up to now there has been almost no experience there of co-operative management of national security and arms policies. These kinds of measures, with their soft constraints on the military, seem the most appropriate for introducing co-operation into an area that, as a rule, is one of the most sensitive in which the state operates—namely, national security. In so doing, however, account must be taken of the specific conditions which obtain on the continent, particularly in Southern Africa, and which place constraints on any straightforward transference of models of confidence-building from other regions of the world. Before discussing concrete measures, it is therefore necessary to examine some theoretical problems of confidence-building and to clarify the goals that are associated with such measures elsewhere, and their preconditions. For practical purposes, this discussion will concentrate on military confidence-building, although national security—particularly in countries of the Third World—should be regarded as embracing more than this.

Confidence and Confidence-building: General Remarks

In its broadest sense, trust is a fundamental element in human relations:

> It is true that in many situations, a person has the choice of whether or not to be trusting in this or that particular regard. If they did not have any trust at all, however, they could not get up out of their beds tomorrow. They would be overcome by an unaccountable fear, a paralysing horror.[5]

In other words, trust means reducing the unintelligibility and complexity of reality to an extent where one is able to function (in collaboration or agreement with others). One trusts that particular events will (not) take place, and one adapts one's behaviour accordingly. In the language of sociological theory, trust may thus be defined as a "speculative advance concession."[6] It is an advance concession, because the consequences of one's own action cannot be calculated with certainty. And it is speculative, because in principle the possibility exists that the concession will be frustrated, that the positive expectation will not be realized. Trust, therefore, is to be located in the broad terrain between certainty and uncertainty, because if there is certainty, there is no need for trust, but if there is ignorance, it is not possible to trust. But trust has also to be distinguished from mere hope, because it is based essentially on a weighing-up of various alternatives for action—on "confident expectation"—the validity of which becomes evident only *post festum*, according to the degree of success.

It is in the lack of information about the consequences of one's own action that both trust and mistrust are rooted. But the latter is far from being the mere negation of the former. Mistrust is rather a functional equivalent of trust, given that it also seeks to improve the ability to act by reducing complexity, in this case by overstating the negative aspect of expectations. Mistrust makes a foe out of a potential friend, leads to a defensive recourse to strength, or, conversely, causes a negation of needs:

> Combative strategies, liquidatory strategies and abnegatory strategies make a mistrustful existence manageable and define the situation in such a way that it is possible to operate expediently within the defined area. Not infrequently, there is a loss of awareness of the mistrust, and the reductionist strategies take on an independent existence as a habitual philosophy of life, as a routine.[7]

The converse is also true: the more expectations are fulfilled, trust confirmed and interaction made intelligible by the application of norms and rules, the more co-operative relations based on trust will become accepted.

In a world of states which has, not unjustifiably, been described as anarchical, the sociological definition of confidence as a "speculative advance concession" transfers without great difficulty to international relations. International law provides an increasing number of norms and rules, intended to keep the behaviour of states in their dealings with one another on an orderly track. But there is no overall power that is able to enforce respect for these norms and rules—a fact that has become painfully obvious following the collapse of the hegemonial bipolar order brought about by the East-West conflict. As a result, trust—and mistrust—acquire crucial importance in the grey area, typical of international relations, between legality and opportunity, between collectively agreed norms and their individual implementation in decision-making. Given that, under these kinds of conditions, there cannot be any certain expectations, inter-state co-operation must rely on trust—in other words on "advance concessions" and the readiness to enter into "risks." But uncertain expectations also produce mistrust, and mistrust tries to avoid risks and generally seeks its salvation in defensive measures, particularly of a military kind.

Taking as a basis the definition of confidence as a "speculative advance concession," it may be said that its corresponding import in international relations is a function both of the risk of suffering damage from a potential adversary and of the calculability of that adversary. The lower the risk of damage and the higher the calculability, the better the prospects for confidence. Conversely, a high risk of damage in combination with high uncertainty will be very unlikely to produce confidence. In military terms, this means that confidence may be conceived of as a function of military capability (i.e., the risk of damage) and military intention (i.e., calculability), as mutually perceived by potential opponents. It is these two variables which, in the security realm, independently determine the actors' readiness to trust.

It follows that "confidence" and "confidence-building" describe a process rather than a state of affairs. Thus, confidence-building in the military sphere is "a dynamic concept, for the creation of a situation in which a State no longer regards another State as threatening."[8] However, the situation is constantly changing, and, if one is not to raise concerns and create new threat-perceptions, any alteration on one side of the equation must be made with due regard to its effect on the other side. There is little dispute about this. A much more controversial issue, however, is the relevance and effectiveness of confidence-building measures as one means among several of enhancing confidence.

The Relevance of Confidence-building Measures: The Conceptual Background

Nowadays, when there is talk of confidence-building measures (CBMs) or, alternatively, confidence- and security-building measures (CSBMs),[9] the model implicitly or explicitly underlying such exchanges is that of European arms control. In this connection, one should not overlook the fact that even in Europe the question of whether CSBMs actually have contributed to confidence-building (and if so, to what extent), is still largely unresolved—at best a subject of heated debate.[10] One should also bear in mind that the controversies about the form and conceptual basis of confidence-building measures have their roots in the specific conditions of East-West confrontation, with its clash between two antagonistic blocs. That situation certainly offers lessons that are of significance for other regions of the world, particularly since the Cold War not only provoked an unprecedented degree of armament, but also prompted considerable intellectual activity. But it would be utterly wrong to try to export the resulting European CSBMs to other areas as a universally applicable model—not least in view of the fact that, since the end of the East-West conflict, they have lost something of their relevance even in Europe and are beginning to give way to new approaches.

Although confidence between potential adversaries is influenced by military capabilities as well as military intentions, the focus of CSBMs has been much narrower. As predominantly interpreted, such measures do not address military capabilities, but instead focus on military intentions:

> In marked contrast to those arms-control measures which concentrate on quantities of weapons and their physical characteristics (and thus, on capabilities), Confidence-building Measures operate on the perceptions of those in confrontation (and particularly on their perceptions of intentions).[11]

Their aim is the exchange and collection of evidence, showing that a perceived threat does not in reality exist, thereby reducing incentives for entering into an arms race and providing reassurance in times of crisis. Thus, it is the increase of knowledge by means of CSBMs which lies at the heart of confidence-building, and this implies that as long as intentions are not sufficiently transparent, any constraints on military capabilities are likely to be rejected, in order to retain safeguards and reduce, or indeed completely avoid, the risk of damage. Advance concessions without risk, however, result not in trust but in mistrust. This curious symbiosis of trust and mistrust, which, on the side of what used to be the West, came to enjoy considerable popularity, becomes understandable when viewed against the background of the conflict which it was intended to contain, namely the irreconcilable confrontation between two highly armed military blocs whose relations with one another were founded on cast-iron military deterrence. The conceptual equivalent of this is the interpretation of arms control which developed at the end of the 1950s in the United States and which found its way from there into the negotiating methods of the Western alliance.

According to this interpretation, arms control is a way of helping prevent war by military means, a method of enforcing the maxim *si vis pacem para bellum*.[12] It does not seek to eliminate either military instruments or the political causes of international conflicts and wars. Thus, arms control is to be seen as a strategy for dealing with the "security dilemma," a strategy aimed at preventing war by reducing crisis instabilities and tensions arising out of the very existence of weapons and arms races. Its object is to stabilize the system of reciprocal military threat through joint efforts and control. Against this background, it may be seen that this kind of arms control is concerned primarily with politically unintentional wars and hence with the risks that result from the individual momentum developed by modern weapons-systems. At a later stage, this situation resulted in a division of labour, whereby arms control was given the task of meeting these challenges by imposing quantitative and qualitative limits on capabilities, whereas CSBMs were to exert an influence through transparency, communication and control.

However questionable this conceptual delimitation was in relation to the overall goal of confidence-building, it did have the advantage of being able to be implemented in modest stages—with CSBMs being accorded the function of ice-breakers. None the less, these kinds of pragmatic or technocratic delimitations were met with considerable reservations, especially in Eastern Europe. In that area of the world in particular, there was a plea for more complex solutions. Critics from the East not only pointed to the limited contribution which CSBMs made to the security of states and to the overall objective of confidence between states, since they were only able to change perceptions, not military realities; they also perceived CSBMs as a diversion from genuine arms-control and disarmament. It is, after all, the size of arms inventories which constitutes the threat to potential adversaries and provides the decisive evidence of benign or hostile intentions. One should not, it was argued, put the cart before the horse: only "together with a series of broader diplomatic, arms control and disarmament measures" can military CSBMs "perform a useful and stabilizing function," since "they are inherently unable, by themselves, to address the underlying causes of suspicion and mistrust, i.e., the deeply rooted contest of specific national and alliance interests."[13]

The clash between this holistic approach and the gradual strategy not only effectively blocked any substantial progress in European confidence-building for some thirty years. The all-or-nothing solution, coupled with the initial *penchant* for little more than symbolic gestures, resulted in the expression of a mistrust so great that it precluded any readiness for risk-taking in either East or West. Until the successful conclusion of the Stockholm Conference on Disarmament in Europe (CDE) in 1986, there was little change in this situation, with the result that the confidence-building agreements that did come about were either of an isolated nature (like the Hot Line established between Washington and Moscow in 1963) or very limited in their effect (e.g., the CBMs detailed in the Final Act of the CSCE in 1975). Ultimately, a fundamentally different political environment was required to break the vicious circle of deep mistrust and pave the way towards considerably more ambitious negotiations and agreements. This reflects the broader dilemma of arms control: in an environment of high tension and deep mistrust, arms control is likely to remain meaningless, and in the opposite case it becomes superfluous. In other words, "arms control is hardest to negotiate when most needed and easiest to negotiate when least needed."[14]

Though one has to be aware of the inherent limitations of arms control and to take note of the overall conflict-formation, one would be ill advised to dismiss arms control on these grounds. If pursued with care and with a readiness to compromise, arms control can have an indirect bearing on the conflict-formation itself. Defining norms, rules, and procedures for regulating the military conduct of the parties involved helps to transform the overall political relationship—as was demonstrated to some extent during the East-West conflict in Europe. Thus, arms control is an essential part of any attempt to foster peace, and the more compatible the political interests of the parties, the more promising such attempts will be.

Making Intentions Explicit: Practical Aspects

Broadly speaking, the purpose of CSBMs is to provide reassurance by making intentions explicit. This actually works both ways. According to the traditional understanding of arms control outlined above, the task of CSBMs is to eliminate misperceptions and misunderstandings which might propel adversaries into an unintended war. CSBMs may thus help foster mutual confidence in a relationship between states that do not harbour aggressive intentions but nevertheless exhibit a varying degree of suspicion and hostility.

But CSBMs should not be confined to situations in which there is a high measure of common political ground between potential adversaries. Even where one is confronted with the danger of premeditated aggression, CSBMs may be a thoroughly sensible step, in that they may provide early warning and thereby reduce the risk of surprise attack. In conditions such as these, intelligence culled through CSBMs may provide reassurance and increase one's own confidence in one's ability to withstand the pressures involved (notwithstanding the intelligence gathered by one's adversary). However, it is scarcely conceivable that one would be able to negotiate sufficiently intrusive CSBMs with aggressors such as

Adolf Hitler or Saddam Hussein. Potentially negotiable CSBMs of an insignificant kind, on the other hand, play into the hands of the aggressor, since they harbour the danger of provoking precisely that which they are intended to prevent, namely misperceptions that ultimately lead to blind confidence, gullibility or, in political terms, appeasement.

Conditions such as these, which allow neither for meaningful CSBMs nor for any other arms-control measures, underline the usefulness of having a regime in place before threatening developments occur. A CSBM regime would provide safeguards in two respects—either by the fact of its implementation, which would make the intentions of the adversary transparent, or by the fact of non-compliance, which in itself would cause concern and might prompt joint action. Thus, the timing of negotiations on CSBMs is critical. Experience shows that the prospects of success are best when political relations are set to change for the better and CSBMs are perceived as underpinning the process of improvement.

There are a number of principles which ought to be taken into account when designing CSBMs. First and foremost, they should be miltarily significant. Thresholds for, say, the notification of military manœuvres make no sense if they do not affect anybody. The same applies to observation of military activities, the aim of which—i.e., confirmation of compliance with the agreed rules and provision of a clear picture of the nonthreatening character of the activity—will be fulfilled only if the requisite conditions in terms of timing and technical considerations exist. Similarly, declaratory measures expressing the good intentions of the parties concerned are irrelevant if not matched by deeds.

Secondly, CSBMs need to be symmetrical in the sense that risks should not outweigh advantages in the perception of the parties concerned. In multilateral agreements, CSBMs will almost always have an asymmetrical impact on the parties involved. However, placing greater restrictions on the powerful parties to an agreement, for example, is acceptable, and indeed desirable, as long as the security of those parties is not undermined.

Thirdly, gradual approaches are to be preferred, in order to avoid overload. Ambitious CSBMs look good on paper but often lack any dynamic in reality because they are hard to implement and are likely to give rise to new, unwarranted concerns. This is also true of CSBMs as the "junk food" of arms control. In conditions, such as those prevailing during the East-West conflict, a gradual approach was needed in which CSBMs were the least demanding point of entry—even though the contribution of the latter were not really measurable in quantitative terms. A holistic approach that essentially called for the removal of the sources of mistrust—i.e., the East-West antagonism that had found visible expression in the European arms race—would only have prolonged the deadlock.

Fourthly, agreements should be binding and the scope of voluntary measures limited. Such measures—like the invitation of observers to large-scale military manœuvres, as provided for in the CSCE Final Act of 1975—harbour an acute danger of arousing new mistrust and of prompting renewed military reinsurance.

Fifthly, CSBMs should have a clearly demarcated area of application, preferably determined by a "security complex," i.e., "a group of states whose primary security concerns are sufficiently closely linked that their national securities cannot realistically be considered apart from one another."[15]

Finally, adequate provision for verification of compliance with agreed CSBMs should be included. This involves, for example, exchange of information about military capabilities and plans, and of military activities below a certain agreed threshold. In this case, it would be sensible to envisage inspection rights, in order to reduce mistrust and in order to limit "contractually permissible" circumventions of the CSBM regime.

Whereas these principles have some universal relevance, the package of specific CSBMs needs to be designed according to the conditions prevailing in a given "security complex." In principle, the following categories of CSBMs may be considered:

(1) *Declaratory Measures.* Declaratory measures, such as the commitment not to use force or the recognition of existing borders, define the common basis on which the parties to a CSBM regime are ready to co-operate. Such declarations of intent are an essential complement to substantial measures, in that they provide a sense of direction and define the principles and norms on which any international regime is to be founded.

(2) *Transparency Measures.* This category forms the core of CSBMs and entails a large variety of measures such as:
- communication measures (designed to facilitate rapid exchanges on urgent matters);
- information measures (designed to increase transparency of military hardware and ensure proper threat-assessment in planning);
- monitoring measures (designed to allow for reconnaissance on a regular basis or in specific conditions of a threatening nature);
- notification measures (designed to signal the distinction between routine and unusual, potentially threatening, military activities);
- observation measures (designed to provide additional insights into the threatening or non-threatening character of the adversary's armed forces and their activities);

- contact measures (designed to enhance mutual knowledge and understanding).

As stated earlier, transparency measures not only help to clarify other states' intentions, they also operate as early-warning systems. These may be of particular relevance to states not in possession of sophisticated technical surveillance systems.

(3) *Constraining Measures.* Constraints may be applied to military activities, force deployments, certain weapons-systems and the state of readiness of particular armed forces. Their basic aim is to increase warning-time in respect of surprise attack and to reduce the danger of a rapid escalation of military conflict. Even more far-reaching are concepts of non-offensive or non-provocative defence, which entail constraints on force structures and on certain categories of weapons, and which may, if mutually agreed, completely eliminate the risk of attack.

Can Confidence- and Security-building Measures Operate in Africa?

Before dealing with the specific conditions in Southern Africa, I should like, for the purposes of contrast, to recall the context in which European endeavours in the field of confidence-building took shape. The readiness to agree confidence-building measures for Europe, within the framework of the CSCE process, was founded on two crucial preconditions: recognition of the territorial status quo and the military stalemate between East and West. Both found expression in the CSCE Final Act of 1975, which established the inviolability of existing borders. This represented an explicit mutual guarantee by East and West of that which both sides had in any case been unable to change in thirty years of Cold War: it was agreed that established spheres of influence should be recognized. This happened in the mutual knowledge that in the nuclear age, with near-parity in military power, the first one to shoot would be the next to die, and that, in consequence, war as an instrument for attaining political objectives was now ruled out.

The CSCE agreements were thus part of a *modus vivendi* whose dominant feature was a supposed balance of power and which believed it could leave any future transformation to the course of history. These agreements brought no change to the ideologically masked power-rivalry. This was also true of confidence-building measures, which were essentially limited to affirming the certainty that war no longer had any place in the arsenal of East-West conflict. They were intended to furnish convincing proofs that both sides had accommodated themselves to the military stalemate, on the basis of reciprocal threat. The East-West conflict on the European continent is thus the prototype of the "realist" paradigm in which states seeking to defend a uniformly interpreted national security and operating in what is in principle a hostile environment have recourse to the classical instruments of power politics (and of the balance of power), namely armament, military deterrence and alliances. With the ending of the Cold War, which both resulted from and was accompanied by the disintegration of state structures and the mobilization of social forces (both of which were expressed in a "rehabilitation" of war as as an instrument of politics) fundamental premises of the realist theory were called into question even in Europe—as were the strategies for cooperative arms-management that were associated with it. In the Third World, however, and particularly in Africa, these premises and strategies could never claim to have been effective, however much the East-West conflict had left its mark in those areas too.

This is not to say that the classical "security dilemma," whereby states operating in conditions of anarchy seek to promote their own security unilaterally—and hence, willy nilly, to the detriment of other states—has no place in Africa. Ethiopia, Somalia and—not least—South Africa have demonstrated, with action up to and including armed conflict, that it is indeed present. However, there are special conditions which mean that the dilemma has a different status here. The most obvious of these is that in broad areas of the African continent one of the central premises of the dilemma is not satisfied: the state as territorial sovereign and as guarantor of the internal and external security of the people living within its borders simply does not exist. The functions of control and order in the "weak states," typical of Africa, frequently extend no further than the limits of cities (capitals), with the result that the post-colonial *étatiste* constructs have proved to be "very leaky vessels" in which territorial delimitation is often no more than a mark on the map, sovereignly ignored by the population supposedly in the state's charge.[16]

A variety of explanations has been given for this fact. They range from lack of time for nation-building and state-formation since independence to the absence of necessary social preconditions, in the form of the recently much-quoted "civil societies."[17] It has also been described as an inevitable and regrettable consequence of "nation-statism"—"Europe's last gift to Africa." It is no accident that out of the legacy of colonial rule—externally imposed, authoritarian and bureaucratic, and "to which any thought of people's participation was damnable subversion"—there arose states which largely failed to fulfil their purpose:

> The state was not liberating and protective of its citizens, no matter what its propaganda claimed: on the contrary, its gross effect was constricting and exploitative, or else it simply failed to operate in any social sense at all.[18]

In the African states and societies of today, urban bureaucracies developed, hand in hand with clientelism and rent-seeking economic activities from which the country, founded on traditions of kinship (or tribalism), increasingly turned away.

In this kind of environment, where states "lack effective institutional capacities to provide peace and order, as well as the conditions for satisfactory physical existence for the population," where, as a result, the regimes in power do not enjoy popular legitimacy and instead, in the absence of "a socially cohesive society," a variety of kinship groups contend for their own securities and for supremacy over their competitors, the security dilemma does indeed have only secondary importance. It has therefore been suggested that one should talk instead of an "insecurity dilemma," though strictly speaking there is no dilemma involved.[19] It is not only that, in the circumstances described, no singular notion of national security exists; it is that the security needs of individuals, social and national groups, the regime and the state as a whole are in some cases acutely at odds with one another. In addition, perceptions of threat are concentrated to a large extent on internal dangers to and from the regime in power and far less on external threats to the existence of the state, even though in principle the latter's weakness makes it easy prey to external covetousness.

Compared to the classical security dilemma, the "insecurity dilemma" has paradoxical consequences, particularly in Africa. Whilst most states on the continent feel anything but safe from an internal point of view, they have up to now been exposed to few external threats—leaving aside a limited number of violent inter-state conflicts. This is all the more surprising in view of the much-quoted (post-)colonial "arbitrary borders" —a notorious expression, but one which overlooks the fact that border-demarcation is inherently arbitrary where there are no agreed principles of order.[20] The reason why, in contrast to Europe, the African states have none the less allowed their individual conduct to be made subject to international convention and, in line with the OAU Charter, have up to now, despite widely expressed discontent, sought (almost) no revision of borders, must therefore lie elsewhere—particularly since the OAU has repeatedly demonstrated that it has no deterrent mechanisms of sanction at its disposal.

The crucial factor here is undoubtedly the nature of African statehood, as described above. And it is no accident that the most obvious source of inter-state conflict to date—the Republic of South Africa—represents a significant exception in this regard. In the case of weak states, the narrow constraints on external adventure reflect the obstacles which the weak economic bases—the result of rampant clientelist appetites—constitute when it comes to acquiring the necessary military resources. An additional aspect is the peculiar nature of "African" nationalism as what is primarily an ideology of anti-colonial emancipation:

> As it happened, African nation-statism almost entirely escaped the turbulent hysterias of Europe: it was far too much concerned with earthy practicalities to be fired by metaphysical yearnings of the Kleistian sort.[21]

And finally, one should not overlook the fact that although the East-West conflict sometimes added fuel to the flames of regional disputes, its protagonists were in fact primarily interested in maintaining control in the established spheres of influence in that area, as determined—in Marxist-Leninist terminology—by the "international correlation of forces." As a result, the superpowers saw themselves as guarantors of the international order, and thus "the Cold War had the effect of providing African countries with patrons when their boundaries were challenged."[22] Also related to this was the peculiar feature of "dependent militarization" in Africa, which, through arms exports, the provision of training and advice, and also through direct intervention, imposed marked limits on the scope which national military apparatuses had for autonomous action.

The end of the East-West conflict and the consequent withdrawal of the superpowers from their African outposts means that the tutelage over the African system of states which had been dictated by the international balance of power has been done away with. This is not to say that the way is now clear for territorial expansionism—although in the current volatile period of transition to an as yet unknown new order, and in the absence of external constraints, this possibility cannot be excluded. More significant, however, is the fact that in the new overall international framework, conservative defence of the territorial status quo is increasingly coming under pressure from revisionist demands for national self-determination—with consequences such as may currently be observed in Sarajevo, Sukhumi, Stepanakert and elsewhere. It is true that up to now, national self-determination has been a primarily anti-colonial byword in Africa (with South Africa having become again the exception). However, it would be rash to assume that African citizens feel more closely bound to their states than did the citizens of the multi-national federations of Europe. On the contrary, the endemic weakness of the central power, and the latter's clientelist bonds with what is all too often only one among countless ethnic groups, create positively ideal conditions for irredentist and secessionist movements. In addition, there are the side-effects of structural adjustment and democratization. Implemented as part of a global wave of economic and political liberalization, and as a response to the atrocious record of failed regimes, these measures entail one thing in particular: a wide-ranging redistribution of power and influence, with serious implications for the African system of states. It is these fundamental challenges, and not the inherent risks of the arms race, as was the case in Cold War Europe, which must be addressed by any effort at regional confidence-building.

Devising Confidence- and Security-building Measures for Southern Africa

At first glance, the situation in Southern African displays considerable similarities with that which prevailed in Europe for four decades. In both cases, two blocs stood in opposition to one another: the South African apartheid regime on the one hand, and, on the other, the Frontline States, joined together in a military alliance in order to safeguard their security, and the members of the SADCC, joined together for the same purpose in an economic association. And it is in Southern Africa that the East-West conflict, with its proxy wars, has left the most obvious marks on the African continent, even though, as became clear *post festum*, the causes of conflict could by no means be regarded as relating solely to the Cold War.[23] In the meantime, however, contrary developments have, paradoxically, taken place in the two regions. Whereas on the European continent the end of the Cold War brought a simultaneous upheaval in the system of states in the eastern regions, but in the west helped to deepen existing supranational integration, developments in Southern Africa followed precisely the opposite course. Here, the state order remained intact and, what is more, as a result of Namibian independence and the peace process in Mozambique, African "nation-statism" was rehabilitated and perfected. On the other hand, very little remains of the former military alliance, now that its purpose has gone, and even economic co-operation, ambitiously extended with the foundation of the SADC, is still in its infancy.

Given this situation, confidence-building in Southern Africa faces two crucial tasks. First, the Republic of South Africa, which, as the dominant power, is the only one with the military and political capability unilaterally to shape the region to its own design, must be integrated multilaterally—and contained. This must be done in every area of mutual relations, and, in view of the loose ties between the other states in the region and of the inadequate institutional basis, it will probably prove no easy task, even with a co-operative majority government in place in Pretoria. Secondly, account must be taken of the peculiarities of the "insecurity dilemma" that is also a characteristic feature of Southern Africa, namely the weakness of the majority of states and the primacy of internal threat-perceptions. The situation is made even more acute by the legacy of more than two decades of military conflict, which manifests itself in continuing flows of refugees (most recently in the form of a renewed exodus from Angola to Zambia and Namibia) and in the endemic illegal trade in obsolete weapons and the appearance of bandits operating across national borders.

Weak states are confronted with a special problem in the case of confidence-building. Confidence presupposes self-confidence, since advance concessions can only be made where there is the capacity to cope with frustrated expectations. This was a source of considerable problems even in the case of East-West relations: given the reciprocal capacity for threat, both sides were worried that by allowing inspection of their military capabilities, they would suffer a degree of damage which they could not calculate. In the case of weak states, which do not even have full control over their own territories, this problem arises in acute form—although it is in principle conceivable that the élites in such states are quite capable of collaboration in exclusive dealings with each other in cases where their interests are similar. An added difficulty is that weak states do not really have the material and institutional resources needed to implement CSBMs in a way that will enhance confidence. One may therefore doubt whether the application—called for from some quarters—of "stronger measures than those applied in a divided Europe" is really what is needed.[24] It would probably be more appropriate to be talking about a different type or set of CSBMs, of a kind that would take account of the specific conditions and restrictions in the region and did not run the risk of being negated by the pressure of exaggerated ambitions.

This takes us on to the second aspect of the "insecurity dilemma," namely the predominance of internal threats (to and from the regime) as opposed to external threats (to the state). Of course, it is not the task of inter-state CSBMs to solve the internal problems of the parties to the agreement. These problems must, however, be taken into consideration, and, more importantly, account should be taken of indirect connections. Thus a CSBM regime—looking at it from a negative point of view—should help ensure that internal problems are not aggravated by inter-state conflicts and that, conversely, inter-state relations do not fall victim to internal conflicts. In addition—on the positive side—efforts should be made to see that the type of CSBM in question also includes arrangements for the joint resolution of internal conflicts. This in turn links in with the condition that the parties to the agreement are following common principles in shaping their internal orders. In the military sphere, for example, this should include democratic control of the armed forces and the guarantee of basic rights for members of the military as for others. These kinds of regulations are, in principle, a matter for sovereign decision by the participating states, and as such are not the proper subject of inter-governmental CSBMs. None the less, fruitful regional co-operation will only be possible, and collective action justifiable, if founded on, and serving to safeguard, common principles.

This brings us to the chief task facing CSBMs in the conditions currently prevailing in Southern Africa. In contrast to their function in Cold War Europe, where they served to stabilize an order perpetuated by the balance of power and by nuclear deterrence, CSBMs in this part of the world constitute "building blocks" in the creation of a new regional order. They are part of a regional security regime (that must be worked towards), whose principles, norms, rules and procedures for regulating political-military relations in their turn underpin regional efforts at co-operation, as evinced in institutional form in the foundation of SADC in August 1992 in Namibia.[25] The changed function of CSBMs produces a changed content. In Cold War Europe, the transparency of military capabilities and activities occupied centre-stage, in order, as already mentioned, primarily to counter the mutual fear of surprise attack.[26] In Southern Africa, on the other hand, where this fear does not exist, the spotlight should be on different areas, notably the intensification and institutionalization of contacts between armed forces. This should include joint military education and, ideally, the harmonization of operational principles and joint exercises, so that troops could, for example, assume regional peace-keeping tasks. This could be supplemented by a continual exchange of information about military capabilities, plans and activities. Measures such as these, which aim at the gradual multiplication of links and, in the more advanced stages, at regional conflict management, would seem to be the most suited to preventing the current "insecurity dilemma" from one day turning, after all, into a "security dilemma."

Up to now, I have not broached those problems caused by deviations from the norm, notably the problem of South Africa. Despite the fact that the country's military budget has already been substantially reduced over the last four years, and despite the fact that further cuts are to be expected in the wake of the ongoing reorientation of government spending, South Africa will continue, for the foreseeable future, to be the only country in the region that is in a position, in terms of both personnel and equipment, of indulging in power projection far beyond its national borders. After years of an active policy of destabilization, the majority government can hardly be expected to revive this option. Yet, South Africa's neighbours, however close their attachment to the liberation movements, are very well aware that intentions can change; and the possibility of this happening without any change in capabilities—in just the way exemplified in the security dilemma—is hardly likely to put anyone's mind at rest. All the more so since there are real notions of guaranteeing regional security through the exercise of a kind of trusteeship—in a way analogous to Russia's role in the Commonwealth of

Independent States. Finally, it should not be forgotten that the imponderables of a highly volatile transition could easily cause shock waves that are unlikely to stop at South Africa's borders.[27]

The question, therefore, arises as to how South Africa's potential can be contained, in the interests of regional stability and security, and how, at the same time, it can be made fruitful. There are, in principle, two ways of doing this: multilateral integration and singularization. Since SADC has without much hesitation admitted the new South Africa, and since the countries of the region, constrained by their deplorable economies, expect to gain much more from co-operation with South Africa than from confrontation with it, the second alternative is excluded merely on practical grounds. However, the institutional basis for regional multilateral co-operation will, for the foreseeable future, remain too weak for South Africa to be accommodated properly and to remove the incentive for it to engage in preferential bilateralism. It would, therefore, seem sensible to provide for "singularizing" safeguards. Thus, for example, something akin to the "sufficiency rule" in the Treaty on Conventional Forces in Europe could be instituted: ceilings for personnel and equipment would be agreed which in principle applied to all parties but were designed in such a way as to fix South African forces at a level that seemed acceptable to everyone in Southern Africa. The CSBM regime should also include regulations that would have only a marginal effect on countries that have only small armed forces—such as Lesotho, Swaziland or Botswana—but which become more binding and more restrictive the greater the capabilities become.[28]

Draft Proposal for
Confidence- and Security-building Measures in Southern Africa

Appended is a draft proposal containing a detailed description of a CSBM regime applicable to the area covered by the SADC states (including South Africa). The proposal is based on practical experience culled in other parts of the world, and it seeks to adapt this in a fruitful way to the specific conditions obtaining in Southern Africa. Although it follows a certain internal logic, in line with the arguments presented above, the proposal is not by any means intended to be adopted wholesale. Selection of individual elements is equally possible.[29]

The practical measures proposed are based on guiding principles (declaratory measures), which do not differ fundamentally from comparable statements.[30] The sovereignty and territorial integrity of all the participating countries is affirmed, together with the principles of the renunciation of violence, the peaceful settlement of conflicts and respect for human rights. More specifically, stress is laid on the need for security in the region to be indivisible and equal for all participating states, and, accordingly, for states not to pursue their security objectives to the detriment of others. This requires regional co-operation, as well as respect for, and the implementation of, international arms-control agreements; it also precludes the formation of exclusive alliances.

There are two areas in which the proposed principles go beyond catalogues of a similar kind. The first relates to the principle of the inviolability of borders, which, whilst proscribing the alteration of borders by violent means and approving collective countermeasures, also explicitly allows peaceful, contractually agreed border-revisions. This is significant in so far as the recent revival of demands for national self-determination have led to internal and external borders intermittently being declared sacrosanct. Although prescriptions of this kind are intended to help steer the unregulated collapse of individual states along an orderly path, and potentially to contain that collapse, it should not be forgotten, following the experiences in Eritrea and former Yugoslavia, that unconditional insistence on the territorial status quo may well aggravate and prolong conflicts.

The second area relates to what is in principle the sovereign regulation of internal affairs, and in particular the role of the armed forces in the internal politics of participating countries. Here, the principles postulated are intended first to ensure that armed forces are not used to oppress ethnic or religious minorities or as a means of blocking the legitimate exercise of fundamental rights by the citizens or political organizations of a country. Secondly, it is intended that by imposing democratic parliamentary control on the armed forces, increasing their accountability and ensuring the effective exercise of human rights by their personnel, a contribution will be made to containing individual political ambitions and the danger of military *coups*. These added features do not do away with the two cornerstones of the OAU—recognition of existing borders on the African continent and non-interference in internal affairs—but they do qualify them and make them more specific in a way which means that the countries of Southern Africa now have a set of guide-lines that no longer preclude collective (re)action in cases where the guiding principles are violated.

The guiding principles embody a code of conduct which, if it were adhered to, would make further measures redundant. In practice, however, these principles will probably represent no more than a signpost to an ideal state of affairs to be aspired to in relations between the countries of Southern Africa. In order to smooth the path to that goal, the declaratory measures therefore need to be supplemented with concrete measures of a kind that will reduce existing mistrust by furnishing convincing proofs.

These include classic measures to render national military capabilities and military planning at the regional level transparent (transparency measures). Also incorporated is a continual exchange of information which embraces not only existing weapons systems, manpower and force structures, but also data about the objectives of future defence-planning, defence budgets and any large-scale weapons procurements. In addition, advance notification of military activities has been introduced, covering out-of-garrison land activities, mobilization and alert activities.

Both items follow the basic pattern of the relevant European models, but there are some modifications to take account of the specific conditions in Southern Africa, notably the limited institutional capacity to implement these kinds of measures. Thus, countries with armed forces below a manpower threshold of 20,000 are required to make military information available only every four years. In the case of larger armed forces, this is to be done every two years—a provision that would apply to six of the eleven countries in Southern Africa.[31] Again, notification thresholds have been adapted to the size of the armed forces in the region, with a further reduction in regard to possible threat-scenarios along national borders (width 50 km in each case). In the zone along the borders, there are, in addition to a generally applicable absolute ceiling for military activities (20,000 personnel), individual constraining measures; in these areas, alert activities and regular military activities involving extra-regional troops are prohibited. Finally, in a departure from the European model, the obligatory invitation of observers to military activities is dispensed with, as are special verification provisions. Instead, it is intended that more informal understandings will result from the intensification of military contacts (ranging from visits to individual units to the reciprocal provision of training-places at national military academies), detailed as an objective in the draft proposal.[32]

Another major area of confidence-building in Southern Africa relates to the creation of joint regimes for the management of borders. The object here is not so much the solution of territorial conflicts, although these can sometimes play a role—as was recently the case in the dispute between Botswana and Namibia over "Swampy Island." A more significant aspect at present is joint control of the trans-border activities stemming directly from the "insecurity dilemma" described above and from the fact that most of the states in question are "very leaky vessels." Not only does this have wide-ranging economic implications for the countries concerned. More importantly, the growing illegal trade in arms and the attacks by armed gangs which are increasingly affecting border regions between Malawi and Mozambique and between Zambia and Angola, are creating serious security problems. Both can be combated by joint surveillance of borders and joint border-patrols.

Whereas military contacts in Southern Africa can acquire weight and substance without extensive formalization, since they are able to build on the collaborative efforts and experiences of the erstwhile Frontline States, institutions and skills for the collective safeguarding of security or for the resolution of conflicts do not exist even in embryonic form.[33] The fact that Southern Africa continues—apart from individual actions, notably by the president of Zimbabwe, Robert Mugabe—to rely on initiatives and support from the North in this area provokes criticism from every quarter and is regarded as a major cause of the crumbling solidarity in the region. It is therefore important, for the sake of regional confidence-building also, that the capacity for collective action should be strengthened. For this reason, the draft proposal includes a mechanism for the settlement of disputes which can also be activated in the case of domestic conflict in a participating country. It begins in moderate terms with a call for bilateral clarification of a disputed point, raised by a particular participating country; in a further stage, it provides for the involvement of all the member states; and finally it authorizes the latter, within the framework of their collective efforts at conflict management and resolution, to approve actions, such as aerial observation flights and fact-finding missions, for purposes of elucidation or as part of peace-keeping operations, the aim being to create the preconditions for a political solution based on the consent of all the parties to the conflict. Coercive measures are not provided for.

As has already been mentioned, the measures set out in the draft proposal are neither exhaustive nor to be regarded as forming an indivisible unit. They simply represent an attempt to provide as comprehensive and detailed as possible a statement of the options, in line with the generally expressed interest in the creation of a CSBM regime in Southern Africa. The decisive factor is, and will continue to be, what appears possible and reasonable to the political actors in the region in the gradual process of *rapprochement* and understanding. Confidence cannot, after all, be distilled from the promises contained in grand proposals; it is the product of practicable experience.

Notes

1. For a discussion of this, see Gino J. Naldi, *The Organization of African Unity: An Analysis of Its Role* (London: Mansell, 1989), pp. 19–26.

2. Abdu Kinana, "The Relevance of Confidence- and Security-building Measures for Africa," *Disarmament: A Periodic Review by the United Nations*, Vol. 14, No. 4, 1991, p. 100.

3. The document reads: "To restore a lasting state of national and continental security, confidence-building measures between African countries are called for under the CSSDCA process to cover, inter alia, exchange of information on troop locations and movements; joint military training; joint military manouvres; joint naval patrols; joint studies and seminars on sub-regional, regional and continental security issues." Quoted from: Laurie Nathan, *Towards a Conference on Security, Stability, Development and Co-operation in Africa*, Southern African Perspectives, No. 13 (Bellville: Centre for Southern African Studies, UWC, 1992), p. 26.

4. The latest of these conferences took place on 24–26 February 1993 in Windhoek, Namibia. See *Confidence- and Security-building Measures in Southern Africa*, Disarmament: Topical Papers, No. 14 (New York: United Nations Department of Political Affairs, 1993).

5. Niklas Luhmann, *Vertrauen: Ein Mechanismus der Reduktion sozialer Komplexität* (Stuttgart: Enke, 1968), p. 1.

6. *Ibid.*, p. 21.

7. *Ibid.*, p. 70.

8. Eric J. Grove, "The Law of the Sea, Ocean Management and Confidence-building," *Disarmament: A Periodic Review by the United Nations*, Vol. 13, No. 4, 1990, p. 104.

9. This term was employed in the run-up to the 1984 Stockholm Conference to indicate the more ambitious scope and objectives, as opposed to the measures adopted in the CSCE Helsinki Final Act of 1975.

10. See James Macintosh, "Confidence- and Security-building Measures: A Sceptical Look," in: *Confidence- and Security-building Measures in Asia*, Disarmament: Topical Papers, No. 7 (New York: United Nations Department for Disarmament Affairs, 1990), pp. 80–2. Macintosh makes a distinction between a "process"—i.e., confidence-building—and a "procedure"—i.e., CSBM—as a means of fostering confidence.

11. Jonathan Alford (ed.), *The Future of Arms Control, Part III: Confidence-building Measures*, Adelphi Papers, No. 149 (London: The International Institute for Strategic Studies, 1979), p. 5.

12. Disarmament, on the other hand, starts out from the conviction that weapons are wrong in themselves and need to be eliminated. However, one should note that there are overlaps, for instance when it comes to the elimination of whole categories of weapons systems (which may be considered particularly threatening, hazardous or self-defeating) or in the case of constraining measures in the realm of CSBMs.

13. Adam-Daniel Rotfeld, "Developing a Confidence-building System in East–West Relations: Europe and the CSCE," in: Rolf Berg, Adam-Daniel Rotfeld, *Building Security in Europe: Confidence-building Measures and the CSCE*, East-West Monograph Series, No. 2 (New York: Institute for East–West Security Studies, 1986), p. 74.

14. Andrew Mack, "Confidence and Security-building Measures and Military Security," in: *Confidence- and Security-building Measures...*, *op. cit.*, in note 10, p. 114.

15. Barry Buzan, *People, States and Fear: The National Security Problem in International Relations* (Brighton, Sussex: Wheatsheaf, 1983), p. 106.

16. Basil Davidson, *The Black Man's Burden: Africa and the Curse of the Nation State* (New York: Times Books, 1992), p. 203.

17. See, for instance, Mohammed Ayoob, "State-Making and Third World Security," in: Jasjit Singh and Thomas Bernauer (eds), *Security of Third World Countries* (Dartmouth: United Nations Institute for Disarmament Research, 1993), pp. 27–9; Peter M. Lewis, "Political Transition and the Dilemma of Civil Society in Africa," *Journal of International Affairs*, Vol. 46, 1992, No. 1, pp. 32–45.

18. Davidson, *op. cit.*, in note 16, pp. 208, 290.

19. See, for instance, Brian L. Job, "The Insecurity Dilemma: National, Regime and State Securities in the Third World," in: Brian L. Job. (ed.), *The Insecurity Dilemma: National Security of Third World States* (Boulder, Col. and London: Lynne Rienner Publishers, 1992), pp. 17–8. In contrast to what happens in the "security dilemma," the political actors here do not face the problem of their action bringing about unintended—and possibly counterproductive—consequences. Rather, there is a complete absence of the preconditions that would enable them to act as in a "security dilemma."

20. Africa may be unique only to the extent that virtually all the borders on the continent were externally imposed by the Congress of Berlin in 1884-1885. A similar process went on in Europe, though on a smaller scale, until this century, when waves of national self-determination broke out (see, for instance, the post-World War I settlement, which, amongst other things, deprived the newly founded state of Hungary of one third of its original Hungarian population—with consequences which were, however, quite different from those in Africa).

21. Davidson, *op. cit.*, in note 16, pp. 171–2.

22. Jeffrey Herbst, "Challenges to Africa's Boundaries in the New World Order," *Journal of International Affairs*, Vol. 46, No. 1, 1992, p. 19.

23. See, for instance, Keith Somerville, "The Failure of Democratic Reform in Angola and Zaire," *Survival*, Vol. 35, No. 3, 1993, p. 52.

24. Laurie Nathan, "'With Open Arms': Confidence- and Security-building Measures in Southern Africa," in: *Confidence- and Security-building Measures..., op. cit.*, in note 4, p. 123.

25. On the continuing institutional differences and the possible solutions, see the chapter by Peter Meyns in this volume.

26. Since this fear has now almost completely disappeared, differences of approach may be observed in the debate about a new generation of CSBMs. Thus, the CSCE "Forum for Security Co-operation" in Vienna is discussing topics such as a joint "code of conduct," "subregional measures," problems of non-proliferation, etc. Given that the sense of urgency has now been lost, however, few results have so far been recorded.

27. See, for instance, Thomas Ohlson, Stephen John Stedman, "Security in Post-Apartheid Southern Africa," *Security Dialogue*, Vol. 24, No. 4, pp. 419–20.

28. This would happen on the assumption that more capable countries—in contrast to those named above—are more likely to be able to implement more demanding CSBMs in accordance with treaty requirements.

29. Which elements are the most amenable to consensus in the region may be gleaned from the policy proposals of the Midgard Conference, which brought together numerous high-ranking militaries from Southern Africa. See Hans-Joachim Spanger and Peter Vale, *Security, Development and Co-operation in Southern Africa: The Midgard Conference*, PRIF Reports, No. 31 (Frankfurt: Peace Research Institute, 1993).

30. For a recent example, see the Kampala Document in: Nathan, *op. cit.*, in note 3.

31. Angola, Mozambique, South Africa, Tanzania, Zambia and Zimbabwe. See table in Appendix.

32. The right to request a visit to a military facility for the purpose of inspection is nevertheless retained as a safeguard.

33. The bilateral commissions for security co-operation instituted between a whole series of states, mostly during the 1980s, are not a viable substitute here. They either never functioned or else have more pending conflicts to solve than they can cope with.

Appendix 1

Table 6.1: Armed Forces in Southern Africa

	Angola*	Botswana	Lesotho	Malawi	Mozambique*	Namibia	South Africa*	Tanzania	Zambia	Zimbabwe
Personnel										
Total	45,000	6,100	2,000	10,400	50,000	8,100	67,500	49,500	21,600	48,200
Army	35,000	6,000	2,000	10,000	45,000	8,000	47,000	45,000	20,000	47,000
Air Force	6,000	100		200	4,000	100	10,000	1,000	1,600	1,200
Navy	4,000			200	1,000		4,500	3,500		
Paramilitary Forces	20,000	1,000		1,500			147,000	1,400	1,400	21,000
Reserves				10,000			360,000	85,000		
Equipment										
Main Battle Tanks	(+) 200				(+) 300		(+) 250	65	30	40
Armoured Vehicles	200	(+) 50	18	43	300	some	(+) 4,800	(+) 200	131	(+) 200
Fighter Aircrafts	65		2	9	43		130	24	24	34
Artillery	300	12	2		(+) 300	some	370	285	96	30

* Government forces only. The figures do not include UNITA armed formations (40,000 personnel), RNM troops (20,000) and the armed forces of the former BVTC homelands (7,000 personnel strength) or the ANC combat wing "Umkhonto we Sizwe" (an estimated 6,000 trained).

Source: The Military Balance, 1993-1994 (London: The International Institute for Strategic Studies, 1993), pp. 199-222.

Appendix 2

Confidence- and Security-building in Southern Africa
Draft Proposal

I. Guiding Principles

A. Commitments Governing Relations Between the Member States

(1) Every State in Southern Africa is sovereign. Every State respects the rights inherent in the territorial integrity and political independence of all other States in Southern Africa.

(2) The member States reaffirm their obligation to refrain from the use or threat of use of force against the territorial integrity or political independence of any member State.

(3) They reaffirm that non-compliance with the obligation of refraining from the threat or use of force constitutes a violation of international law. They will not allow their territories to be used in contravention of this principle.

(4) They will refrain from any promotion of wars of aggression. They reaffirm in particular that war of aggression is a crime against peace. Aggression entails international responsibility.

(5) The member States recall the inherent right of individual or collective self-defence in the event of an armed attack, as set forth in the Charter of the United Nations.

(6) They reaffirm the inviolability of borders and reiterate that frontiers can only change in accordance with international law, through peaceful means and by agreement.

(7) No occupation or acquisition of territory resulting from the threat or use of force in contravention of international law will be recognized as legal. The member States will not recognize the validity of any other acts undertaken in contravention of this principle.

(8) The member States reaffirm the universal significance of human rights and fundamental freedoms. Respect for and effective exercise of these rights and freedoms are essential factors for international peace and security, justice and economic development, as well as for the evolution of friendly relations and co-operation among all States.

(9) They reaffirm their commitment to the principle of the peaceful settlement of disputes, which is an essential complement to the duty of States to refrain from the threat or use of force, both being essential factors for the maintenance and consolidation of peace and security.

(10) Each member State will ensure that all domestic disputes that may arise between groups of its population and their organizations are settled by peaceful means. The member States will not recognize changes in the status of their internal territorial entities and their borders which result from the use of force.

(11) They will co-operate with each other with the aim of containing and preventing the spread of an internal conflict in accordance with the requirements and requests of the democratically elected legitimate government of the State concerned.

(12) The member States reaffirm their commitment to prevent and combat terrorism, including the prohibition of illegal activities on their territories, for example, in the subversion of legitimate governments. They will refrain from organizing or encouraging organizations of irregular forces or armed units, including mercenaries, for the purpose of invading another member State. They undertake to co-operate in establishing effective international instruments in this respect.

(13) No foreign forces will be stationed on the territory of a member State without that State's explicit consent. They will be withdrawn immediately if such consent has been invalidated.

(14) They will promote arms control, disarmament, confidence- and security-building through full implementation of their international commitments and the elaboration of new measures.

(15) They will conduct regular bilateral and multilateral consultation and permanent security dialogue, maintain close contact and co-operate on matters related to security.

B. Commitments Maintaining and Enhancing Regional Security

(16) The member States recognize that security is indivisible and that the security of every member State is inseparably linked to that of all the others.

(17) They will pursue their security interests as sovereign and independent States and on the basis of full equality. They will respect the right of each of them to enjoy all rights inherent in full sovereignty both in the field of security and in accordance with international law.

(18) The member States will, at all times, be guided by the principle of full respect for the legitimate security needs of each other. They will ensure that the security of each of them is not adversely affected. No State will seek to strengthen its own security at the expense of that of others.

(19) The member States recognize the role of regional arrangements in dialogue and co-operation. In developing regional and other forms of co-operation in the security field, they will ensure that their aims and actions are in full conformity with the objectives and principles of the Charter of the United Nations and OAU documents.

(20) Notwithstanding the right of States to freely choose their own security arrangements, the member States will undertake not to conclude treaties or agreements, or enter into security arrangements with any State, aimed at adversely affecting the security of other member States. This includes, inter alia, transfers of armaments, expertise, technology, financial assistance.

(21) They will keep the levels of their armed forces to the minimum commensurate with legitimate common or individual security needs within Southern Africa and beyond. They will determine those needs in accordance with their obligations under international law, taking into account legitimate security concerns of other States, in particular their neighbours. They will refrain from any attempt to build military superiority.

(22) They will base their military doctrines on defensive principles. The structure, equipment, state of readiness and training of the armed forces will be oriented to serve defensive purposes. They will approach with restraint their defence needs in planning military expenditures, arms procurement, infrastructure upgrading and in other aspects of the maintenance and development of their military potential.

Promoting Arms Control and Disarmament

(23) The member States are committed to the full implementation of existing arms control and disarmament agreements and will pursue further such measures with the aim of enhancing security and stability.

(24) They will undertake and support efforts to conclude a treaty on a Nuclear Weapons Free Zone on the African Continent.

(25) The member States will also adhere, and if they have not already done so, become parties to international arms control and disarmament treaties concluded within the UN framework. They will also co-operate closely with a view to furthering disarmament efforts worldwide, including the strengthening of UN arms control and disarmament fora and regimes.

(26) They exercise and promote due restraint in and transparency about arms transfers and the transfer of sensitive military know-how, particularly in situations of tension and conflict. They will regularly provide data on imports and exports to the United Nations Register of Conventional Arms. Armaments transfers for the sole purpose of obtaining economic benefits is hereby declared an irresponsible behaviour.

(27) They will prevent, through regional co-operation, coordinated border control, appropriate legislation and enforcement procedures, illegal arms transfers.

Conflict Prevention and Peaceful Settlement of Disputes

(28) The member States will seek effective ways of preventing, through political means, conflicts that may emerge among themselves or within their territories. They reaffirm their existing undertakings on conflict prevention, crisis management, peaceful settlement of disputes and commitments to use OAU mechanisms.

(29) The member States will promptly consult among each other on how their commonly shared values of democracy, respect for human rights, the rule of law, economic development and others have been affected by the conflict immediatly after it has arisen. In order to promote the application of dispute settlement and crisis management and to obtain just and viable results, they will actively co-operate with a view to helping the parties

concerned to generate the will and desire to put into use available mechanisms, with their free choice.

(30) The member States will consider possibilities for concerted action in defence of the above values and, if such action is deemed appropriate, will determine specific forms and mechanisms for conducting it.

(31) They will consult on how best to use the peace-restoring mechanisms of the United Nations and the OAU and to co-operate in implementing them. They reaffirm their commitment to use best efforts to provide material or financial assistance to peace-keeping and peace-enforcement operations.

Democratic Control of the Armed Forces

(32) Each member State will maintain an effective constitutional and legal framework for the status, functioning and use of the armed forces.

(33) The member States will ensure that functions, responsibilities and activities of regular armed forces, militia and paramilitary forces are fully controlled by legitimate constitutional authorities.

(34) They will ensure the primacy of the democratic civilian institutions over all military and paramilitary forces, as well as internal security, intelligence services and other law enforcement institutions. They will, in particular, ensure that the government decision-making process extends to all aspects of the functioning of the armed forces and that decisions applying to the armed forces and their implementation are subject to parliamentary control.

(35) Each member State will ensure, with due regard to the specific requirements of military matters, transparency of and public access to matters related to the functioning of its armed forces.

(36) Each member State will ensure the effective exercise of human rights and fundamental freedoms by personnel serving with its armed forces in conformity with the reqirements of the military service.

(37) Each member State will ensure that its laws and practice relating to the recruitment of personnel to serve in the armed forces are in conformity with humanitarian principles and international law.

(38) No member State will allow its armed forces to serve the interests of a single particular political grouping.

(39) They will ensure that their armed forces are trained, staffed and equipped in accordance with international instruments governing the conduct of war, and are aware of those instruments. Orders violating those principles will not be recognized as valid. Persons responsible for violating those principles will be held accountable by each member State.

Norms Guiding the Domestic Use of the Armed Forces

(40) The member States will not use armed forces to limit the exercise of the civil rights of their people and, in particular, the right of political organizations to advocate any constitutional change they consider appropriate, provided they do not use or encourage recourse to violence. They will not use or encourage violence against such organizations.

(41) The member States will refrain from using armed forces or undertaking acts of coercion to deprive people of their national, religious, cultural, linguistic or ethnic identity. States have a duty to refrain from acts of reprisal involving the use of force and to protect the populations, groups or national minorities against such acts.

(42) Each member State will use its military personnel for domestic purposes, in particular to assist in relief operations or in restoring public order, only on the basis of strict constitutional procedures and within the limits prescribed by international law. Such forces may use force only when strictly necessary and to the extent required for the performance of their duty.

(43) The member States underline their commitment that if armed forces usurp political control in any member State, appropriate joint action will be considered.

(44) They reaffirm that international humanitarian law of war must be applied in civil wars and domestic conflicts.

II. Policy Measures

A. Global Exchange of Military Information

(45) The member States will provide to all other member States information concerning their military forces and their defence planning as specified below. The frequency of the information exchange will be set as follows: States possessing regular armed forces in excess of 20,000 active personnel every two years; States posessing armed forces below above threshold every four years.

Information on Military Forces

(46) The information will be provided in an agreed format not later than [...] of the relevant year. It will reflect the situation as of 1 January of that year.

(47) Subject of information shall be armaments and equipment, personnel strength, peacetime location, rank structure and operational concepts. This applies to all land, air and naval forces stationed both within their national territories and beyond on the territories of third States.

(48) The information will include data on:

(a) Armaments and Equipment

Total equipment holdings, in the categories listed below. The information will include the type names or national nomenclature and general descriptions of characteristics and capabilities. The information will be exchanged once for each type of equipment and will be amended as required in the next information exchange if new types enter into service:

- battle tanks,
- armoured combat vehicles,
- anti-tank guided weapons, mounted on armoured chassis,
- artillery (75 mm caliber and above),
- multiple launch rocket systems,
- combat aircraft (including trainers),
- helicopters (attack, combat support, transport),
- ships greater than 100 tons loaded displacement,
- submarines greater than 50 tons submerged.

(b) Personnel

The information will include:

- total authorized personnel on active duty,
- total authorized personnel in reserve status,
- total authorized conscripts,
- total authorized personnel in paramilitary formations,
- total authorized professional officers/enlisted,
- total authorized number of personnel in general staff,
- command organization specifying the designation and subordination of all formations and their normal peacetime location,
- rank structure,
- concept of operations.

(49) The information subject to global exchange will be disaggregated as follows:

- for all ground forces stationed within the land territory of the reporting State to the level of brigade or equivalent;
- for all other forces stationed within the land territory of the reporting State to the level of service;
- for all military forces stationed beyond the land territory of the reporting State to the level of service.

(50) To resolve misperceptions and misunderstandings, each member State will be entitled to obtain timely clarification from any other member State concerning the information on their military forces. Questions may be submitted at any time following the receipt of a member State's information. Member States will make every effort to answer such questions fully and promptly. They may also offer visits to military facilities as referred to below to be used for the purpose of evaluating the information provided.

Information on Defence Planning

(51) The member States will exchange information on their defence planning for the forthcoming five fiscal years. The information will be provided not later than [...].

(52) In a written statement they will describe the following:

- the national defence policy, including military strategy/doctrine as well as priorities for allocating financial, human and material resources;
- planned major changes in the size, structure, equipment and deployment of its armed forces, including information on major changes in paramilitary forces;
- major investment projects, in particular the procurement of major equipment;
- budget figures for the forthcoming fiscal year and provisional budget estimates for the forthcoming five-year period, itemizing defence expenditures on the basis of the categories set out in the United Nations Instrument for Standardized International Reporting of Military Expenditures adopted on 12 December 1980;
- a general overview of the realization of plans notified in earlier information exchanges.

(53) In order to facilitate an evaluation of the information provided, the member States may include any information they deem necessary on the constitutional procedures for defence planning, including the stages of defence planning and the institutions involved in decision making.

(54) To increase transparency, each member State will be entitled to ask any other member State for clarification of the information provided on defence planning. Questions should be submitted within a period of four months following the receipt of a member State's information. Member States will make every effort to answer such questions fully and promptly. It should be understood that these exchanges are informational only. The questions and replies may be transmitted to all other member States.

(55) The member States may hold every two years a meeting to discuss relevant issues, such as implications originating from the information provided or the realization of defence plans notified in earlier information exchanges.

B. Communications

(56) The member States will establish a network of direct communications between their governments for the rapid transmission of messages relating to agreed measures. The network will complement the existing use of diplomatic channels.

(57) Each member State will designate a point of contact capable of transmitting and receiving such messages from other member States. Each member State will notify this designation in writing to other member States not later than [...] and will notify in advance any change in this designation.

(58) The technical characteristics of the network are to be agreed upon.

(59) Communications will be in the English language.

C. Contacts and Co-operation in Military Matters

(60) To increase transparency and to improve further their mutual relations in the interest of strengthening the process of confidence- and security-building, the member States will, as appropriate, promote and facilitate mutual visits to military formations and their facilities as well as exchange programs and contacts between military personnel.

Visits to Military Facilities

(61) Upon request by a member State, each member State will arrange visits for liaison teams to any of its major peacetime military facilities in order to provide the visitors with the opportunity to view activity and see major weapon and equipment systems of respective formations.

(62) The host State may invite additional representatives of other member States, if deemed appropriate. As a rule, up to two visitors from each member State will be invited.

(63) No member State with overall force levels below 50,000 active troops will be obliged to accept more than five such requests per caldendar year. Member States with force levels in excess of above threshold are obliged to accept up to ten requests per calendar year. No more than one request per caldendar year from the same member State will have to be accepted.

(64) A visit will not be counted against the active and passive quotas if it cannot be carried out.

(65) The visit to the military facilities will last for a minimum of 48 hours. In the course of the visit, the visitors will be given a briefing concerning

the personnel as well as the major weapon and equipment systems and on current activity. They will have the opportunity to communicate with commanders and troops and will be provided free access to all military equipment located at the facility. Access will not have to be granted to sensitive points.

(66) The visitors will be provided with appropriate transport and accommodation during the visit by the host State. Travel expenses to and from the place will be covered by the invited State.

Exchange Programmes and Military Contacts

(67) The member States will arrange exchanges and visits between senior military and defence representatives on a regular basis. Similarly, exchanges between military commanders and officers of commands down to battalion or equivalent level will be initiated.

(68) Member States are encouraged to provide, in a spirit of reciprocity, places for military personnel from other member States on command and general staff training courses or seminars.

(69) They will make available student slots for their military academies and general staff schools, in particular with a view to support collectively States not in possession of adequate training facilities.

(70) They stipulate the need to facilitate exchanges and contacts between relevant military institutions as well as between academics and experts in military studies and related areas.

(71) Recognizing the importance of maintaining stable border regimes, member States will take the necessary steps, on a bilateral basis, to facilitate joint supervision and patrol of existing borders.

(72) As a further move towards a common security space in Southern Africa, member States will also consider and encourage joint military exercises. They will take the necessary steps in military education and training to get prepared for joint peace-keeping operations.

D. Notification and Observation of Military Activities

(73) The member States will give notification in writing through diplomatic channels in a standardized format to all other member States at least 30 days in advance of the start of the notifiable military activities in the zone of application for confidence- and security-building measures. Notification will be given by the member State on whose territory the activity in question is planned to take place.

(74) Each of the following military activities conducted as a single activity at or above the levels defined below will be notified:

(a) Out-of-Garrison Land Activities

When military formations involving 5,000 or more ground troops, or forces comprising more than 50 main battle tanks or armoured personnel carriers, are carrying out a common activity under a single operational command, whether independent or combined with air or naval components.

When military formations involving 2,000 or more ground troops, or forces comprising more than 30 main battle tanks or armoured personnel carriers, are carrying out a common activity under a single operational command, whether independent or combined with air or naval components within 50 kilometers from national borders.

(b) Mobilization Activities

When 10,000 or more troops (reservists, paramilitary forces) or the major combat elements of two or more brigades or equivalent formations are involved.

(75) When a notifiable out-of-garrison land activity or mobilization activity is carried out on short notice as an alert activity, it will be notified at the time it begins, that is, when troops are ordered to carry out the activities.

(76) Notifications will contain the following essential information:

- the type of military activity and its designation,
- general characteristics and purpose of the military activity,
- the name of the States involved in the military activity,
- the area of the military activity, indicated by geographic features, where appropriate, and defined by geographic coordinates,

- the planned duration of the military activity, indicated by envisaged start and end dates,
- the envisaged total number of troops engaged in the military activity,
- the types of armed forces involved in the military activity,
- the level of command, organizing and commanding the military activity.

(77) The member States will invite the other member States voluntarily to send observers to attend notifiable military activities. Respective requests by any member State will be considered in a spirit of goodwill.

(78) The inviting State will determine in each case the number of observers, the procedures and conditions of their participation, and give other information which it may consider useful. It will provide appropriate facilities and hospitality.

E. Stabilizing Measures

(79) Military activities subject to prior notification, involving more than 20,000 troops (armed forces, reservists, paramilitary), are prohibited.

(80) Alert activities subject to notification within 50 kilometers from national borders are prohibited.

(81) Military activities subject to notification, involving armed forces from outside respective member States, are prohibited within 50 kilometers from the national border of a non-participating State.

F. Mechanism for the Settlement of Disputes and Conflicts as regards CSBMs

(82) Member States will, in accordance with the following provisions, consult and co-operate with each other in the event of:

- a violation of one of the Guiding Principles endangering peace, security and stability;
- non-compliance with the confidence- and security-building measures contained in this document;
- unusual and unscheduled activities of military significance;
- hazardous incidents of a military nature.

(83) The member State which has security concerns about any such event may transmit a request for an explanation to another member State which is deemed responsible. The request will clearly state and explain the cause of the concern.

(84) The reply will be transmitted within not more than 48 hours. It will contain answers to questions raised, as well as any other relevant information which might help clarify the case giving rise to concern.

(85) The requesting as well as the responding State, after considering the reply provided, may then request a meeting to discuss the matter. Such a meeting will be convened within not more than 48 hours. It will be held at a venue to be mutually agreed upon or, alternatively, at [...]. The responding State is entitled to ask other interested member States to participate in the meeting.

(86) Depending on the nature of the disputed case, the requesting as well as the responding State may subsequently call for a meeting of all member States. Such a meeting will be convened within not more than 72 hours, provided one third of the member States have given their consent. It will be held at [...].

(87) In a situation of emergency, the meeting of all member States may be convened immediately after a security concern has been raised. An emergency meeting requires the consent of half of the member States.

(88) The meeting of all member States will have the overall responsibility for managing the crisis with a view to its resolution. It will determine the procedure to be applied and establish a precise mandate for action. It will initiate and promote the exercise of good offices, mediation and conciliation.

(89) With due regard to the principle of non-intervention in internal affairs it may adopt the following measures:

(a) Aerial Observation Flights

The requesting State or other member States may be authorized to carry out observation flights over any portion of the territory of the responding State. State parties carrying out observation flights are entitled to use their own equipment (reconnaissance aircrafts, cameras, video cameras, on the basis of commonly available technology). At the point of entry, aircraft and sensors to be used will be examined by the State party to be observed in order to prove that the equipment confirms with required standards.

On this occasion, the observing party will submit a mission plan, specifying the area to be flown over. Findings will be reported immediately to all member States. This measure requires the consent of half of the member States.

(b) Fact-finding Missions

The meeting of all member States may decide to dispatch a fact-finding mission to the responding State to clarify the contentious issue on the ground. The establishment of fact-finding missions will in every case contain a clear mandate. The receiving State will make every necessary effort to ensure that the mission is able to fulfill its mandate. Fact-finding missions will transmit their report to all other member States without delay. This measure requires the consent of a two-third majority of the member States.

(c) Peace-keeping Operations

Peace-keeping constitutes an integral part of conflict prevention and crisis management. It may be undertaken in cases of dispute and conflict to help maintain peace and stability in support of ongoing efforts at a political solution. Peace-keeping operations require the consent of all member States and will be undertaken with due regard to the responsibilities of the United Nations in this field and in conformity with the purposes and principles of the Charter of the United Nations.

(90) Member States will designate officials of their foreign and defence ministries to serve as liaison officers and as representatives in the settlement mechanism. Similarly, they will earmark units in their armed forces to be made available, when requested, for service in peace-keeping operations.

7

Establishing Democratic Defence Forces in Mozambique: A Case Study

Joao Bernardo Honwana

The search for peace and security is intimately connected with the destiny of a country's armed forces. This search is a difficult process in most cases, but experience suggests it is most problematic when regular and guerilla forces have to be fused into one army. The countries of Southern Africa, forced to address the legacy of past conflict, have built an impressive and possibly unique body of knowledge around the complex questions associated with the integration of armed forces. Quite clearly, the nature of the regional conflicts has made it imperative that this be tackled with great urgency. In Zimbabwe and Namibia, the creation of truly national armed forces has been carried out more or less successfully; Angola, however, is a different matter. There integration remains incomplete, and this has allowed the contending parties to the Bicesse Peace Accord to return to war after the elections. This case study reflects the complexities of the issue and examines the difficult choices that have to be made in the period leading to integration. In addition, it suggests that success and failure in this process are never far apart.

The 1992 Rome Peace Accord between the Mozambican government and the Resistência Nacional Moçambicana (Renamo) produced a cessation of hostilities that has now lasted for two years and, despite its shortcomings and omissions, has created an atmosphere of hope for millions of Mozambicans. However, post-conflict reconciliation and the transition to peace are fraught with difficulties, as recent developments in Angola demonstrate. In particular, the Angolan tragedy illustrates how important and difficult it is to devise adequate strategies for the post-conflict demobilization, disarmament and integration of armed forces.

With that lesson in mind, all major parties to the process of peace-building in Mozambique have agreed that elections should not take place before demobilization and disarmament are complete, and the new defence force is in place. Assisted by the United Nations, Great Britain, France and Portugal, government and Renamo forces are being integrated to form a 30,000-strong new defence force, the Forças Armadas de Defesa de Moçambique (FADM), defined as a non-partisan and professional democratic force.[1] For various reasons, this has proved an extremely complex task.

The officers and soldiers who will comprise the FADM belonged until very recently to armed forces which were neither designed nor oriented to serve a democracy and were the main antagonists in a particularly vicious and cruel conflict. Therefore, they need to be educated in patterns of legitimate interaction with society in a democratic environment. Moreover, despite the introduction of a new constitution in 1990, which formally defines Mozambique as a liberal democracy, it will certainly take more than a constitutional change to transform the political culture of Mozambican society. The institutional weakness of the state, the absence of civil society and the severe economic, social and psychological legacy of the war will inhibit the democratic transformation of the armed forces. Mozambique's extreme poverty means that the implementation of the Rome Peace Accord depends heavily on foreign assistance, which comes with conditions impacting severely on national sovereignty. One of these is the demand for urgent "internationally acceptable results," such as free and fair multi-party elections, good governance and democratic armed forces. However, there is a danger that in the attempt to establish democratic institutions as quickly as possible, the importance of developing democratic values in Mozambican society and within the state administration may be neglected. A "democratic" Mozambique could then amount to a mere parody of democracy. Equally, "democratic armed forces" might be just another fashionable expression with no practical meaning. In many countries in Africa, Asia and Latin America, the military has tended to interfere in the political affairs of the state, even though its officers were trained in Western democracies. The training of the new Mozambican defence force by officers from Western democracies, however important, is not sufficient to ensure that FADM will be a democratic defence force. What else, then, should be done?

In this chapter, I attempt to identify the obstacles to the establishment of democratic armed forces, to outline the essential features of armed forces in a democracy, and to explain why it is important that an informed public debate in Mozambique on the future of the military should take place.[2] This is based on the assumption that democracy is a prerequisite for enduring peace and national reconciliation. Thus, the current transition should essentially be about the democratic transformation of the state and its institutions. In this process, the creation of democratic armed forces is a crucial component. More specifically, the integration of the armed forces needs to address critical issues regarding the nature of civil-military relations, the role of the military and its professionalism and legitimacy.

A number of broad issues will not be touched on here. These include the impact of ethnic tensions on the military, the role of international assistance and the impact of regional dynamics on the defence and security concerns of Mozambique. However, this chapter will have served its purpose if it contributes to a debate on the place and role of armed forces in a democratic Mozambique at an early stage of the transition process.

The Political Background

The peace agreement signed by the government and the rebel movement Renamo in Rome on 4 October 1992 established the framework for peace-building in Mozambique. It contains guiding principles for the general elections, eventually held in October 1994, and for the activities of political parties, as well as an agreement on a cease-fire and a timetable for its implementation. It also defines the role of the United Nations Operation in Mozambique (ONUMOZ) as general monitor of the implementation of the agreement, with a focus on the cease-fire, the electoral process and the coordination of humanitarian assistance. Protocol IV of the Rome Peace Accord deals with the formation of the Mozambique Defence Force (FADM), determining its force levels and command structure and setting a timetable for the assembly, selection and training of the new army before the inauguration of the new government.

The accord has to be implemented in a situation characterized by profound domestic and international changes. Mozambique is in a transition from war to peace and in the process of replacing an authoritarian one-party system and its centralized command economy with multi-party parliamentarianism and a market economy. The instability, inherent in a change of such magnitude, is compounded by the legacy of the war: a fundamental social disintegration and the attendant loss of basic moral values. The situation has been further complicated by the draconian Plan for Economic Rehabilitation (PRE), a structural adjustment programme for the economy introduced in 1987 when the country joined the International Monetary Fund.[3]

In addition, attempts to consolidate national unity and cohesion have been adversely affected by a two-year long electoral campaign in which ethnic, regional and religious loyalties have been increasingly exploited by the emerging opposition parties in the hope that this will win them popular support. Inevitably, this approach undermines national reconciliation, long-term nation-building and development. Many observers agree that the opposition in particular seems more concerned with gaining access to political power and the associated material benefits than with promoting a political programme substantially different from that of Frelimo.

To make matters even worse, Renamo's commitment to peace is questionable: it maintains a de facto dual territorial administration and often threatens to resume the war.[4] Renamo's reluctance to abandon its militaristic posture is hardly surprising, since its bargaining power rests on the threat or use of violence. Some of my sources have asserted that Renamo's behaviour also indicates its dependence on external support and its inability to follow an independent agenda.

The fact that the government is one of the parties to the conflict has had a severe impact on its ability to govern effectively. Its authority is seriously undermined by pervasive social instability and the country's extreme dependence on external assistance. There is a particular danger of dissatisfied military personnel disrupting the peace process. Government soldiers have been complaining in increasingly violent ways about inadequate salaries, poor living conditions and insufficient support for the reintegration of demobilized personnel. Discipline and morale are rapidly declining, and the officers are unsure about whether to join the new army.

Obstacles to a Democratic Defence Force

The political regime in Mozambique and the effects of South Africa's destabilization have seriously hindered the processes of democratization and of nation-building in the country. In this regard, three points should be considered: first, a weak state inevitably experiences serious difficulties in managing the "naked power" of the military; second, a weak civil society is inherently unable to influence policy-making and to exert control over the state's defence policy; third, the past experience and current perceptions of the military personnel who will comprise the FADM are likely to make the establishment of a democratic defence force more difficult.

Political Factors: The Weakness of the State and the Absence of Civilian Society

When it came to power in 1975, the Frente de Libertação de Moçambique (Frelimo)[5] was confronted with the fact that while a state called Mozambique already existed, a nation had yet to be built. National unity was considered a prerequisite for saving the country from underdevelopment, and a strong centralized state apparatus was deemed necessary to achieve it. Some former guerilla commanders and cadres were appointed to civilian posts, to guarantee that the nascent party's policies were implemented in those sectors. This followed a tradition developed during the war of independence (1962-1974) in the liberated areas, where Frelimo had sought to address the immediate concerns of the peasantry in order to consolidate its power base. At that time, the guerillas understood the importance of the voluntary adherence of the peasantry to the struggle and the peasants were convinced that the struggle would bring their own liberation. This interdependence and mutual respect produced a political tradition that can best be described as "grassroots participatory democracy."[6]

In the course of the attempt to implement this experience nationwide, Grupos Dinamizadores (GDs, literally: galvanizing groups) had been created to keep the country going and to deal with the crisis created by the massive exodus of (mainly Portuguese) skilled labour during the transition to independence in 1974-1975. The GDs were democratically elected bodies in the communities, factories, administrative divisions, schools and hospitals, and were initially meant to have an advisory role. They soon became very influential as their activities ranged from mediating in domestic and community disputes to providing intelligence on acts of economic sabotage and managing factories.

The war of liberation and its immediate aftermath were a period of intense democratization which contrasted sharply with Mozambique's colonial past. According to Hanlon: "Frelimo gave Mozambicans a voice. In colonial times they had little to say; in the first years of independence there were meetings everywhere in which people spoke their minds."[7] At its third congress in early 1977, however, Frelimo transformed itself from a broad nationalist front, legitimately representative of the vast majority of Mozambicans, into a Marxist-Leninist vanguard party. Frelimo believed that, once the economic and social decline that followed the end of colonial rule had been halted, Mozambican society and the state needed to be organized to undertake the battle against underdevelopment. This meant that the GDs, with their almost spontaneous origins and fairly independent methods which implied the idea and practice of direct democracy and contradicted the concept and discipline of the vanguard party, had to be abandoned.

At the same time, the administrative structures of the new state were developed through the election of people's assemblies at all levels, from local to national parliament, and the training and appointment of officials for the administration at district and local levels. By 1980, the socialist option seemed to be working quite successfully, as long as one ignored its democratic shortcomings. The government enjoyed a great measure of legitimacy:

> The first five years of independence produced dramatic gains for most Mozambicans. Freedom and a measure of democracy changed people's lives; women especially gained rights for the first time. Health and education became much more widely available. Mozambique did not suffer the racial and other ethnic tensions seen elsewhere. The economic decline had been reversed and the economy was growing. Victory over underdevelopment seemed possible.[8]

However, the system was not designed to be democratic and did not encourage the emergence of a strong and independent civil society. The party set the agenda for debate in state and non-governmental "mass organizations" alike, and all these bodies increasingly became simple conduits for party instructions. Since political opposition was prohibited, there was no political pluralism, no free press and no freedom of opinion. And finally, there was no clear separation between the legislative, the executive and the judiciary.

The bold plans to construct a strong state apparatus and develop the country along a socialist model were doomed to fail, principally because they became the prime targets of Renamo between 1980 and 1989. As a result of the war, the early economic and social gains proved unsustainable by 1983. These difficulties were compounded by ill-advised agrarian policies and the constraints imposed by inadequate foreign assistance, on which Mozambique became increasingly dependent. Frelimo's manifest intolerance of the traditional cultural practices of the peasantry further alienated important sectors of the population from the new regime.[9] Renamo, in turn, managed to exploit the government's vulnerabilities.[10] The rapidly weakening Mozambican state, whose effective presence became increasingly confined to cities and towns, was more and more preoccupied with security. As a result of the crisis, the political leadership became dependent on the armed forces, which gave existing authoritarian tendencies an additional boost and led to a gradual militarization of society.

At its fifth congress in 1989, Frelimo decided to reform itself and the state and to initiate direct negotiations with Renamo to end the conflict. Adherence to Marxism-Leninism was replaced by a return to the posture of a broad national front, and intransigence towards Renamo by a discourse on peace and national reconciliation. Besides the global and regional changes taking place at this time, two internal factors were central to this decision: the social and economic disruption caused by destabilization and the realization that there could be no military solution to the war.

Consequently, a new multi-party constitution was adopted in 1990, establishing the freedom of the press, the independence of the judiciary, basic democratic liberties and the separation of the party from the state. The People's Republic of Mozambique was renamed the Republic of Mozambique, reflecting the abandonment of the ideal of a socialist state. The political liberalization that followed was characterized by the mushrooming of political and civic formations, as well as the separation of the trade unions and the "democratic mass organizations" from the party. Without party and state patronage, however, these organizations have remained weak and uncertain about their social and political role. Their activity is generally limited to the major urban centres where it has attracted more curiosity than substantial support. This limited interest indicates that political pluralism and civic activism are not high priorities for the Mozambican population, whose immediate concerns have more to do with the devastation and insecurity caused by the war. So far, it appears, political liberalization simply addresses the need to accommodate Renamo and the external pressures for good governance and democracy.

From the above discussion and my earlier observations about the fragility of the state, it follows that the main protagonists of the process of change in Mozambique are a weak state, an almost non-existent civil society and political parties whose adherence to democratic principles is rather questionable. Therefore, political democratization is occuring without the mutually reinforcing interaction of a strong state with a strong civil society. More pertinently, the establishment of democratic armed forces and democratic civil-military relations have proved more difficult, since a weak state is less effective in controlling the power of the armed forces. This creates a potential for the development of interventionist tendencies within the military which, in turn, may undermine the state and democracy. Lesotho and Nigeria, where weak states are held hostage by highly interventionist armed forces, are cases in point.[11] Equally, a weak civil society is unable to make substantial inputs to policy-making or to keep the state and its agencies in check. In the defence realm, this means that the state is more at liberty to formulate and implement unpopular defence policies, or, to put it crudely, to use military power against the public interest. Zaire, where an unpopular regime is maintained with the active complicity of the military, is a clear illustration of this point.[12]

Military Factors

The conflict in Mozambique had its origins in the national liberation struggle against Portuguese rule. After independence, the conflict evolved from a Rhodesian aggression to a South African-supported destabilization, and came to an end as a civil war between the government and the rebel movement Renamo with the signing of the Rome Peace Accord on 4 October 1992.

The rise of the Mozambique National Resistance (MNR, later Renamo)[13] as a pseudo-liberation movement which was trained and logistically supported by, and operationally subordinate to, the Rhodesian Special Air Service, is well documented.[14] At its inception, Renamo served a twofold purpose: to assist Rhodesian forces in their operations against ZANLA inside Mozambique and to implement the agenda of those resentful and frustrated Portuguese settlers who wanted to unseat the "communist" Frelimo government.

In response, Maputo reshaped the Forças Populares de Libertação de Moçambique (FPLM) to become the regular Forças Armadas de Moçambique (FAM), introducing conscription in early 1978, organizing the army into mechanized brigades and creating new services—the air force, air defence, navy and the borderguard troops. Former guerilla commanders were retrained in Soviet military academies, and with the assistance of Soviet military advisers they presided over the transformation of an all-volunteer guerilla force into a conventional defence force. The thinking was that a strong, modern and politically reliable regular military was needed to counter the "racist aggression" against the young revolutionary state.[15] To ensure military loyalty to Frelimo's socialist project, the defence minister and his two deputies (all serving soldiers) were made full members of the party's ruling body, the politburo; senior commanders were appointed to the central committee, and all officers were urged to join the party. An extensive network of political commissars was established to undertake the ideological education and political mobilization of the troops. Moreover, the country's constitution stated unequivocally that the FPLM was Frelimo's "armed wing" and answerable to the party. Its primary mission was "the defence of the Mozambican revolution."

The military leadership not only participated in all areas of political decision-making but also, given their senior positions in the party hierarchy, played a leading role in that process. It should be noted that such military involvement in politics was generally accepted by Mozambican society during this period (1975-1980), since the FPLM enjoyed a high degree of legitimacy within society as a whole. Its image as the national liberator, its effectiveness in countering Rhodesian military incursions and its acknowledged role in the liberation of Zimbabwe certainly helped to enhance the prestige of the FPLM. The respect and social status enjoyed by the military was indicated by the September 1980 decision to introduce ranks and insignia in the armed forces. Ten members of the eleven-men strong ruling politburo were given military ranks (major-general and colonel) for "their merits in the liberation struggle," although most of them had been civilian "politicos" with no military experience or expertise.

In early 1980, shortly before Zimbabwe gained independence and when it was clear that the Rhodesian regime had collapsed, South African military intelligence took over control of the MNR.[16] South Africa's patronage allowed Renamo to expand its activities from the provinces of Manica, Tete, and Sofala, in 1979-1980, to Gaza, Inhambane and Maputo in the south, and to Zambezia and Nampula in the north, by mid-1983. From an original group of a few hundred men, Renamo grew to 5,000 in 1981, and to more than 8,000 by 1983.[17] The targets of Renamo's onslaught ranged from development and aid projects, roads, bridges and railways to schools, hospitals, rural shops, farms and entire villages. Naked cruelty against the civilian population became Renamo's hallmark, with systematic massacres the rule rather than the exception in vast rural areas, particularly in the south of the country. The aim of this campaign of destruction and terror was clear: to disrupt the rural infrastructure, isolate the government in garrison towns, render the country ungovernable through economic and social collapse and bring Frelimo to its knees.

As the security situation deteriorated, an intensified militarization of the state and society took place: military methods were used to deal with non-military issues, criticism was unwelcome and was labelled as enemy-inspired. Thus FAM/FPLM became increasingly unaccountable for their actions, and corruption and human rights abuses increased. This fall in standards, coupled with the failure to win a clear military victory, explains the dramatic loss of prestige of the armed forces by the time of the cease-fire in October 1992.

FAM/FPLM was essentially the military expression of Frelimo, created to defend the socialist state. The general perception is that this close connection between FAM and Frelimo remains strong, despite some recent measures of political disengagement, such as the abolition of the political commissariats and all party structures within the military and the withdrawal of all senior commanders from Frelimo's central committee. Renamo, essentially the military conduit of foreign interventionist interests, was effectively a mercenary army in its own country. Despite its notorious cruelty against the civilian population, however, Renamo drew some internal support from the peasantry, which had been disempowered by the government's antagonism to the rural cultural heritage and practices and by the policy of forced villagization.[18] In this connection, Hall has commented:

As the war has progressed, destabilization, externally mounted, has tipped over into an internally self-generating process of violence, to which the Mozambican government has been compelled to seek accommodation.[19]

This brief examination of the history of the conflict in Mozambique clearly indicates that neither FAM nor Renamo's guerillas were conceived to serve a democratic state. It is essential to educate the FADM members to develop democratic values, to enable the new military to make a consistent contribution to the current process of transformation.

The Military's Uncertain Future

The provisions of the Rome Peace Accord on the future of the military seem to have caused different reactions within the ranks of the opposing armies. Renamo soldiers and officers are reported to have generally expressed readiness to do as they are told by their leaders—most of them will probably join the new army.[20] In contrast, FAM officers and soldiers do not display the same degree of discipline and unanimity.

As opposed to the successful struggle for national liberation and the war of resistance against Rhodesia's aggression, which contributed to the independence of Zimbabwe, the end of the war in Mozambique brought neither tangible victory, nor glory, nor any sense of accomplishment. FAM was not defeated, but it did not win the war either. As a result of this impasse, both Frelimo and the Mozambican state became so fragile that they had to reshape themselves completely, in order to survive as viable political entities. Privately, members of the FAM leadership blame the "civilian" government for lack of support for the defence forces during the war. Victory would have been possible, so the argument goes, if only the government had been more sensitive to the needs of the military. Frelimo would not then have been forced to give in to Renamo's humiliating demands. For instance, the agreed ceiling of 30,000 men for the FADM, comprising government and Renamo troops in equal proportion, means that only 15,000 FAM men will find a place in the new defence force.

Most (conscript) soldiers, disillusioned with low salaries and poor logistics, have expressed their unwillingness to join FADM and prefer to go home. The same is true of a number of relatively well educated junior officers, who believe they will be better off as civilians. But the majority of senior officers and generals take a different view. Most of them, as veteran guerilla commanders and cadres, gained positions of relative power and status more by virtue of their political loyalty to Frelimo than through professional skills and competence. Demobilization threatens their current living standards by exposing them to the "unprotected" and ever-shrinking civilian labour market. FAM officers, selected for the new defence force, face the troubling prospect of the end of the privileged relationship with a Frelimo single-party government and legislature. In this regard, it may be indicative that sources close to the process of integration report that Renamo officers, who recently participated in a leadership course together with their government counterparts, expressed the view that having "won" the war they should be given the top command of the FADM. The same sources also report that despite public statements to the contrary, officers in the new army remain bitterly divided along lines that oppose Renamo to Frelimo.[21]

In other words, the leadership of the new defence force views military integration as a profoundly unsettling exercise and is mainly concerned with immediate personal job security rather than with the future of the military institution. More importantly, the officer corps lacks internal cohesion, since the loyalty of its members is to their former political masters rather than to the constitution or the state as such. Consequently, a worst-case scenario, whereby part of the new defence force is used by one political party to undermine the democratically elected new government, thus jeopardizing the entire democratic process, cannot be ruled out.

Towards a Democratic Defence Force in Mozambique

A viable democracy in Mozambique is only conceivable if the country's people and institutions acquire democratic values and develop a democratic culture. This is particularly relevant for the military and raises a number of questions:

- What are democratic armed forces in the Mozambican context?
- How can the military acquire a democratic culture in a society with no Western democratic traditions and come to accept the principles of civilian control, accountability, transparency, and public scrutiny?
- How can it develop the qualities and project the image of professional competence and political legitimacy, needed to serve in a democratic order?
- Should its members, especially those guilty of outright terrorism, play an active role in the reconstruction of the country's physical infrastructure and social fabric?

Civil-Military Relations

As a state agency with exclusive access to the means of violence, armed forces are normally a major source of power. Therefore, all states seeking to establish democracy have to ensure that such power is legitimately used to serve society as a whole rather than misused to promote sectional interests. This relates critically to the nature of civil-military relations, "the distribution of power and influence between the armed services and the civilian authority."[22]

It is a commonly held view that in a democracy civil-military relations are stable when the military is subordinated to civilian political control. This entails the notions of accountability and transparency in military affairs, respect for the rule of law and a clear separation between civilian and military power.[23] These principles confer the necessary political legitimacy on the armed forces. Civilian political control of the armed forces means that the armed forces respect the authority of the government of the day and accept that they are accountable to this government. The military leadership provides its technical expertise to the elected representatives in the process of decision-making on defence matters. This implies that armed forces operate within the legal framework established by the constitution, the relevant defence legislation and military regulations. Accountability, in turn, requires transparency and the satisfaction of the public's right to know, as a means to counter the military's frequent inclination towards excessive secrecy. In this regard, a balance is to be sought between transparency and freedom of information, on the one hand, and the confidentiality, often imposed by the sensitive nature of defence- and security-related issues, on the other.

A number of mechanisms are commonly used to establish and develop a democratic civil-military interaction. These relate to the strictly military realm, the executive and legislative branches of the state and the general public. The armed forces are encouraged to practise democratic civil-military relations through education in democratic values. Thus, their members come to understand the need for civilian control and refrain from taking actions which may undermine or threaten the elected civilian authorities. But internal self-restraint alone is not sufficient to prevent military elites from interfering in politics. Edmonds, for instance, argues that "armed services should be seen for what they (are) in reality: a politicised, highly active and motivated interest group, one that not infrequently also (has) strong political views."[24]

For this reason, governments and parliaments frequently introduce legal instruments of control over the military which normally include legislation defining the mission, role and composition of the armed forces; an accountable civilian ministry of defence with overall responsibility for the activities of the military; multi-party parliamentary control over the defence budget, weapons procurement and the main directions of defence policy; legislation preventing excessive secrecy and ensuring the "right to information" about military matters. These arrangements require that civilian decision-makers in both executive and legislature have sufficient knowledge of defence and security issues to exert effective control over the armed forces, particularly in emerging democracies. This has proved extremely hard to achieve:

> A central problem in these countries is that, after years of authoritarian rule, the new ministries of defence and parliamentary defence committees do not have the skills and knowledge to manage military affairs effectively. Their lack of experience gives rise to frustration within the armed services and creates the space for soldiers to engage in politics.[25]

The formal mechanisms of civilian control simply set the rules in the struggle for power and influence between the civilian and the military elites. But governments, armed forces and parliaments are there to serve, defend and promote the development of the citizens who pay for their existence. Therefore, defence and security policy-making and management must be as transparent as possible and open to public scrutiny. This enables society to have a degree of control over matters, such as military doctrine, threat perceptions, the defence budget, weapons procurement and military co-operation, through informed public debate, academic research and the media. Moreover, the public has the power to vote out of office a government whose defence policies are detrimental to the nation's interest.

Implications for Mozambique and the FADM

The above discussion suggests that for democracy to become established in Mozambique, the FADM should at least not pose any threat to a democratic state and should, if possible, make a positive contribution to peace and nation-building. This makes the need to manage and "guard the guardians" particularly acute.

Mozambique is characterized by poverty, underdevelopment and inefficient administration, and the armed forces are the only state agency capable of undermining or opposing the ongoing political transformation. For these reasons, the FADM should be democratic rather than just politically neutral. Edmonds stresses:

> As a state institution, itself a political construct, the armed services have a permanent political label and are symbolic of, and stand for, the political ideology upon which the political and juridical principles of the constitution and the political regime, or system, is based.[26]

Therefore, and in view of the characteristics of both the government and Renamo forces, the FADM needs to acquire democratic values. Specifically, the officer corps should be educated in concepts of peace and security, the constitution, the principles and mechanisms of democratic civil-military relations, international law on war and the use of force and human rights. Frelimo's experience of educating its guerillas to respect the people during the struggle for national liberation (1962-1974) could also play a role in this endeavour. Additionally, the ministry of defence needs to be "civilianized," its civil servants and the members of the parliamentary defence committee need to develop an expertise in defence and security issues, and the general public debate on defence and security must be encouraged.

Finally, a stable civil-military interaction also depends on the government's willingness and ability to fulfill its responsibilities with regard to the armed forces. Here mutual respect and trust between the political and civilian elites is crucial. Just as the military should avoid taking actions which may undermine the position of democratically elected politicians, so politicians and bureaucrats should respect the military chain of command and not interfere in the tactical and operational aspects of defence. Besides ensuring that the military observes the law, the government itself should also operate legally, refrain from using the armed forces for partisan purposes and respect their professional input and corporate interest in defence policy-making. In particular, the government should provide the necessary material and financial resources to guarantee the effectiveness of the armed forces.[27]

The Future Role of the FADM

The Rome Peace Accord states that the "general purpose" of FADM is to guarantee national sovereignty, independence and territorial integrity. During the period between the cease-fire and the inauguration of the new government, the FADM may be called upon to protect civilians against "crime and violence of all kinds" in co-operation with the police force. The accord also defines some additional functions of the FADM: the provision of assistance in natural disasters and support for reconstruction and development.[28]

Defence Against External Threats. Historically, the only external threat to the security of Mozambique and the other independent states in Southern Africa was posed by the white minority regimes in Salisbury and Pretoria. With the demise of apartheid and of the "total strategy," this threat no longer exists. Nevertheless, South Africa will remain the dominant regional power and will retain a considerable offensive military capacity which may be perceived as a potential threat by Mozambique. Solutions to this problem, or to any other external threat which may emerge within Southern Africa, should be sought through means other than military confrontation.[29] To ease international tension and prevent the emergence of violent conflicts in Southern Africa, Mozambique should promote the establishment of bilateral and collective security co-operation arrangements within the framework of the broader regional integration process, as reflected in the Southern African Development Community (SADC). This would allow the member states to concentrate their energies on the reconstruction and development of their countries in peace and stability. In this scenario, the FADM would have no foreign threat to fight against.

Internal Deployment. While in stable democracies internal peace and stability are normally unchallenged and the maintenance of law and order can be left to the police, this does not necessarily apply to emerging democracies. Mozambique is clearly an emerging democracy where national unity and cohesion and internal stability have yet to be consolidated. The level of instability and violence in the country will most probably remain high, given the prevailing socio-economic conditions. In addition, it is the general opinion of observers that demobilized soldiers and guerillas may resort to violence as a means of survival. So far, little has been done to contain residual banditry. Moreover, a post-electoral worst-case scenario must be considered, whereby the loser cries fraud and resorts to violence to destabilize the new government. Given the high level of animosity and distrust still prevailing between the government and Renamo, the military's key function is likely to be action against internal unrest and violence.

But armed forces are trained to defeat the enemy on the battlefield and not to maintain law and order in a civilian environment. They should be employed exclusively to fight external threats and not their fellow citizens. Internal deployment often undermines an army's legitimacy and has a negative impact on its cohesion and morale, as was the case in Zimbabwe after independence.[30] Furthermore, such internal deployment may lead the military to become increasingly involved in political decision-making which, in turn, may bring about a militarization of society. Apartheid South Africa is a case in point, and the same tendency has been observable in Mozambique since the early 1980s. In order to minimize these risks in case of the FADM's deployment in a counter-insurgency and a policing role, its training needs to pay particular attention to subjects like appropriate rules of engagement, human rights education and the use of minimum force.

Emergency Assistance, Reconstruction and Development. If all goes well, regional stability may be preserved and Mozambique may face no external threat; the outcome of the elections may be accepted peacefully; and the problem of crime may not require extraordinary measures. Under these circumstances, Mozambique can concentrate all its energy on internal peace-building, i.e., national reconstruction and development.

The reconstruction of the roads, bridges, hospitals and schools destroyed during the war, the provision of health care, education services and environmental protection are all actions that help to consolidate peace. These actions also have a direct bearing on the security of the citizens. The participation of the FADM in such undertakings would contribute to enhancing its legitimacy within society as a whole. However, while the employment of armed forces in disaster relief is generally accepted in view of the military's capacity for rapid response, the desirability of military involvement in non-military activities is questionable. Opposition to the involvement of the military in civilian affairs is based on the belief that it undermines military professionalism and combat readiness, that it may help self-interested military elites to argue in favour of a large force and an inflated military budget, and, more significantly, that it may lead them to believe that they are better able to manage society than are civilian politicians.

In summary, the key roles of the FADM are likely to be deployment in counter-insurgency and internal policing missions, and involvement in reconstruction and development activities. Both functions may be critically necessary to the process of immediate peace-building in Mozambique, but they may also place civil-military relations under considerable strain and impact severely on the democratic nature of the military. Mozambican policy makers will have to consider these concerns when deciding how to employ the armed forces. Specifically, the internal deployment of the FADM in counter-insurgency and policing functions should be a temporary measure to allow the police force to be trained and equipped to deal with internal stability, law and order.

Military Professionalism. Military professionalism has been differently understood in a variety of countries in distinct periods, reflecting the interaction of largely indigenous factors, such as political culture, military traditions and the complexity of state bureaucracy.[31] However, it is generally accepted that modern military professionalism includes the broad features of any profession—specialization, authority, responsibility, an ethical code and a professional culture—plus the possession of legitimacy in the wider society. These features demand further elaboration.

Specialization implies that the military profession is a specialized occupation, with the expertise that results from extensive training. Professional expertise confers on the military the authority to provide a service and the autonomy to admit, train, promote and discharge its members. The military also enjoys a degree of independence in determining how best to implement defence and security policies. Such autonomy is, however, limited by the notions of legitimacy and responsibility in democratic societies.

Establishing Democratic Defence Forces in Mozambique

In effect, the role of the military as the state agency responsible for the management of organized violence gains legitimacy in a society for as long as that society feels that the military expertise exists in an area which is crucial to the well-being and integrity of the entire community and is exercised in conformity with established principles, norms and regulations. The military leadership must be responsible, both individually and collectively, towards the state and the community. Another element of professionalism is the code of ethics which regulates the professional's relationship with society and with his or her peers. In the armed forces, the ethical code demands that the serviceman is unconditionally committed to the defence of society and is permanently ready to carry out orders from a higher authority. Finally, a professional culture reflects all the above attributes and involves adherence to a set of values, norms and symbols, such as uniforms, insignia and the use of a distinctive professional language.

In order to prepare the new army for its role before the October 1994 elections, and to make up for the delays in selection, FADM units and officers were given accelerated training by British, French and Portuguese instructors. This provides them, at best, with only the basic foundations of professional military expertise. According to well-informed sources, it was decided that the officers from both sides who took part in a leadership crash-course will not be forced to undergo any tests or evaluation, in order to avoid perceptions of bias towards either the government or Renamo. Completion of the course will be enough to qualify them for appointments as generals and senior officers. Such a political compromise, necessary as a way of securing national reconciliation and peace, does nothing to guarantee the professionalism of the FADM. Further training and education will be required after the elections and the inauguration of the new government. This will help to establish the right balance between competence and efficiency in the use of force, and the indispensable awareness of the moral and ethical implications of carrying this responsibility. Only then will the FADM be able to "serve the country with professionalism and respect the democratic order and the rule of law," as defined in the Rome Peace Accord.

Legitimacy. The full achievement of legitimacy by the FADM may depend on the attitude of both the new military and Mozambican society towards those soldiers who were responsible for terrorism and human rights abuses during the war. There seem to be three broad options for approaching this issue, none of which is totally free from undesirable political and ethical consequences.

First, the government could decide that it is in the interest of national reconciliation and of the internal cohesion of the FADM to ignore past human rights abuses. This seems to be the current trend in Mozambique which may create the perception that war criminals have escaped justice entirely. More importantly, this would mean entrusting them once again with the very means of organized violence they abused so gravely in the recent past. In this case, the credibility of the FADM could be seriously undermined from the outset, and the expectations of justice held by vast sections of Mozambican society would be frustrated. Moreover, the healing of the wounds of war demands that such wounds be unambiguously acknowledged; only after the crimes have been exposed and the perpetrators identified can amnesty and forgiveness be considered.

A second option would be to tackle the issue uncompromisingly in the interests of justice and transparency, investigate all allegations of atrocities, exclude those involved from the new military and bring them to justice. This would give the FADM a high moral and ethical standing, but it would entail considerable political and practical difficulties. The investigation would necessarily lead to the re-opening of the still very fresh wounds of war, with serious effects on the internal cohesion of the FADM. Moreover, it would probably render most of Renamo's military leaders and soldiers ineligible for the new army, since Renamo forces perpetrated acts of pure terrorism against the population as a matter of policy. Taken to its logical conclusion, this policy would raise the whole issue of the ultimate responsibility for the behaviour of the men on the ground, with destabilizing results for the peace-building process.

Laurie Nathan suggests a compromise between "total amnesia" and the quest for "total justice" concerning war crimes. This would mean either the exclusion of a group of "notorious individuals and units" from the new military, rather than a complete purge, or the creation of a "truth commission" to investigate alleged violations, without the imposition of sanctions upon those found guilty of misconduct.[32] Whichever option is chosen by the Mozambican authorities, this extremely complex and sensitive issue is likely to be one of the most challenging tasks in the process of creating a legitimate FADM, trusted and respected by the citizens it is meant to serve.

To realize the hopes of millions, peace and national reconciliation must be reflected in changes that go far beyond a simple cease-fire and regular, free and fair elections. Peace and national reconciliation must enable all Mozambicans to contribute freely to the creation of the legal, political and social institutions that will frame their own participation in national reconstruction and development. In short, democracy is an essential prerequisite for enduring peace and real national reconciliation in Mozambique. And, conversely, democracy will not be viable in the country unless the armed forces are trained to recognize and embody democratic values.

Notes

1. See *General Peace Agreement of Mozambique* (Amsterdam: African-European Institute, AWEPAA, 1992), p. 28.
2. The chapter reflects my understanding of the Mozambican political transition, based on the experience of nearly twenty years of service in the Mozambican armed forces. It also draws on interviews I conducted in Maputo with military officers, government officials, officials of the United Nations Operation in Mozambique (ONUMOZ) and local political observers in December 1993 and March 1994.
3. For an overview of the social effects of the PRE, see J. Hanlon, *Mozambique —Who Calls the Shots?* (London: James Currey, 1991), pp. 133-44. Maria Florinda, a peasant member of parliament, is quoted as saying with respect to the 60% of Mozambicans who live in extreme poverty: "We are tightening our belts too much, and now our bodies are about to be divided in two. We ask the government to look for a way that will permit us to loosen our belts, at least by one centimeter" (p. 144).
4. See, for instance, *Mozambique Peace Process Bulletin* (AWEPAA, Amsterdam), No. 9 (April 1994), p. 2.
5. Frelimo was the nationalist movement that led the struggle for independence from Portuguese colonialism between 1962 and 1974. After the military coup of April 1974 in Portugal and through skilful negotiation, it was acknowledged by the new Portuguese regime as the only legitimate representative of the Mozambican people to whom the colonial authorities should hand over power.
6. See J. Hanlon, *Mozambique: The Revolution Under Fire* (London: Zed Books, 1990), p. 29.
7. See Hanlon, *op. cit.*, in note 3, p. 13.
8. See Hanlon, *op. cit.*, in note 3, p. 16.
9. For an interesting account of how the peasants of Erati reacted to Frelimo's agrarian policies and entered into an alliance with Renamo, see C. Geffray, *La Cause des Armes au Mozambique: Anthropologie d'une Guerre Civile* (Paris: Karthala, 1990).
10. See G. Morgan, "Violence in Mozambique: The Case of Renamo," *Africa Insight*, Vol. 20, No. 2, 1990, p. 79.
11. See, for example, S. Baynham, "Security Issues in Africa: The Imperial Legacy, Domestic Violence and the Military," *Africa Insight*, Vol. 21, No. 3, 1991, pp. 180-89.
12. See S. Baynham, "The Subordination of African Armies to Civilian Control: Theory and Practise," *Africa Insight*, Vol. 22, No. 4, 1992, p. 262.
13. MNR was the initial acronym for Mozambique National Resistance and was replaced with Renamo after 1982, when the movement adopted the Portuguese version of its name, Resistência Nacional Moçambicana.
14. For a survey of the Rhodesian Special Air Service's involvement in early Renamo operations, see M. Hall, *The Mozambique National Resistance Movement (Renamo) and the Reestablishment of Peace in Mozambique*, paper submitted to the Centre for African Studies (London, School of Oriental and African Studies)

August 1991; B. Cole, *The Elite: The Story of the Rhodesian Special Air Service* (Transkei: Three Knights Publishing, 1984).

15 . See Samora Machel's "8th of March Speech" in: *Noticias*, 9 March 1977.

16 . For a detailed description of Renamo's transfer to South African control, see A. Vines, *Renamo: Terrorism in Mozambique* (London: James Currey, 1991), pp. 11-31.

17 . See Hall, *op. cit.*, in note 14, p. 3.

18 . See Geffray, *op. cit.*, in note 9.

19 . See Hall, *op. cit.*, in note 14, p. 1.

20 . See *Mozambique Peace Process Bulletin* (AWEPAA, Amsterdam), No. 8 (February 1994), pp. 2-10.

21 . Author's interview with FADM officers in Maputo on 24 March 1994.

22 . See L. Nathan, *The Changing of the Guard: Armed Forces and Defence Policy in a Democratic South Africa* (Pretoria: Human Sciences Research Council, forthcoming), chapter 5.

23 . For an overview of theories on civil-military relations, see M. Edmonds, *Armed Services and Society* (Leicester: Leicester University Press, 1988), pp. 70-92.

24 . *Ibid.*, pp. 81-2.

25 . See Nathan, *op. cit.*, in note 22. Although these remarks were made with reference to Latin American countries undergoing a transition to democracy, such as Nicaragua, they are equally applicable to Mozambique.

26 . Edmonds, *op. cit.*, in note 23, p. 95.

27 . See Nathan, *op. cit.*, in note 22, chapter 8.

28 . See *General Peace Agreement of Mozambique* (Amsterdam: AWEPAA, 1992), p. 28.

29 . Certain political and military circles in Mozambique have constructed threat scenarios (highly unrealistic in the view of the author), whereby Zimbabwe and Malawi may have territorial ambitions and, therefore, should Mozambique be perceived to be very weak, could consider military action to redraw the common borders.

30 . See A. Seegers, "Revolutionary Armies of Africa: Mozambique and Zimbabwe," in: S. Baynham (ed.), *Military Power: Politics in Black Africa* (London: Croom Helm, 1986), pp. 129-65.

31 . See Edmonds, *op. cit.*, in note 23, pp. 38-43, 78-86; R. Williams, "Of Skills and Subordination: Revisiting Professionalism," *South African Defence Review* (Institute for Defence Politics), No. 4, 1992, pp. 22-30.

32 . See Nathan, *op. cit.*, in note 22, chapter 7.

8

Towards a Security Regime in Southern Africa: Some Working Suggestions

Hans-Joachim Spanger and Peter Vale

The ending of white minority rule on the African continent in 1994, and the prior abrupt end of the global bipolarism between East and West in 1989, have opened a new era with profound implications for the security landscape in the Southern African subregion. The antagonism, which pitted members of the Organization of African Unity and the South African liberation movements against the apartheid regime, has as much disappeared as the African outposts of the two camps, which were considered part of the global confrontation between capitalism and socialism. This has created unprecedented opportunities for resolving long-standing and violent conflicts in the region, as was demonstrated by the peace accords in Namibia and Mozambique as well as by the negotiated—though failed—settlement in Angola.

However, opportunities seldom produce automatic results. The ongoing civil war in Angola suggests that the road to a stable and lasting peace in Southern Africa is fraught with dangers and numerous uncertainties. In conditions of economic despair and social unrest—so widespread throughout the region—it has proved extremely difficult to overcome the legacy of armed struggle, destabilization and apartheid. Additionally, other, more traditional, sources of conflict lie just below the surface. The recent border conflict between Namibia and Botswana over a small, unpopulated riverine island, for instance, suggests that the solidarity generated among the frontline states may easily fade, giving rise to quite different, and occasionally hostile, responses. The central and abiding tragedy for the region, however, is that its peoples know each other only through conflict.

That the process of change in Southern Africa entails both opportunities and risks is neither unique nor surprising; in every corner of the globe change has proved turbulent and worrisome. As a result, the joint management of transition has become of utmost importance and urgency. In order to avoid "Balkanization" on the Bosnian trajectory in Southern Africa, it is not only necessary to overcome narrowly construed national interests. Equally, it is important to create mutual transparency and the mechanisms for developing co-operation and managing conflict.

Southern Africa neither possesses adequate multilateral institutions nor has it developed a tradition of crisis prevention and conflict resolution. The co-operation between the frontline states—for more than a decade the effective tool for tackling an imminent threat—has lost its cohesion. The grouping is now searching for a new role. As a result, it lacks the critical mass to become an anchor of stability, as represented by, for example, NATO in the European context. And bilateral agreements on security co-operation, concluded among various frontline member states, have hardly proved a substitute. Only a multilateral framework, consisting of improved and extended inter-state organs, exchange systems, communication links and negotiation procedures in the military, economic, social and political fields can help to develop the mutual trust and co-operation necessary for building and preserving regional security. If Southern Africa simply flounders without formal restructuring, the spectre will plunge the region into further crisis.

Much depends on the future role of the new democratic South Africa, which is set to become a fully integrated part of Southern Africa. The ANC-led majority government has frequently reiterated the importance it attaches to peaceful and development-oriented co-operation with its neighbours. Moreover, conscious of the prevailing asymmetries in economic and military capabilities, it has explicitly renounced all hegemonic ambitions and promised to follow the principles of equity and mutual benefit. The same applies to the construction of a new regional order, which will be based on collective endeavours.

However, these are nothing but expressions of good intent on the part of the dominant regional power. Though important as a point of departure, they still await the test of real life. Equally, it is true that only on the basis of a stable multilateral framework will it be possible for the neighbouring countries to accommodate South Africa and benefit from its size. But there are impediments to regional regime-building. Within South Africa, the amazing—and rather unexpected—success of the first democratic elections hardly obscures the shaky nature of the domestic transition with its many imponderables. And it has proved equally unsettling that individual countries did not hesitate to establish early, or even premature, relations with South Africa, thereby demonstrating a desire for preferential relations with the dominant power over regional solidarity.

From Collective Defence to Collective Security

In the 1970s and 1980s, the frontline states were compelled to join forces against an external threat. So, apartheid and destabilization provided the background for the formation of a classical military alliance. In a regional security system, the order of priorities is bound to change. As circumstances shift, alliance partners join hands to prevent members of the security system from violating the established principles and rules. In these conditions, peace-keeping and peace-enforcement become as important as joint intervention in protracted civil wars. This addresses the major source of instability in today's Southern Africa. But it requires different military training, logistics and equipment, and also calls for established procedures and institutions for authorizing any such employment of forces.

Even though direct military threats have receded, this does not justify an attitude of benign neglect in Southern Africa. It is true that the root causes of conflict are non-military in nature and that the danger of interstate military conflict seems remote. But even in a region where military expenditures are relatively limited, the militaries still disproportionately draw on scarce resources. This set against the escalatory potential of threat perceptions and instabilities which directly result from the existence of armaments and military apparatuses in respective nation states, is very unsettling. This applies to all the countries of the region, but in particular to South Africa which—irrespective of its intentions—is the only state with capabilities to project power far beyond its borders. So procrastination may have adverse effects in the longer run. Instead, the current easing of military tension represents a perfect opportunity for negotiating a security regime as an important ingredient to regional peace.

Many questions arise: what geographic area should be covered; what institutional framework is appropriate; what specific measures should be designed; and, finally, what sequencing of the steps should be taken when conceiving and implementing a security regime in Southern Africa? As a precaution, it is necessary to emphasize that in prevailing circumstances overly ambitious approaches might easily produce adverse results. The region not only suffers from a large array of crippling problems, but also from the inability of respective authorities to tackle these effectively.

Regional co-operation has been characterized as "weak commitments by weak states to weak regional organizations." These constraints should be given adequate attention when designing a security regime which requires firm commitments by individual member states and vigorous efforts to implement agreed measures.

Regarding the area of application and the institutional framework, the Southern African Development Community (SADC) and the geographical area covered by it, is the most appropriate for security co-operation in Southern Africa. Although its predecessor, the Southern African Development Coordination Conference (SADCC), was limited to economic co-operation, it proved its effectiveness in mobilizing resources and realizing joint projects in the energy and the transport sectors—areas of strategic importance at that time. SADC is set to move beyond this limited purpose. In its founding treaty, adopted in Namibia in August 1992, SADC aimed at becoming a community of Southern African states with overall responsibilities in the economic, political, social and cultural fields. Though it has not formally assumed security functions, the treaty sets down the desire to "promote and defend peace and security" (Article 5) and identifies, as areas of co-operation, "politics, diplomacy, international relations, peace and security" (Article 21), for which relevant protocols may be concluded and appropriate institutions may be created.

In theory, this also applies to the newly founded Common Market for Eastern and Southern Africa (COMESA, formerly PTA). The relevant treaty also states that the common market shall pursue the objective of promoting peace, security and stability among the member states (Article 3); this, in the medium term, might also allow for the creation of adequate instruments. The pursuance of similar aims in an overlapping membership has given rise to some controversy as to which should be given preference. However, there is a degree of complementarity with respect to the underlying rationale of the two organizations—functional co-operation to further joint development projects in the case of SADC, versus functional integration to promote free trade in the case of COMESA—which might facilitate a compromise solution.

Even though a solution to the dispute is not yet in sight, there are at least two reasons which strongly favour SADC in the security realm. Firstly, it has a tradition of security-related co-operation. Secondly, and more important for security co-operation to be effective, it requires a "security complex" in which the primary security concerns of individual countries are linked to such a degree that they cannot realistically be considered apart from one another. This is true for SADC, but not for COMESA which extends much further in a north-easterly direction, thereby comprising at least three "security complexes" (i.e., Southern Africa, East Africa/Horn of Africa, Indian Ocean). Even SADC may, in the medium term, not be entirely appropriate, since SADC member Tanzania is gradually turning back to East Africa whereas Zaire, though deeply entrenched in the Angolan civil war, has not yet been admitted to either of the two organizations.

Providing the Framework: Institution-building

Within SADC, the institutions charged with security functions will have to reflect the changed nature and purpose of the military in the region. They should guarantee the necessary transparency and military co-operation to prevent the generation of unjustified threat perceptions. They should also facilitate joint action in the face of emergencies. Finally, they need to develop adequate mechanisms of crisis prevention, conflict management and conflict resolution among (and possibly also within) respective member states. Simple structural procedures and cost-effective working mechanisms are required for these institutions to become effective. In light of these principles and with due regard to the fact that the potential for inter-state conflict is intimately linked to instability on the domestic level, the establishment of the following organs are recommended: an Inter-State Committee for Defence and Security, a Mechanism for the Settlement of Disputes and Conflicts with attendant bodies and a Southern African Institute for Security and Development Studies.

Establishing an Inter-State Committee for Defence and Security

The establishment of an Inter-State Committee for Defence and Security, which will form the core of military co-operation in Southern Africa, has encountered support throughout the region. This committee will not exist in isolation; it is conceived as the regional equivalent to institutions such as the OAU Defence Commission and the relevant bodies instituted in the framework of the ECOWAS Protocol on Mutual Assistance on Defence. Most importantly, however, the committee draws on the fruitful experience of a similar body which was established in the framework of the Frontline States Alliance—even though this has largely lost its clout and has become rather ceremonical. In order to reinvigorate it, the proposed committee will therefore have to assume responsibilities other than the erstwhile defence coordination. It ought to consist of senior military officials who meet on a regular basis and in contingencies on ad hoc basis. To facilitate its work, the establishment of a small secretariat, possibly equipped with its own system of communication, is appropriate. The inter-state committee should also be entitled to convene expert meetings to deal with specific issues.

The duties and responsibilities of the inter-state committee will be carried out on the basis of relevant protocols to be concluded by the SADC member states. Conceivably, these might include the following:

- the regular exchange of information on military expenditures, force levels, weapons acquisitions, training of armed forces and military activities on an agreed format;
- the sharing of information and expertise on common concerns, such as demobilization, integration of regular and guerilla forces, civil-military relations;
- the elaboration and supervision of protocols and annual calendars on military exchanges between the member states;
- the formulation and implementation of common positions in the field of arms control and military confidence-building;
- consultations on unusual military activities;
- the planning and supervision of joint military operations;
- the harmonization of standard operational procedures and coordination of weapons procurement.

With a view to becoming a regional arrangement under Chapter VIII of the UN Charter and because of the limited resources and capabilities of the member states, SADC will have to approach the United Nations for supporting and funding the work of this committee. In present circumstances, this appears to be the only way for overcoming the constraints, which have effectively undermined the operation of similar bodies on the continent. Though one might think of South Africa providing most of the necessary funds and thus performing a role similar to Nigeria within ECOWAS, this does not seem suitable in light of both the West African experience and the attendant perpetuation of existing asymmetries in Southern Africa.

Enhancing SADC's Role in Conflict Resolution

Because conflicts in Southern Africa, as in other parts of the continent, could only be tackled by involving external powers from the North, has raised a great measure of concern. The states of the region, however, have begun to respond; the decision in late January 1994 to send a regional task force into troubled Lesotho—albeit symbolic—signals the region's determination to pursue peaceful mechanisms to end regional conflict. Zimbabwe's Foreign Minister Nathan Shamuyarira called the decision the beginnings of regional security co-operation to ensure stability and peace. It was, he concluded, "an arrangement to defend democratic trends in our region and to ward off the dictatorship and militarism present in other regions of the world."[1]

This is a promising beginning, but there is a long way to go. To reduce its reliance on foreign involvement, SADC therefore needs to develop a dispute-settlement and conflict-resolution capacity. This will require both an adequate mechanism for decision-making within the community and sufficient capabilities for joint peace-keeping and peace-enforcement operations. To achieve this objective, a separate *Mechanism for the Settlement of Disputes and Conflicts* needs to be established. This institution might operate within the structure of SADC to discuss and clarify any issue which has raised security concerns and to authorize joint action, such as fact-finding missions or peace-keeping operations. Provisions concerning the employment and the operation of the mechanism shall be layed down in a protocol attached to the SADC treaty. In this regard, the OAU Mechanism for Conflict Prevention, Management and Resolution, enacted at the summit meeting of the organization in 1993, is a useful model.

In the framework of the mechanism, a *Permanent Committee of Wise Persons* might be established to act in a mediator and possibly an arbitrator role. In the African context, the authority and undisputed impartiality of such groups has often proved an effective ingredient in reconciling conflicting interests. Such a committee may be engaged on short notice and in an informal way. Additionally, use should be made of the good offices provided by non-governmental organizations. Here, the role of the churches is of great importance. With their region-wide networks, the various religious communities could augment the process which aims at underpinning the region's security.

With respect to the pressing nature of domestic conflicts, prone to international involvement, the mechanism should in any case not be confined to inter-state conflicts. It is common knowledge that the roots of contemporary conflicts in Southern Africa lie primarily in the domestic sphere. While these may have been exacerbated by inter-state strife—South Africa's destabilization of Mozambique is a good example—their solution requires domestic accord. Unfortunately, however, there is no single source to internal strife in Southern African countries; the only common thread is that they all have structural roots.

In light of the scope and multifaceted character of domestic conflicts in the region, it probably needs specific institutions which—on a regional level—help to address these from an early stage. Because the ombudsman concept enjoys wide support and has proved its relevance in many parts of the world, it is appropriate to give the idea of an *Office of Regional Ombudsman* an airing in Southern Africa. Such an institution could, for instance, act as the first court of petition in the resolution of domestic conflict. In proposing this, one has to be mindful of the fact that an ombudsman needs to enjoy particular legitimacy and that this institution will have to be representative of the region's people in order to become effective. These requirements can only be met in conditions of democratic representation which, apart from setbacks, is still advancing in Southern Africa.

The continent-wide push for democracy also holds some promise for the resolution of many disputes in the region. Nevertheless, it is important to recognise that building democratic culture is an ongoing process; as seriously, without sound governance and sustained development, the region's prospects for democracy are bleak. To carry forward the current democratic impetus and give the concept of an ombudsman some backing, the establishment of a *Standing Conference on Governance, Democracy and Development* could be considered. To nourish the roots of democracy and the traces of civil society, the standing conference should not be located in government structures but in the NGO sector. It should aim at spreading the democratic ideal throughout the region by linking with established institutions of this kind at the national and continental level. But governments themselves are not absolved from the responsibility of promoting democracy and the rule of law. For this to succeed more than lip-service is needed; thus individual governments should be held accountable to the conference.

Developing Regional Expertise

For regional institutions to become an effective tool for building and maintaining security in Southern Africa, an intellectual foundation is required which is not bound up with narrow national interests. Hence the need to strengthen regional expertise by jointly looking into the causes of conflict and by developing concepts and strategies aimed at addressing these. This can best be done by a regionally-based institute which will devote its energies to researching and publicising areas of concern in the field of security. The Midgard Conference, and other gatherings of that kind, therefore recommended that a *Southern African Institute for Security and Development Studies* should be established to conduct research, organize regular conferences and publish a journal. At the time of writing, work on this project has reached an advanced stage. Details of these preparations are included in the Appendix to this chapter.

Areas of Concrete Action

Confidence- and Security-enhancing Measures

Regional security can only be achieved if mutual trust governs relations between the states in Southern Africa. There are several ways to pursue this objective. Joint institutions are best suited for building confidence, because they provide a basis for regular contacts and assist common understanding, eventually leading to joint action. No less important, however, are complementary measures, which define the scope and content for the operations of these institutions. In this regard, it may be advisable for SADC to adopt a document on confidence- and security-building measures. This may be considered an initial step aimed at laying ground for more ambitious and intrusive measures in the field of military co-operation.

There is broad consensus in the region for a CSBM regime. Many in politics and in the military have even expressed a sense of urgency on the issue. At the same time, it is widely believed that in the conditions pertaining in Southern Africa, regional CSBMs will have to be substantially different from the models applied elsewhere. They ought to reflect specifics: that in Southern Africa the root causes of conflict are primarily located in the domestic sphere; that the relatively weak states and governments in question suffer from serious constraints when it comes to implementing any set of measures; that the range of military capabilities puts respective countries on a profoundly different footing; that a great deal of common problems result from cross-border activities which need to be tackled jointly; and finally, that the majority of states can build its future co-operation on a tradition of mutual understanding, generated in an erstwhile military alliance.

A CSBM regime tailored along these prerequisites should contain the more traditional measures, known, for instance, from relevant international accords. These might include, with the aim of increasing mutual transparency, the regular exchange of military information on the seize, structure and deployment of forces, as well as on military planning and weapons procurement. Transparency as regards military activities seems equally relevant for building confidence. Emphasis should, however, be put on measures facilitating communication, contacts and a regular exchange on all levels of military hierarchies. Regular visits between military units of, for example, neighbouring countries would be as conducive to increased mutual understanding as joint military education through staff schools and military academies. Arguably, measures of this nature contribute most effectively to building a regional network of personal contacts, which is considered essential for tackling threatening contingencies.

The recent insurrection of military units against the government in Lesotho, like the past involvement of the South African Defence Force in the domestic political process with its deeply disruptive effects on peace and prosperity, point to the precarious civil-military relations in the region. In order to ensure that these events were not repeated, or effectively contained, safeguards need to be employed. As a matter of common concern, states in the region should, consequently, be persuaded to ensure democratic control of the defence and security forces. This will only be possible if each serving member undertakes to safeguard the human rights of individuals throughout Southern Africa. Such an undertaking will, all things being equal, underwrite civil society in individual states in the region. Through this, military forces would be more accountable to political bodies, and citizens would not fear a violation of their rights by military forces.

This also applies to the discontinuance of covert action in Southern Africa, be it authorized by state agencies or by insurgent groups of disbanded military units. Irrespective of past divisions as to whether cross-border activities of liberation movements and respective government agencies constituted a violation of, or were justified by, international law, in present circumstances this legacy has become a matter of pressing concern for most countries in the region. The containment of irregular activities calls for reinforced and joint border controls, preferably encouraged and supervised by a regional body. Government-sponsored operations, such as intelligence gathering, may require a two-track approach. One issue concerns the public accountability through control at the parliamentary level where rules and parameters might be established, which may also allow for other, more open, methods to ensure accountability and transparency. The second encourages an increased cooperation between the relevant state agencies throughout Southern Africa, based on the assumption that this may contribute to easing mistrust and constrain thinking in worst-case scenarios.

In a special category, the region might also pursue mechanisms for security on the high seas. A beginning might be made by sharing information on the movements and activities of foreign fishing trawlers in the waters around the region. This may gradually move from confidence-building towards securing common regional assets.

Arms Control

Arms control is an important prerequisite for military stability. Within the SADC structure the rationale for specific force levels and structures of its member states might conceivably be discussed with a view to agreeing on levels commensurate with the requirements of both national and regional security. In addition, SADC might encourage unilateral arms reductions of its current (and future) members with particular emphasis on offensive capabilities. And, finally, SADC might also act as a coordinator of the arms-control policies of its member states. This would entail the adherence of its members to international arms control and disarmament treaties concluded within the framework of the United Nations, such as the Non-Proliferation Treaty, the Biological and Toxic Weapons Convention, the Chemical Weapons Convention or the United Nations Register of Conventional Arms. There might also be a role to play in the ongoing efforts at concluding a treaty on a nuclear weapons free zone on the African continent.

There is a set of peculiar problems which again are a legacy of the region's unhappy past and deserve special attention today: the side effects of demobilization. As recent experience in countries such as Zimbabwe, Namibia, Angola and Mozambique has revealed, times of military demobilization hold particular dangers for all democracies, not only democracies-in-forming. Unless the socio-economic conditions and political repercussions of large-scale demobilization are taken seriously, acute security problems will inevitably arise. It is certainly the prime responsibility of the countries concerned to develop and employ the appropriate ways and means. But without serious and sustained support by the international community, demobilization in Southern Africa is bound to threaten the rehabilitation of the region.

In the same vein, the endemic circulation of arms—the AK-47 in particular—has become a major source of instability. Only if strict measures are brought to bear can this effectively be contained. Though small arms are not particularly conducive to traditional arms control, some important principles should, however, guide efforts to control their spread. Thus, the relevant authorities will have to undertake responsibility to curb gun-running by formulating, enacting and enforcing domestic gun control legislation. The same applies to multilateral efforts at the inter-state level which are badly needed to contain the spread at all possible stages. This could be augmented by encouraging national police forces to share their experiences.

Peace-keeping

As elsewhere in the world, peace-keeping should be a part of the regional arsenal. It would also help Southern Africa secure a role in the wider international community. There are, however, considerable obstacles in the way of a coherent regional programme aimed at this ideal; for instance, the militaries of the region are not compatible. Nevertheless, it is strongly recommended that Southern Africa's militaries, as a matter of urgency, overcome their national preoccupation and prepare themselves for peace-keeping missions, both in the region and beyond. In the light of the prevailing international experience, preparedness is absolutely essential—the lessons of Somalia, Rwanda and ECOMOG are sobering ones. Under no circumstances could the regional superstructure withstand the kind of experience which has marked the tragedy in Liberia.

Of prime importance is the question of military education and training, which are not yet sufficiently geared towards such a task. However, some pools of international expertise exist. United Nations advisors, for instance, may be consulted. But peace-keeping is not easy, and it cannot be detached from the realities in the region. Therefore, it may be appropriate to set up an advisory group—from the academic, military and security communities—to advise governments and regional institutions on the pitfalls and promises of both, peace-keeping in the region and the region's role in wider peace-keeping efforts.

In a near miraculous way, Southern Africa appears to have been relieved from the apocalyptic destructions to which it seemed programmed in the 1980s. History teaches, however, miracles cannot sustain themselves; the divine intervention needs, it would appear, to be nourished by a commodity often in short supply—human rationality. The challenge for Southern Africa is therefore to find the courage to move forward in the joint project of securing the region in a world in which insecurity is the normal state of affairs.

Notes

1. "Regional Break-through as SA Invited to Help Lesotho Mutiny Task-force," *Southscan* (London), Vol. 9, No. 4 (28 January 1994), pp. 2-3.

Appendix

The Southern African Institute:
A Forum for Security and Development Concerns

The United Nations Conference on Confidence- and Security-building Measures in Southern Africa, held in February 1993, ignited a number of promising suggestions.[1] Our concern is to take forward one of these: the need to establish a regionally-based institute which will devote its energies to researching and publicising areas of concern in the fields of security and development. The deliberations of a similar gathering, the so-called Midgard Conference, independently touched upon the same idea—urging the need to strengthen regional expertise.[2] The conference recommended that "A Southern African Institute for Security and Development Studies should be established to conduct research, organize regular conferences and publish a journal."

The present document drawing on the findings of an international task force proposes the establishment of the Southern African Institute: A Forum for Security and Development Concerns (SAI).[3] The SAI will aim at creating a climate in Southern Africa which will be conducive to the building of long-term security for all the peoples of the region. It will do so in the following areas of interest:

- *Research*. It will provide the facilities for serious investigation of Southern African issues to scholars, journalists and policy-makers. It will support a fellowship programme for suitable qualified senior professionals.[4]
- *Study Groups, Task Forces and Focused Research*. These would draw together political, business, labour, media and academic leaders to brief themselves and to make policy recommendations on salient questions affecting Southern Africa. By using a mix of these approaches, innovative answers may be found to a host of new questions which, as yet, have not been asked.
- *Outreach*. It will disseminate its work and research findings to a variety of publics. Traditional approaches, like conferences and publications, will be augmented by accessing the electronic media.[5]
- *Policy*. It aims to influence public policy in the region by inputs into the decision-making process. This will take place at the government and the non-governmental level.[6]
- *Training*. It will offer relevant, high-calibre education to various regional stake-holders. This will support the process of multilateral co-operation in Southern Africa.[7]

Tasks and Purpose

In researching the establishment of the SAI, this task force has canvassed a number of opinions and visited institutions in Africa, Europe, North America and Asia. Our investigations have led us to conclude that the SAI should not be located in a university. Not only would this entail having to choose one Southern African university, but institutions situated within universities suffer a number of administrative drawbacks. Neither do we believe that the SAI should be linked, as often happens, to any government department. Our view is that this relationship—notwithstanding the most vigorous efforts to feign independence—becomes too binding. Changes of government alternatively weaken or strengthen the funding base of institutes; overall, this is not conducive to open and free engagement, which is imperative if the institute is to be credible. It is necessary, therefore, to stress that only an institution which is free from external interference can face up to the challenges of the times.

The SAI will direct itself towards improving the security atmosphere in sub-Saharan Africa by promoting an informed discussion on regional security concerns through serious research, exchange of ideas and publications. This would be interdisciplinary in nature and international in scope. It will be non-partisan and non-sectarian in approaching its work.

No single programme can help nourish and sustain the SAI. Indeed, the imperative to engage Southern Africa's leadership in the processes of global change, suggest that multiple approaches at different levels of society are necessary. The SAI will need, therefore, to mix traditional approaches to policy work with a range of initiatives which are in keeping with the times:

- *Fellowships.* Senior academics, policy makers, journalists, diplomats, military officers will be encouraged to spend periods of residence in the SAI. This prestigious fellowship programme will initially be the core of the SAI's activities. Although they will pursue their independent research, fellows would, in the course of their year-long residency, contribute to the overall work of the institute.
- *Periodic Retreats.* These would bring together opinion leaders and policy makers to deliberate on issues concerned with regional relations, in general, and security and development issues, in particular. On an informal basis, these occasions might provide moments for fecund exchanges of views on the manifold issues which confront Southern Africa's peoples as the twentieth century closes.
- *Regional Affairs Briefings for Parliamentarians* on Southern African issues which touch the levels of their jurisdiction. All too often parliamentarians are not able to spend sufficient time on the issues

which are beyond their immediate attention. Not only would this ensure that the SAI is more engaged with the formal political process, but cultivate a deep appreciation amongst legislators for Southern African issues.
- *An Annual Seminar on Southern Africa.* This would be aimed at promoting a public interest in security and development issues in the region. It would not hope to replace the profusion of gatherings on regional questions which are underlay. Nevertheless, the SAI conference should gain the reputation of the foremost and publicly relevant gathering on the topic.
- *Networking.* The SAI needs to engage sister organizations throughout the world, but more particularly in Asia and in Africa. A notable feature of global change has been how similar problems are revealing themselves in different parts of the world. Never before has the need for global exchange become as important as today.
- *The Media.* Energetic efforts should be made in public education through the print and electronic media. The institute ought to contribute to the press and by organizing specialist training programmes on regional affairs with practising or trainee journalists.
- *The Community.* Systematic efforts need to be made to connect regional issues with the needs of the community—those in public education, community organizations, trade unions, environmental and human rights groups. Civic organizations, far more than political parties, are the greatest hope for policy consensus on a range of Southern African issues.
- *Outreach.* The fruit of the research of SAI fellows will be published in a reputable publication series which—modelled on the Adelphi Papers of the International Institute for Strategic Studies, London—will be the flagship of the SAI's work. The sheer accessibility of working papers suggest their importance as a means of putting to the public —for wider debate and dissemination—ideas at the work-in-progress stage. The institute should publish such a series. Experience shows the importance of creating a series which lies between the academic and the journalistic. Written in clear, accessible language with little or no footnotes, advancing the implications of unequivocal policy options, such digestible policy documents have recently been successfully pioneered by the Carnegie Endowment for International Peace. Leaving aside communication associated with interactive video, fibre-optic networks and tele-conferencing techniques, SAI should be active in the production of television and radio programmes. The prospects for this will increase, as the region's air-waves are further deregulated and integrated. The SAI has a major role to play in the development of new understandings of regional questions at the

school level. Almost every text which touches upon international relations will be re-written; the SAI should help to shape the international images which will fashion the region's young. The SAI should aim to produce at least one edited volume a year; this should be on a policy-related topic. Ideally, the Institute ought to be involved in the publication of a scholarly series with a reputable publisher.

Other Institutions

This document argues for the establishment of a new body, but critics —with very good reason—will point to the plethora of institutions throughout Southern Africa. How do these measure against the SAI? To begin with a general point: all the countries of the region have institutes which deal, in general terms, with international and regional issues; but —and this is the overall point—Southern Africa has no regional institute which focuses on these themes. If the regional integration process is to be fostered, an institute of this kind will be vitally important.

The greater concentration of institutions are within South Africa: four bodies claim to have a specialized interest in Southern African issues. The business-linked *South African Institute of International Affairs*, for example, claims to have a particular interest in the region; the University of Natal-based *Economics Policy Unit*, the free-standing government-oriented *African Institute of South Africa* and the University of Western Cape-based *Centre for Southern African Studies*. Additionally, the following specialist strategic studies institutions have an interest in regional security questions: the University of Pretoria-based *Institute for Strategic Studies*; the recently formed free-standing *Institute for Defence Policy* and the newly renamed *Institute for Conflict Resolution* which is situated at the University of Cape Town. The same university has an *Institute for African Studies*, which periodically shows an interest in regional issues, and finances a named academic chair in *Southern African Studies* which, however, is not really concerned with regional questions. The university also has a strongly focused *Southern African Labour and Development Unit*, which has done pioneering work in regional labour issues. The same university's *Institute for the Study of Public Policy* has recently published a collection of essays on "critical choices" for the region. The University of the Witwatersrand in Johannesburg also has an *Institute of African Studies* which, however, is not primarily concerned with regional questions. Notwithstanding— perhaps, because of—apartheid, development issues have been studied with great interest in South Africa. For instance, the *Development Bank of Southern Africa* has a strong policy research unit; despite its name, however, little direct interest is shown in Southern African issues. The main preoccupation is with development questions, as these touch upon South Africa itself. Development issues are researched at universities as far apart—politically and geographically—as *Rhodes*, the *Free State*, *Natal*, the *North* and *Potchefstroom*, a university for higher christian education. South Africa also has a *Development Studies Society of South Africa*; this is a quasi-professional body made up of individuals with an interest in the broad area of development. The society hosts a conference every second year.

Elsewhere in Southern Africa, institutions concerned with regional questions are also to be found. In the mid-1970s, the University of Lesotho, for instance, established an *Institute for Southern African Studies*. Other institutions with an interest in international and regional studies are found in Mozambique—an *African Studies Institute* and an *Institute for International Relations*; Zimbabwe, which is home to the *Southern African Political Economy Series (SAPES)* (a region-wide network of researchers), a newly-established *Institute for International Affairs* and the free-standing *Zimbabwe Institute for Development Studies*; Botswana—the university-based *Institute for Development Studies*; Namibia—a university-based *Faculty for Research* (which includes a strong development component from the old Namibian Institute for Social and Economic Research) and the *Namibian Economic Policy Research Unit*, known by the acronym *NEPRU*. The University of Zambia hosts an *African Studies Institute* which, amongst other issues, shows a keen interest in regional transport issues. In Tanzania, there is a university-based *Institute for Development Studies* and the free-standing and, in the region, uniquely sponsored (by both the governments of Tanzania and Mozambique) *Centre for Foreign Relations*. The CFR has organised seven in a series of conferences under the theme "Peace and Security in Southern Africa." It is widely regarded that these gatherings are the most important venues for the deliberations of security and development questions in the region. This observation illustrates the inter-dependency of the institutions in the region and suggests how important it is for their work to be drawn together through the SAI.

This survey reveals that a large number of institutions are concerned with regional, or security, or development issues, but no single one draws these issues together. In addition, no institution is concerned with these issues at the regional level; each one operates with regional questions at the national or university level. In our opinion, therefore, the work promised by the SAI will be unique. In this way, the SAI does not intend to replace these institutions but will augment the energetic effort at research and policy-understanding, which is underlay throughout the region.

Funding

It will not be possible to contemplate an undertaking as ambitious as the SAI without substantial financial commitment by the participating countries. The formal impetus for the SAI will come, we envisage, through the Inter-State Defence and Security Committee of the frontline states grouping. An initial engagement with the issue will help the region's militaries and administrations with the necessary commitment of resources to the project. Without a strong financial guarantee from the states involved, efforts to launch the project are doomed to fail. The amounts needed will include the purchase of a building, the equipment necessary to ensure that the organisation is operational and a building suitable for the residential aspect of the SAI's work. Of central importance in this regard will be the creation of a library to carry and support the research necessary to make the SAI a world-class institution. Without an excellent library, frankly speaking, there will be no Southern African Institute.

The costs of establishing the SAI will have to be carried by the participating countries; regular and running costs will have to be drawn from separate and reinforcing budgets, associated with the work of the SAI. Even though funding for work of this kind is proving exceptionally difficult in the 1990s, there are funds to be found outside of government. Consider these:

- A not insubstantial amount can be garnered from the *international donor community*. USAID has set aside funding for the training of South African diplomats and is looking carefully into the funding of projects which will enhance Southern African regional relations. The European Union can also be tapped for development, affirmative action-type funding. NORAD (Norwegian Development Aid Agency) and SIDA (Swedish International Development Agency) also come to mind as possible sources;
- *Partnerships with sister institutions* can be very successful. Conferences or joint study projects generate not only activity and interest, they can, through careful costing, help with core-funding;
- Innovative and imaginative *research proposals* will be favourably considered by the international foundation community. This is not an endless source of funds, however; as a result, it requires careful understanding of the quickly shifting fads in the field and, as importantly, the development of a sound track record in the delivery of the final product;
- Conferences and the like have to be *self-funding*. In other words, the fiscal management of the SAI has to be geared to the generation of

funds needed both for project and core funding. Tight financial control has to mark its activities if the SAI is to survive and prosper;
- Government funding on a non-permanent basis can cover a range of activities. Think, for example, of an annual retreat of the region's leaders which would be funded by the offices of the heads of state. The scope for this kind of funding has to be innovatively explored within the parameters of the SAI's central purpose.

Conclusion

We, therefore, recommend the establishment of an independent centre for research into, and a forum for information, discussion and debate on security, strategic change, conflict prevention, and development in Southern Africa. This new institution will be called *The Southern African Institute: A Forum for Security and Development Concerns*. While its chief focus will be on Southern African concerns, where global questions touch these regional preoccupations, the SAI will research these issues.

Our recommendation is that the SAI should be established in a regional capital. A city which has a pleasant climate and a fairly robust intellectual life. We also believe that it is important that the SAI should be located in a country with good communications.

We further recommend SAI to be governed by a two-tier structure. First, a *Board of Governors* drawn from the states of Southern Africa. Each participating country will nominate one representative. The Chairman of Board of Governors will be a prominent and respected Southern African who shares the ideals of the SAI and has a demonstrable record of interest in the field. The body will be responsible for the legal personality of the SAI and will help establish and maintain the direction of the SAI's work. It will be responsible for the appointment of the SAI's senior staff, including a director and other senior directing staff. This board will be accountable for the SAI's sound financial management. Second, a *Board of Advisors* who will be responsible for the academic, intellectual and policy directions of the SAI. They will set the framework of the work of the SAI, advising on the topics to be researched. This board will be responsible for the identification of research fellows and will, with the director, support the permanent staff of SAI in the discharging of their academic work. We recommend that the SAI enjoy diplomatic status and a legal personality. Its accounts shall be audited each year and its legal affairs shall be incorporated in the country where it is located.

We recommend that the process of establishing the SAI continues to be canvassed among the governments and the militaries of the region; without their support, the project cannot succeed. As a result, once this proposal has been developed, this concept should be put before the Interstate Defence and Security Committee of the frontline states and the appropriate structures within SADC. Additionally, that an international conference be organized to launch the idea of the SAI. We do not want to minimize the difficulties of these initial tasks. Aside from developing a document which will be acceptable to all the militaries of the region, we will need to explain the idea to the region's publics and to the region's leaders. Setting aside the obviously important questions of deepening understanding between the militaries of the region, the SAI will considerably strengthen the debate on security and development issues throughout the region. Only an informed debate can help to prevent conflict.

Its multilateral flavour, we hope, will widen the scope for a growing regional consensus on these issues; only this will enable the region to face the problems associated with old wars, like Angola, and the emerging security debates of the 1990s. These issues will heighten, as the millennium approaches. The inherent weaknesses of African states will deepen the threats posed by post-Cold War security questions. The SAI's focus on the dynamic of change will enhance the prospects that the peoples of the region can, as the Bible charges, turn swords into ploughshares. The spark which ignited these ideas was the notion that no other regional forum exists which can facilitate discussion of the kind envisaged in this document.

Notes

1. See *Confidence- and Security-building Measures in Southern Africa*, Disarmament, Topical Papers, No. 14 (New York: United Nations Department of Political Affairs, 1993).

2. Hans-Joachim Spanger and Peter Vale, *Security, Development and Co-operation in Southern Africa: The Midgard Conference*, PRIF Reports, No. 31 (Frankfurt: Peace Research Institute, 1993).

3. The task-force was led by Major-General (rtd.) Herman Lupogo, Managing Director of the Arusha International Conference Centre, Tanzania. The other members of the team were Dr Abillah Omari, Director of the Centre for Foreign Relations in Tanzania and Professor Peter Vale, Co-Director of the Centre for Southern African Studies, University of the Western Cape. The project was located in the Centre for Foreign Relations in Dar es Salaam and in the Centre for Southern African Studies, University of the Western Cape. Because of the ease of communications, the task-force was administered by the latter institution. DANIDA and the Danish Foreign Ministry, through that country's representative in South Africa, generously assisted with funding to complete the investigation. Ambassador Peter Bruckner and his colleague, Peter Hansen, were particularly helpful.

4. The universally acclaimed success of the London-based International Institute for Strategic Studies (IISS) rests largely on the quality of their research output. We believe that the creation in Southern Africa of an institution which provides the opportunities for serious minds to spend periods investigating a topic and writing up their findings is vital.

5. In the 1990s, academic and policy-oriented research is senseless if it fails to reach popular communities. This has become especially important in the face of the broad thrust towards democracy in Africa. Additionally, there can be no development of a Southern African community, unless the citizens of the region are enthusiastic about future co-operation. Energetic efforts should be made towards public education through the print and electronic media. The institute ought to contribute to the press and by organizing specialist training programmes on regional and international affairs with practising or trainee journalists.

6. The decade-long period of destabilization was promoted by bureaucrats—in this case, soldiers—who were not receptive to alternative perspectives on policy. Without encouraging a robust exchange of views between policy makers, academic communities and the public, policies are likely to be one-dimensional and will not enjoy wide popular support. However, the SAI will *not* be prescriptive; it will offer, instead, a series of policy considerations that will allow governments themselves to choose or to disregard.

7. Experience elsewhere, most notably South-East Asia, teaches that regional understandings are best promoted by engaging bureaucrats in the joint endeavour. The best mechanism to achieve this is to ensure an appreciation for the importance of the common objectives: joint training in multilateral issues paves the way for greater understanding and cohesion and will help to foster professional unity and *esprit de corps* among Southern African bureaucrats. The SAI should also strive to train leaders from the private and public sectors to understand and manage the growing range of regional issues.

About the Book and Editors

With the ending of white minority rule in South Africa, the democratic elections in Mozambique and the renewed efforts at a negotiated settlement of civil war in Angola, Southern Africa has entered a new era. Much more is required, however, to ensure lasting peace and security. The states on the subcontinent are confronted with the twofold task of creating a sound multilateral framework for conducting mutual relations and for accomodating the dominant power—the new democratic South Africa.

This book examines the potential for—and the obstacles to—regional co-operation and the process of regional institution-building, emphasizing the need to develop a genuine and indigenous capability for managing and resolving conflict. Throughout, the contributors explore ideas about common norms, principles and concrete measures that lend support for building confidence and security. Finally, the specific experiences in organizing collective security in other parts of the African continent are carefully analyzed.

Hans-Joachim Spanger is senior fellow at the Peace Research Institute Frankfurt, Germany. **Peter Vale** is research professor and director of the Centre for Southern African Studies, University of the Western Cape, Bellville, South Africa.

Index

Abuja Treaty for the African Economic Community, 48
Accord de Non-Aggression et d'Assistânce en Matière de Defense (ANAD), 68, 75-77, 80
African National Congress (ANC), 2, 3, 12, 33, 37, 38, 40, 51, 52, 57, 102, 103, 168
ANAD, see Accord de Non-Aggression et d'Assistânce en Matière de Defense
ANC, see African National Congress
Angola, 7, 14-16, 27, 35, 40, 42, 47, 56, 70, 81, 85, 97, 99, 100, 102, 103, 121, 125, 147, 148, 167, 171, 177, 186
Apartheid, 2-5, 7, 14, 16, 20, 26, 34, 36-40, 42, 45-47, 50, 51, 53, 55, 63-65, 87, 93, 97, 108, 120, 160, 161, 167, 169, 182
Armed forces, 8, 71, 74, 77, 82, 115, 116, 121-125, 133, 135-139, 143, 145, 147-149, 152, 153, 155, 157-164, 172, 176
Arms
    control, 8, 107, 108, 111-114, 124, 132, 134, 172, 176, 177
    industry, 8
    limitation, 79
    procurement, 133
    proliferation, 7, 8, 17, 81, 134, 177
    race, 111, 112, 114, 120
    reduction, 79, 177
    trade, 8, 119, 125

Bicesse Accord, 15, 35, 147
BLNS countries, 19, 21, 45, 56
Border, 72, 77, 78, 80, 84, 94, 95, 98, 117, 141, 143, 175, 176
    arbitrary, 118
    colonial, 6, 70, 71
    conflicts, 125, 167
    control, 7, 125, 134, 154, 176

    demarcation, 118
    disputes, 75-77
    inviolability, 116, 124, 131
    national, 121, 122, 125, 142
    physical, 7
    recognition, 115, 124, 132
    regime, 141
    revision, 99, 118, 124
Botswana, 13, 16, 19, 23, 40, 42, 44, 45, 47, 96, 123, 125, 167, 183
Boutros-Ghali, Boutros, 66, 85

CBM/CSBM, see Confidence- and Security-building Measures
CEAO, see Communauté Economique des Etats de l'Afrique de l'Ouest
Chiluba, Frederick, 51
Ching'ambo, Lloyd, 46
Chissano Joaquim, 48
Civil society, 10, 11, 148, 150, 152, 153, 174, 176
Civil-military relations, 149, 153, 157, 158, 160, 162, 172, 176
CMA, see Common Monetary Area
Cold War, 1-8, 11, 35, 36, 63, 91, 93, 97, 101, 103, 104, 111, 116, 117, 119, 120, 122, 186
Colonialism, 12, 71, 84, 93, 117-119
COMESA, see, Common Market for Eastern and Southern Africa
Common Market for Eastern and Southern Africa (COMESA), 34, 39, 42-49, 51-56, 96, 170
Common Monetary Area (CMA, previously: Rand Monetary Area), 26, 39, 44, 45, 52-54
Communauté Economique des Etats de l'Afrique de l'Ouest (CEAO), 75, 77

191

Communication, 9, 10, 40, 107, 112, 115, 139, 140, 168, 171, 175, 179, 185
Conference on Security and Co-operation in Europe (CSCE), 63, 104, 107, 113, 115, 116
Confidence- and Security-building Measures (CSBM/CBM), 114-116, 121-123, 126, 175
Conflict
  armed, 14, 35, 69, 70, 75, 81, 82, 154, 155, 161, 167
  causes of, 35, 61, 92-94, 101, 104, 120, 167, 169, 174, 175
  domestic, 62, 63, 77, 80, 81, 87, 100, 104, 126, 136, 171, 173, 175
  East-West, 34-36, 91, 93, 99-101, 108, 110, 111, 113, 114, 116, 117, 119, 120
  escalation, 65, 71
  ethnic, 5, 63, 64, 93, 94, 98
  formation, 93, 113
  indigenous, 100
  international, 91, 97, 112
  inter-state, 66, 94, 95, 118, 121, 169, 171, 173
  internal, 75, 84, 121, 132
  local, 34, 35
  management, 61, 64-68, 70, 71, 73, 75, 79, 80, 85-87, 91, 92-94, 96-99, 101, 102, 104, 122, 126, 168, 171, 173
  military, 81, 94, 95, 116, 120, 169
  prevention, 66, 68, 71, 76, 80, 92, 93, 99, 134, 145, 168, 171, 173, 185, 186
  racial, 4
  resolution, 65, 68, 70-72, 76, 84-87, 91, 96-100, 102, 104, 126, 148, 168, 171-173, 182
  settlement, 4, 5, 123, 143
  territorial, 84, 125
  types of, 96, 100, 101, 103
  zones of, 97
CONSAS, see Constellation of Southern African States
Constellation of Southern African States (CONSAS), 14, 33, 50
CSCE, see Conference on Security and Co-operation in Europe

DBSA, see Development Bank of South Africa
De Klerk, F. W., 2, 12, 34, 37, 51, 65
Demobilization, 148, 156, 172, 177
Democracy, 5, 6, 10, 80, 92, 93, 134, 148, 149, 151-153, 157-159, 161, 164, 174

Democratization, 66, 81, 82, 85, 119, 150-153
Destabilization, 3, 20, 35, 40, 50, 95, 122
Development, 8, 9, 10, 17-26, 34, 38, 41, 43, 44, 50, 54, 56, 64, 67, 68, 73, 78, 79, 83, 86, 91, 92, 93, 96, 132, 134, 150-153, 155, 159-162, 164, 168, 170, 174, 179-185
Development Bank of South Africa (DBSA), 50
Disarmament, 25, 26, 85, 112, 177

ECA, see United Nations, Economic Commission for Africa
ECCAS, see Economic Union of Central African States
ECOWAS, see Economic Community of West African States
Economic Community of West African States (ECOWAS), 54, 55, 68, 73-75, 82-84, 172
  Monitoring Group (ECOMOG), 75, 83, 178
  Protocol on Mutual Assistance on Defence, 74, 77, 171
  Protocol on Non-Aggression, 73, 74, 77
Economic Union of Central African States (ECCAS), 68, 79, 87
Erskine, Emmanuel, 86
Ethnicity, 5, 6, 94
European Union (EU), 36, 64

FADM, see Forças Armadas de Defesa de Moçambique
FAO, see Food and Agricultural Organization
Food and Agricultural Organization (FAO), 101
Forças Armadas de Defesa de Moçambique (FADM), 148, 150, 157, 159, 160, 161, 164
Forças Populares de Libertação de Moçambique (FPLM), 155
FPLM, see Forças Populares de Libertação de Moçambique
Frelimo, see Frente de Libertação de Moçambique
Frente de Libertação de Moçambique (Frelimo), 102, 150-152, 155-157
Frontline States (FLS), 39, 47, 55, 56, 63, 65, 102, 120, 126

IMF, see International Monetary Fund
Inkatha Freedom Party, 5,7
Insecurity dilemma, 118, 120, 121, 122, 125

Index

Integration, 24-26, 41-43, 45, 46, 48, 49, 52-54, 56, 82, 94, 98, 102, 103, 120, 123, 161, 170, 182
  of armed forces, 147-150, 156, 157, 172
Inter-State Committee for Defence and Security, 171
Interference, 69, 81, 82, 92, 96-98, 101, 108, 124, 180
International Monetary Fund (IMF), 10, 18
Intervention, 74, 76, 82, 84, 98-100, 119, 144, 153, 155, 169, 178

Kampala Document, 108
Kinana, Abdu, 108, 128

League of Nations, 62, 65, 67, 68, 77
Lesotho, 6, 7, 19, 38, 40, 42, 44, 45, 96, 123, 153, 172, 176, 183

Makoni, Simba, 40, 51, 54
Malawi, 19, 23, 40, 42, 46, 95, 125
Mandela, Nelson, 2, 12, 33, 65
Mediation, 65, 69, 74, 76, 96, 97, 101, 144
Midgard Conference, 3, 174
Migration, 7, 16, 17, 95, 101, 103
Military
  academies, 141, 154, 175
  activities, 78, 114-116, 125, 142, 143, 172, 175
  aggression, 14
  alliance, 120, 169, 175
  apparatus, 119, 169
  assistance, 75, 84, 154
  balance, 116
  blocs, 78, 111
  budget, 17, 122, 162
  capabilities, 110, 111, 115, 118, 120-122, 125, 160, 168, 175
  conduct, 113
  confidence-building, 108, 110, 112, 172
  confrontation, 160
  contacts, 125, 126, 141, 172, 175
  co-operation, 171, 175
  coup, 124
  deterrence, 111, 112, 117
  education, 122, 141, 175
  equipment, 141, 169
  establishment, 9, 154, 155, 157-159, 162, 163, 171, 178, 180
  exercise, 141
  expenditures, 15, 108, 133, 139, 169, 172
  facilities, 140
  formations, 140, 142
  information, 137, 158, 175
  intentions, 110-112
  personnel, 122, 136, 138, 140, 141, 150, 157
  professionalism, 149, 162, 163
  service, 135
  stability, 176
  strategy, 133, 139, 159
  threats, 74, 76, 77, 83, 94, 112, 169
  training, 70, 169
MNR, see Renamo
Movimiento Popular de Libertação de Angola (MPLA), 102
Mozambique, 7, 8, 14-16, 19, 35, 38, 40, 42, 46-48, 56, 81, 85, 100, 102, 120, 125, 147-154, 156, 157, 159-164, 167, 173, 177, 183
MPLA, see Movimiento Popular de Libertação de Angola
Mugabe, Robert, 12, 49, 127
Mutharika, Bingu wa, 43, 49, 51, 53

Namibia, 2, 4, 5, 15, 16, 35, 40, 42, 44, 45, 85, 96, 99, 102, 120-122, 125, 147, 167, 170, 177, 183
New York Accord, 34, 102
Nkomati Accord, 102
Nomvete, Bax, 47

OAU, see Organization of African Unity
Office of Regional Ombudsman, 173, 174
Office of the United Nations High Commissioner for Refugees (UNHCR), 101
Organization
  inter-governmental, 65, 96, 100
  international, 66, 78, 97, 98, 100, 101, 104
  non-governmental (NGO), 64, 101, 104, 173, 174
  regional, 23, 24, 26, 34, 39-41, 54, 67, 68, 73, 75, 80, 82, 85, 86, 97, 170, 171
Organization of African Unity (OAU), 6, 35, 40, 42, 61, 65, 68-73, 76, 77, 83-87, 98, 101, 104, 118, 124, 133-135
  Charter, 68, 70, 71, 108, 118
  Commission on Mediation, Conciliation and Arbitration, 68-70, 108
  Defence Commission, 70, 71, 76, 171
  Liberation Committee, 102
  Mechanism for Conflict Prevention, Management and Resolution, 68, 71-73, 173
  Secretary-General, 72, 87

PAC, see Pan Africanist Congress of Azania
Pan Africanist Congress of Azania (PAC), 40, 51, 56, 102
Peace, 17, 18, 79, 81, 83, 85
    building, 71, 79, 148, 149, 162, 164
    enforcement, 75, 135, 169, 173
    keeping, 61, 64-66, 70-73, 75, 76, 79, 81, 82, 84-86, 96, 97, 101, 104, 122, 126, 135, 141, 145, 169, 173, 177, 178
    making, 64-66, 71, 79, 87, 91, 94, 104
    process, 107, 120, 150
Preferential Trade Area (PTA), 26, 39, 42-49, 51-57, 170
PTA, see Preferential Trade Area

Reconciliation, 65, 83, 148-150, 152, 163, 164
Refugees, 15, 75, 81, 95, 121
Renamo, see Resistência Nacional Moçambicana
Resistência Nacional Moçambicana (Renamo/MNR), 7, 147, 149, 150, 152, 155
Rome Peace Accord, 35, 102, 147-149, 154, 156, 160, 163

SACU, see Southern African Customs Union
SADC, see Southern African Development Community
SADCC, see Southern African Development Coordination Conference
SAP, see Structural Adjustment Programme
Salim, Ahmed, 72
Sanctions, 3, 14, 51, 77, 97, 100, 101, 118
Security
    agenda, 1
    arrangement, 61, 75, 77-79, 85, 86, 133
    climate, 17, 78, 180
    collective, 61-63, 65-68, 75, 79-87, 90, 91, 102, 161, 169
    community, 62
    complex, 115, 170
    concept, 82
    concerns, 1, 2, 6, 8, 9, 68, 80, 115, 133, 144, 149, 160, 170, 173, 180
    co-operation, 25, 26, 168, 170, 172
    dialogue, 132
    dilemma, 34, 112, 117, 118, 122
    doctrine, 14, 16
    food, 40, 41
    human, 8, 9, 82, 85, 86, 89, 90
    institutions, 61, 63, 65, 80, 87, 171
    instruments, 67, 69, 74
    international, 62-64, 100, 177
    issues, 7, 9, 34, 128, 158, 159, 180, 181, 183
    management, 68, 91
    mechanism, 65, 68, 70, 72, 73, 77, 80, 82, 86, 90
    national, 83, 108, 117, 118, 177
    regime, 122, 167, 169, 170
    studies, 8, 171, 174, 179, 185
Self-determination, 5, 6, 94, 98, 119, 124
Shamuyarira, Nathan, 172
South Africa, 2-10, 12-17, 19-26, 33-42, 44-46, 50-53, 55, 56, 63-67, 70, 81, 85, 95-97, 102-104, 117-120, 122, 123, 150, 154, 155, 161, 167-169, 172, 173, 176, 182-184
South West African People's Organization (SWAPO), 40, 102
Southern African Customs Union (SACU), 19, 20, 23, 25, 26, 39, 44-46, 51-54, 56, 96
Southern African Development Community (SADC), 14, 15, 18-23, 26, 34, 37-59, 68, 97, 104, 120, 122-125, 161, 170-173, 176, 177, 186
Southern African Development Coordination Conference (SADCC), 19, 20, 26, 27, 33, 37, 39-43, 45-48, 50-54, 57-59, 120, 170
Southern African Institute for Security and Development Studies, 174, 179-186
Sovereignty, 6, 7, 41, 71, 81, 94, 97, 98, 123, 131, 133, 148, 160
Soviet Union, 2, 3, 5, 6, 63, 99, 100, 154
Structural Adjustment Programme (SAP), 10, 18, 19, 25, 93, 95, 119, 149
SWAPO, see South West African People's Organization
Swaziland, 14, 19, 21, 40, 42, 44, 45, 96, 102, 123, 124

Tanzania, 11, 40, 42, 53, 54, 56, 82, 95, 108, 171, 183
Territorial
    expansion, 119
    integrity, 71, 73, 78, 102, 108, 123, 160
    status quo, 116, 119, 124
TVBC homelands, 15, 50

UNDP, see United Nations Development Programme
UNHCR, see Office of the United Nations High Commissioner for Refugees
UNITA, see União Nacional para a Independência Total de Angola

Index

União Nacional para a Independência Total de Angola (UNITA), 7, 97
United Nations, 61, 67, 76, 77, 84, 108, 134, 139, 148, 177
　Charter, 66, 67, 73, 85, 96-98, 131, 133, 145, 172
　conflict management, 65, 73, 104
　Development Programme, 17
　Economic Commission for Africa (ECA), 14, 42, 48, 55
　peace-keeping, 71, 72, 82, 85, 86, 97, 101, 178
　peace missions, 85, 135, 149
　Programme of Action for African Economic Recovery and Development, 18
　Secretary-General, 66, 72, 79, 85, 86
　Security Council, 97, 98, 102
　Standing Advisory Committee on Security Questions in Central Africa, 68, 79, 80, 82, 91
United States of America, 3, 64, 67, 78, 99, 100, 111, 184

Weak states, 10, 26, 117, 118, 121, 122, 153, 169, 175
WHO, see World Health Organization
World Bank, 10, 18, 50
World Health Organization (WHO), 101

ZANLA, see Zimbabwe African National Liberation Army
ZANU, see Zimbabwe African National Union
ZAPU, see Zimbabwe African People's Union
Zambia, 10, 15, 23, 38, 40, 42, 46, 47, 49, 51, 53, 54, 102, 121, 125, 183
Zanzibar, 11
Zimbabwe, 12, 16, 20, 21, 23, 27, 37, 40-43, 49, 53, 54, 95, 97, 102, 126, 147, 154-156, 161, 177, 183
Zimbabwe African National Liberation Army (ZANLA), 154
Zimbabwe African National Union (ZANU), 102
Zimbabwe African People's Union (ZAPU), 12, 102